AQUINAS
ON BEING AND ESSENCE

AQUINAS
ON BEING AND ESSENCE

*A Translation
and
Interpretation*

by

JOSEPH BOBIK

UNIVERSITY OF NOTRE DAME PRESS

TO

TERESA

AND THE CHILDREN

PREFACE

This book has but one aim: to present an intelligible interpretation of the doctrines put forth by St. Thomas Aquinas in his treatise *On Being and Essence*. By "intelligible" in "intelligible interpretation" I mean (1) an interpretation which squares with the observed facts, i.e., one which does the least violence to what is given to a man in sense observation and in introspection, (2) an interpretation which is free of internal inconsistencies, and (3) an interpretation which is in principle capable of coping intelligently with objections, and with other interpretations, one which is thus capable in principle of illuminating its own positions. By "interpretation" in "intelligible interpretation" I mean exactly what one can find in the dictionary, namely, an attempt to bring out the meaning of the treatise by sympathetically entering into it. And this to my mind entails at least two things: not only (1) an attempt to explain, wherever necessary, the sense of the claims made in the text of the treatise but also (2) an attempt to argue, wherever necessary, for or against each of these claims, as each may require.

The aim of this book is not a scholarly one. There will be no attempt, therefore, to take into account each of the many commentaries which have been written on *On Being and Essence*.[1] Nor will there be any attempt to pursue in footnotes, or wher-

ever, any of those extraordinarily uninteresting asides which
are ordinarily found in books of a scholarly sort.

The aim of this book, most simply stated, is to do a bit of
genuine philosophy.

Apropos of the translation, it is to be noted that it was made
from the text of Ludovicus Baur; [2] comparisons were made with
the Marietti [3] text and with that of Fr. Roland-Gosselin.[4] Secondly, the translation, and accompanying interpretation, were
undertaken as (1) an attempt at the beginnings of a removal
from philosophical discourse of the grammatically unpleasant
expression "act of existing," which is employed by Fr. Maurer [5]
to render the Latin word *esse* in his widely used translation of
On Being and Essence (and elsewhere, and by other existential
Thomists as well); and (2) as an attempt at the beginnings of
freeing philosophy from certain unacceptable theses of existential Thomism which hover over its use. The attempt
throughout, both in translating and in interpreting, has been to
use as ordinary an English as possible, and still communicate
the philosophical content intact.

The ideas contained in this interpretation were used and de-
veloped, in part, in conjunction with my teaching of metaphysics, both undergraduate and graduate, at the University of
Notre Dame. In its present form the interpretation is aimed
at serious students of philosophy, whether undergraduate or
not, whether teachers or not. It is nonetheless a version from
which the serious undergraduate can gain much. It is a version,
too, which would have considerable appeal for undergraduate
teachers of metaphysics. For, following the treatise *On Being
and Essence,* it covers the whole of metaphysics in a most economical way, in terms of a reduction to the human intellect's
analytically first concepts, those of being and essence; it considers uses of the words "being" and "essence," it investigates
the essence of natural substances, the immateriality of the human soul, the existence and the essence of God; and it lays the

foundations for avoiding the pitfalls of attributing to things what belongs to our knowledge about them, and of attributing to our knowledge of things what in fact belongs to things themselves. And it is the only interpretation in English of St. Thomas Aquinas' *On Being and Essence* which is anything like a commentary.

For most of what is good in this book, I am indebted to many kind and patient souls, my teachers and students and colleagues and friends, too numerous to call by name. For what is bad, I am indebted to no one.

To my wife and children, a special citation for heroic patience in their respective roles of writer's widow and widow's children.

JOSEPH BOBIK

Notre Dame University

CONTENTS

INTRODUCTION

1. A small mistake in the beginning is a big one in the end, according to the Philosopher in the first book of *On the Heavens and the Earth*. And as Avicenna says in the beginning of his *Metaphysics*, being and essence are what is first conceived by the intellect.
2. Thus, to avoid making mistakes out of ignorance of them, and to become familiar with the difficulties they entail, we must point out what is signified by the words "being" and "essence," and how they are found in diverse things, and how they are related to the logical intentions, genus, species, and difference.

In this brief introduction St. Thomas Aquinas does two things. In (1) he gives the reason for writing this treatise. Being and essence are the beginning points of knowledge by the intellect. One must guard, therefore, against making mistakes about being and essence; for it is obvious that a single and simple error at a beginning point easily turns all that follows after into a multiple and complex one.

In (2) he states the three tasks of this treatise, each task an attempt to lay the foundations for guarding against possible

1

errors apropos being and essence. The first task is to clarify the meanings of the words "being" and "essence"; [1] this is done in chapter one. The second is to investigate the being and essence of the various sorts of real thing.[2] The third is to determine how the being and essence of real things are related to the logical intentions, genus, species, and difference.[3] The second and third tasks are treated in alternating order. Rather than completing the second task before embarking on the third, St. Thomas does part of the second task, then part of the third, then returns to do another part of the second, etc. Thus, chapter two shows how essence is found in material things; chapter four, how the essences of material things are related to the three logical intentions. Chapter five shows how essence is found in the separated substances, i.e., in the human soul, in the intelligences, and in the First Cause. In chapter six, after a review of the way in which essence is found in diverse substances, St. Thomas considers the relation of the separated substances to the three logical intentions. Chapter seven shows how essence is found in accidents, and then how accidents are related to the three logical intentions.

1

Apropos of what he does in (1), we must make clear the sense of the claim that "being and essence are what is first conceived by the intellect." Why does he say that the intellect first conceives both being and essence? Why not being alone, or essence alone? What is the meaning of "first"? What is the content of this first concept?

To begin with, we must notice that in other works he says that what the intellect first conceives is being, making no mention of essence.[4] What, then, does it mean to say that what the intellect first conceives is being? And why is "and essence" added here?

WHAT THE INTELLECT FIRST CONCEIVES IS BEING.

In the *Summa of Theology,* in a context in which he had just mentioned Boethius' distinction between what is *self evident to all* and what is *self evident to the wise,* St. Thomas writes: "In the case of things which are apprehended by all men, there is an order. For what is first apprehended is being, the understanding of which is included in everything, whatever it may be, which anyone apprehends."[5] From this, and from what he writes elsewhere,[6] it is clear that whatever else he may mean by "first," he means not simply temporally first, but, more importantly, analytically first. Thus, the meaning or concept of the temporally first word we learn to use contains, though implicitly, the meaning or concept which we attach later to the word "being." When one's intellect first begins to function, even in a context which is conceivable as temporally prior to one's learning to use his first word, whatever else it may grasp in conception about sensible things, it grasps that concept to which one later on attaches the word "being."

To make this clear, one must consider the following. Human knowledge about real things is by sense and by intellect; knowledge by sense focuses on unique features of individuals, knowledge by intellect on shared features; knowledge by sense is temporally prior to knowledge by intellect, and knowledge about sensible things is temporally prior to knowledge about nonsensible things. Thus, our temporally first knowledge is sense knowledge about sensible things. Knowledge by intellect is dependent on knowledge by sense as on an origin; since this is so, our temporally first knowledge by intellect is about things which are sensed.

At this point two things are to be noticed: (1) that our temporally first concept bears explicitly on a sense experience, and implicitly includes the concept of being; and (2) that the expression "analytically first" in the claim that the concept of being is our analytically first concept can be given a clearer and fuller meaning in terms of a reference to the intellect's three operations. First, since our temporally first knowledge is sense knowledge about sensible things, then the human knower first grasps these sensible things by means of their sensible qualities. By virtue of their sensible qualities these things are first actual for, or present to, human sense. And it is through their first actuality for, or first presence to, human sense that these things become first actual for, or first present to, the human intellect. They become first present to the human intellect as *something-there*, i.e., as something asserting itself, as something different from us and confronting us, as something doing things to our senses. This means that our temporally first knowledge by intellect is a knowledge the content of which is rooted in a sense experience.

Consider, for example, a child who is just learning to talk, and who has just burned his finger on the kitchen stove. His mother, pointing to the stove, says, "Hot!"; the child soon learns to do the same thing. What, now, do both mother and child intend to communicate by the word hot when they point to the kitchen stove and say that it is hot? That that thing, which the child will later learn to call by the name stove, and by many other names—e.g., thing, something, something-there—is a thing which, when one touches it with his finger, burns the finger. They are explicitly concerned with communicating the fact that the kitchen stove burns the finger. They are not explicitly concerned with communicating the fact that the kitchen stove is something-there, though knowledge of this fact is the least possible knowledge presupposed by and implied in knowledge of the fact that it burns the finger. Thus, our temporally first intellectual knowledge can be described as a knowledge whose explicit content is rooted in some sense experience or other, the implicit content of which is at least what can be expressed as something-there, i.e., being. J. Maritain puts it briefly and clearly:

This [being] is the first of all concepts, because it springs in the mind at the first awakening of thought, at the first intelligible coming to grips with the experience of sense by transcending sense. . . . The first idea formed by a child is not the idea of being; but the idea of being is implicit in the first idea which the child forms.[7]

Secondly, knowledge by intellect takes place by three different acts: (1) simple apprehension, the result of which is a concept; (2) composition and division, the result of which is a proposition; and (3) reasoning, the result of which is an argument. These three acts are so related to one another that the second cannot occur if the first does not; or can the third if the second does not; also, if the first does not, either can the third. This is to say that if simple apprehension does not occur, no intellectual activity at all occurs; or that whenever intellectual activity of any sort at all occurs, simple apprehension always occurs. This is also to say that propositions are *per se* constituents of arguments; and concepts, of propositions; i.e., just as propositions are analytically prior to arguments, so too concepts are analytically prior to propositions. Similarly, the concept of being, that which we expressed above as *something-there*, is so related to all our concepts about sensible things that nothing other than it can be conceived if it is not conceived; or whenever whatever else is conceived about sensible things, something-there is always conceived. Thus, something-there is a *per se* constituent of, or is analytically prior to, all other concepts about sensible things; but not vice versa. Thus, further, whenever the intellect does anything at all apropos of sensible things, it conceives something-there. The concept of being is the analytical beginning point of all human intellectual activity apropos of sensible things.

One can make an approach toward establishing that
something-there expresses the content of our analytically first
concept about sensible things by considering the human intellect's natural passing from potentiality to actuality in its
acquisition of knowledge. The human intellect moves from
knowing nothing to knowing something; humans are born with
no knowledge; they are born only with powers for acquiring
knowledge. In moving from no knowledge about sensible
things to knowledge about them, the human intellect functions
through the senses to move first to some (as opposed to a
complete) knowledge; then, as one's sense experience with
sensible things grows, to progressively more and more knowledge about them. But what is the least the intellect can
possibly come to know about sensible things, when it first
comes to know anything at all about them? Perhaps one can
say: next to nothing. But to know next to nothing about
sensible things, and to know this by intellect, is to know about
them something which is at the highest possible level of universality. Knowledge by intellect is from the outset a universal
knowledge; and the least possible knowledge by intellect is the
most universal possible knowledge. It is such, therefore, that it
is applicable to any and every individual sensible thing of any
and every sort, but without expressing anything which is
proper to, or distinctive of, any individual or sort. When the
intellect first conceives the sensible thing, what can the intellect conceive about a sensible thing less than this, namely,
something-there (where 'there' takes on its meaning in one's
recognition, however implicit, that something other than himself is asserting itself, is doing things to his senses). For the
intellect to conceive less than this would, clearly, imply that
the intellect's first concept was uttered at once about things
which are there and about things which are not there. This is
clearly impossible; for 'what is not there' can be taken to mean
(1) absolute nothing, which is of itself inconceivable; it is

conceivable only in terms of a reference to what is there; or (2) something nonsensible, which we conceive only after, and in terms of a reference to, what is there.

One must keep in mind that what is said about what it is that the intellect first (both temporally and analytically) conceives about sensible things—namely, the concept of being—is said by way of analysis. One must, therefore, be careful to remind himself of what this means. It means that in order to come to an understanding of that first concept, one will employ many concepts and distinctions made after that first concept. These concepts and distinctions will have a precision and distinctness which that first concept did not have. And some of these concepts and distinctions will be used in talking about the content of that first concept; one must guard against attributing the precision and distinctness of these to the content of that first concept. For example, one will use the distinction between sense knowledge and intellectual knowledge; the distinction among conceiving, composing and dividing, and reasoning; the notion of the most universal possible; which have already been used in some way in what has been written above.

It means that one will also use other concepts and distinctions, for example, the distinction between a word and the concept to which we attach the word; the distinction between the time when the first concept is formed by the intellect and the time when that first conception is given a verbal formulation; the distinction between signifying things as a whole and signifying them as a part; the different ways in which we know something which is a whole; the distinction between essence and existence. The last three distinctions just named will be used below at a more appropriate place (see pages 199–203).

Since humans use words to give their ideas a more precise, a more elaborated, and a less emotionally hindered expression than can be given them by the crying of a hungry baby, or by a laugh, or by the movement of a hand, one might ask: When is the word "being" attached to the intellect's first concept? We attach words to concepts about sensible things, so that the words stand for these things through the mediacy of the concepts. It would be difficult, impossible perhaps, to determine when, in the lifetime of a given individual, the individual first attaches the word "being" to that which was his first conception about sensible things.

When one says, here and now—i.e., in making an analysis—that the intellect first grasps a sensible thing as something-there, it should be made clear that this first grasp did not, then and there, receive the verbal formulation "something-there." This verbal formulation, like the verbal formulation "being" (and like any verbal formulation in respect to its corresponding conception),[8] is attached to the first conception of the intellect only after one has heard the formulation used by others, and has heard it so used a sufficient number of times to allow him to gather that the user of the word has in his own mind attached the word to this first conception. The first verbal formulation was almost certainly a formulation bearing on the sensible quality through which the sensible things was being grasped by sense when the intellect first began to function; and this first verbal formulation was a formulation given to him ready-made: given to him, most likely, by his parents; ready-made, from the language spoken by his parents. For example, "hot" may have been a given child's first verbal formulation (see page 4).

WHAT THE INTELLECT FIRST CONCEIVES IS BEING AND ESSENCE.

Among all the words we use apropos of sensible things, the meaning of the word "being" is analytically first. But the word "being," used apropos of sensible things, has many meanings, as will be seen below; and its first meaning—i.e., the meaning first conceived by the intellect—is a meaning which one can formulate in this way: what has essence. (It must be noticed that one can also formulate the meaning of the word "essence" in terms of the meanings of the word "being," as is in fact done by St. Thomas in chapter one; see page 44, [5] in the text of the treatise; also page 45.) This—i.e., what has essence—is real being, is something-there (some things have no essence—e.g., blindness—and are therefore not real beings); this is the being of the categories. Things which are not real things are of themselves inconceivable; being which has no essence is of itself inconceivable; it is conceivable only after, and in terms of a reference to, being which has essence.

This can perhaps be made clearer if one considers in some way, at this point, what the word "essence" means (more will be said below). Whatever else it means, it means a certain quality with a twofold aspect: (1) that within things by which things exist independently of our knowing that they exist—i.e., a principle of independent existence—and (2) that within things by which things cause us to know them, i.e., a principle of knowability. We have already in some way expressed this idea above (see page 4; also page 6) in attempting to give a clear meaning to the expression "something-there" as representing the intellect's first concept: something different from us and confronting us (this is rooted in essence as principle of independent existence), something doing things to our senses (this is rooted in essence as principle of knowability). Essence, thus, is simultaneously that in things whereby things *are there* and whereby they *are knowable*. If things were not there, then they could not cause us to know them; the source of their being there is the source of their causing us to know them; this source is called essence. To be sure, things which are not there can be known; but only in terms of something other than themselves, only in terms of things which are there. And this in a way similar to the way in which sight grasps color by virtue of light, but light by virtue of nothing other than light itself. Essence can be described as being related to the human intellect as light is to sight; and what has essence is grasped by the intellect in the way in which what emits light is grasped by sight.

Thus, the analytical beginning point of our intellectual knowledge about sensible things is a grasp of being, but of being which has essence. And this is why St. Thomas adds here: "and essence."

2

Apropos of the tasks he enumerates in (2), it is important to notice that it is one thing to investigate the meanings of the words "being" and "essence," and quite another thing to investigate the being and essence of diverse sorts of real thing. This is clear from the obvious fact that one can know what the words "being" and "essence" mean, and have no idea what the being and essence of some real thing—e.g., man—might be. The same thing is the case with other words. For example, one can know what the word "cause" means, yet have no idea what the cause of some given fact might be; or what the word "existence" means, yet have no idea what existence might be. The following questions are suggested by the things just said: Why does metaphysics bother about investigating the meanings of words, since metaphysics is from the outset an attempt to investigate real things? Why does St. Thomas here limit his investigation of the meanings of words to but two, namely, "being" and "essence"?

The third task mentioned by St. Thomas in (2) suggests the following questions: What are logical intentions? Why does St. Thomas consider the question of the relation of being and essence to logical intentions? Why does St. Thomas choose to consider but three of them, namely, genus, species, and specific difference? What does St. Thomas take to be the difference between logic and metaphysics?

Metaphysics and the Investigation of the Meanings of Words

To begin with, one must notice that there are certain words which have a very wide use in the discourse of daily life, apropos of things like bread and butter, clothes, houses, taxes, who's running for president, how to avoid temptations, in the various sciences like physics, chemistry, biology, psychology, and in the various branches of philosophy like natural philosophy, moral philosophy, philosophy of art. As used in everyday discourse, the meanings of these words are left uninvestigated or unanalyzed. As used in the various sciences and in the various branches of philosophy, their meanings are not differentiated; that is, no one of the sciences, nor any one of the branches of philosophy, takes it upon itself to record, in precise formulations, the different meanings which a same word has as it is used apropos of their (i.e., its own and that of others) proper, but different, subject matters. That a same word might have different meanings as it is used apropos of different subject matters is suggested by the difference itself in the subject matters. But the meanings of these words should not remain uninvestigated; otherwise there will remain a certain indeterminateness, a certain incompleteness, in human knowledge.

Among these widely used words (e.g., principle, cause, element, necessary, contingent, good, true, beautiful, one, many), as they are used in everyday discourse, the word "being" (the more usual English equivalent is the word "thing") is first, analytically first. That is, the meaning of the word "being" is included in the meanings of the others, but not vice versa. And not only is its meaning included in the meanings of widely used words but it is also included as well in the meanings of all (however widely or not widely used) the words of everyday discourse. Thus, the meaning of no such

word will be fully and explicitly understood unless the meaning of the word "being" is fully and explicitly understood. (Of
course, for the purposes of one's everyday life, it is not
necessary to have a full and explicit understanding of the
meanings of the words one uses.) Further, since propositions
and reasonings are composed of words, the truth of no everyday proposition, nor of any everyday reasoning, will be fully
and explicitly understood unless the meaning of the word
"being" is fully and explicitly understood. Since the meaning of
the word "being" is the analytical beginning point of everyday
intellectual knowledge, and since everyday intellectual knowledge is in some sense the beginning point of all intellectual
knowledge, it is desirable and indeed necessary to make no
mistakes about its meaning; for a small error at a beginning
point easily becomes a great one in the end.

Commenting on Aristotle's *Metaphysics*, St. Thomas writes:

Because the particular sciences [i.e., any science about real things
other than metaphysics] put aside the investigation of some things
which need to be investigated, it was necessary that there be a
science, a universal and first science, which would investigate the
things which the particular sciences do not consider. These put-
aside things appear to be both the common notions or aspects
which follow on common being (which none of the particular sciences considers, since they do not belong to any one of the
particular sciences any more than to any other, but commonly to
all of them) and also the separated substances, which transcend
the scope of the consideration of all the particular sciences. And
thus Aristotle, handing down to us such a science, moves on, after
his investigation of the common notions, to a particularized treatment of the separated substances, to the knowledge of which are
ordered not only the things which have been treated so far in this
science [metaphysics], but also things which are treated in other
sciences.[9]

His words lead to this description of metaphysics: metaphysics
is concerned with left-overs, i.e., with pursuits which are left

over in the sense that they are outside, or beyond, the scope, the methods, the interest, of the various sciences and of the various other branches of philosophy. (That metaphysics is beyond them is clear from the simple fact that metaphysics investigates things which depend on sensible matter neither for being nor for being known.) These left-over pursuits are basically two: (1) metaphysics attempts to clarify—i.e., to record and to give clear and precise formulations to—the different meanings of these widely used words, both for the sake of this clarification itself and for the sake of its own metaphysical scientific procedures; (2) metaphysics attempts an investigation of extramental immaterial things (the separated substances), especially of what is first among all things. That the latter is beyond them is obvious. That the former—i.e., the attempt at clarification—is beyond them is indicated by the simple fact that no one of them undertakes this attempt. Further, there is no reason why any one of them, in preference to any other should attempt this task, seeing that these words are used by all of them (or at least by more than one of them). And it would be superfluous for each of them to do this. Hence, this clarificatory task ought to fall to a separate science, to a science whose subject matter includes in some way all other subject matters, to a universal or encompassing science—metaphysics. Thus, it has become a function of metaphysics to observe, and to see what words are such that they are used not only in everyday discourse, but in the various sciences (some or all), and in the other branches of philosophy (some or all), and to clarify their meanings.

But metaphysics does not pursue this clarification only for the sake of the clarification itself. Metaphysics from the outset is an attempt to acquire knowledge about the existence and the characteristics of the first among all things; from the outset its intention is to use these words for its own purposes, that is, it attempts to elaborate for these words meanings which are suitable for metaphysical scientific procedures. It elaborates these meanings in a way such that they represent some sort of continuity in terms of an extension. Extended meanings of this sort, especially those which are extensions of the meanings of words used in the discourse of everyday life, are very valuable because they are extensions of what everybody already knows in some way, and because they are thereby in contact with the something-there which is grasped in our analytically first concept. These extensions have the great advantage of putting us into an uncommon and enviable position: we know at least in some way, and from the very beginning of our attempt at doing metaphysics, what we are talking about; and what we are talking about is things-there, i.e., the things given to us in sense experience.

What makes a meaning suitable for metaphysical scientific procedures? (We referred to such suitability in the immediately preceding paragraph.) One must recall how being as being is established as the subject of metaphysics: [10] if first philosophy, or metaphysics, has as its prime intention to come to a scientific knowledge of the first cause (i.e., of what is first among all things), and if something exists which is immaterial (e.g., the human soul), and if first philosophy is to be a science, then being as being (and not material being, or some other part of the whole of being) must be the subject. This is necessary in order to have an adequately universal effect in terms of which to come to a knowledge of the first cause. Any meaning or notion which, like that of being as being, is independent of sensible matter, and which is known to be realized extramentally apart from matter, can be used as a means through which to acquire more knowledge about the first cause. Any such notion is among the common notions referred to in the text quoted just above from St. Thomas' *Commentary on Aristotle's Metaphysics.*

Thus, the clarificatory function of metaphysics has at least this twofold orientation: (1) toward lessening a certain inde-

terminateness and incompleteness in human knowledge, by
undertaking a task which no other science undertakes; and (2)
toward metaphysics itself for which it elaborates meanings
suitable for scientific procedures.

It is to be noticed that it is the concern of metaphysics to rise
as quickly and as economically as possible to a proved knowledge of the existence and of the characteristics of the first
among all things. If metaphysics can accomplish this by, for
example, simply tracing the meanings of a same word as it is
used in everyday discourse, i.e., without tracing its different
meanings through the various sciences and through the various
other parts of philosophy, there is no reason why it should not.
Metaphysics can complete its tracing of words at leisure, i.e.,
after its primary task has been accomplished. To be sure, it is
hoped that this leisurely tracing will afford additional paths to
a knowledge of the existence and of the characteristics of the
first among all things, paths which will serve to strengthen its
initial economical one.

The tracing which St. Thomas proposes in his treatise *On
Being and Essence* is a highly economical one. He proposes to
trace the meanings of but two words—namely, "being" and
"essence"—and that of the word "being" at the level of everyday discourse. His reason for this proposal is at least twofold:
(1) the fact that the grasp of being, or of something-there, is
the analytical beginning point of everyday intellectual knowledge, and (2) the fact that metaphysics is from the outset an
attempt to rise to a knowledge of a first cause which is something real, i.e., real in a sense at least as strong as the sense in
which the referent of the expression "something-there" is real.

There are other reasons why metaphysics bothers about the
meanings of words, especially that of the word "being." For
example, (1) to avoid errors which come from not being
careful about the ways in which words function, like the claim
of Parmenides and Melissus that being is one; (2) to identify,

in terms of what everybody knows, what metaphysics is primarily about as about a subject (see pages 56–58).

SECOND INTENTIONS, LOGIC, AND METAPHYSICS

The genus, the species, and the difference represent diverse intellectual grasps or expressions of things. Each expresses the thing as to what the thing is—i.e., as to its essence—but each in a different way: the genus expresses the common part of what the thing is; the difference, the proper or distinctive part; the species, the whole thing, i.e., the whole of what the thing is. The two remaining predicables—namely, property and accident—are not expressive of what a thing is. Since St. Thomas' effort in this treatise is a most economical one and since it begins by focusing on the analytical beginning point of human intellectual knowledge, it is clear why he chooses to consider only those logical intentions which relate to the intellect's first operation, simple apprehension. And since the analytical beginning point of human intellectual knowledge is a grasp of being *and essence,* it is clear why he chooses to consider only those logical intentions which relate to our grasp of what things are; it is clear, therefore, why he does not consider the intentions property and accident.

It is precisely because of the fact that we, as human knowers, have many different grasps of things, that logical intentions enter the domain of human knowledge. In an intellect which grasps everything by but one concept, there would be no place for logical intentions. Most simply described (i.e., at the level of the intellect's first operation, simple apprehension), logical intentions are relations discoverable by the mind among its many different grasps of real things.

It is the view of St. Thomas that the things which logic investigates as its subject are intentions which are only secondly known; they have come to be called second intentions. He explains what he understands by such intentions:

What is first known (*prima intellecta*) are things outside the soul, the things which first draw the intellect to knowldge. But the intentions which follow on our mode of knowing are said to be secondly known (*secunda intellecta*); for the intellect comes to know them by reflecting on itself, by knowing that it knows and the mode of its knowing.[11]

Then, in what immediately follows, he offers genus, species (also second substances) as examples of such intentions.

To make clear what logical, or second, intentions are, one must begin by noticing that they are opposed to first intentions. First intentions are meanings or concepts derived from, or at least verified in, extramental, or real, things. For example, the meaning we derive from those things which are men, and to which we attach the word "man," i.e., the meaning "rational animal"; the meaning we derive from those things which are animals, and to which we attach the word "animal," i.e., the meaning "sensitive organism." Second intentions are meanings derived from, or verified in, first intentional meanings; second intentions are characteristics which belong to meanings derived from real things (i.e., to first intentions), not only because of these meanings but also because these meanings are in the grasp of a human intellect. If one compares the meaning which he attaches to the word "animal" with the meaning he attaches to the word "man" (this presupposes a possession of each meaning), it is easy to see that the meaning of the word "animal" is part of the meaning of the word "man." For a meaning to be part of another meaning is a second intention, a characteristic (here a relation) discoverable by the intellect between two possessed meanings, a relation which belongs to first intentional meanings both because of the meanings themselves and because these meanings are known by a human intellect. If we consider the meaning we attach to the word "dog," it is easy to see that the meaning of the word "animal" is part of its meaning as well as part of the meaning of the word "man." It is thus the (or a) common part of the meaning of both. This is roughly what it is for a meaning to be a genus. If some meaning A is part of some meaning D and also part of some meaning M, then A is, roughly speaking, the (or a) genus of D and M.

It is to be noticed that the first intentional meanings being compared exist in a human intellect. Second intentional relations are, therefore, relations between terms which exist in the intellect. The relations themselves, therefore, exist in the intellect. Second intentional relations are not real relations; they are not relations which belong to things outside the mind precisely as outside the mind; for example, Jack's being one inch taller than Paul; Paul's being Jack's father. Nor are second intentional relations characteristics which belong to things because of, and only because of, what these things are, i.e., only because of the first intentional meanings derived from these things; for example, the incorruptibility of the human soul; such characteristics are first intentions. Second intentional relations are characteristics which belong to things as known, not to things as things.

The following points will help to clarify the preceding. (1) If being a genus belonged to animal as animal (i.e., to animal because of, and only because of, what the word "animal" means), then only the meaning of the word "animal" could be a genus. But this is clearly not the case. One can find any number of meanings which are related to other meanings as their genus. For example, the meaning of the word "body" is a genus in relation to the meaning of the word "organism" (i.e., living body) and to that of the expression "nonliving body"; the meaning of the word "organism" is a genus in relation to the meanings of the words "plant" and "animal."

(2) One must notice the difference between (a) what it is to be a genus and (b) that which is a genus. The former is a second intention; the latter, a first intention. To be a genus is to have a relation of a certain sort (genericity) to other meanings. Animal has such a relation to man and dog. And it is because of

this relation that animal is called a genus; and this in a way similar to the way in which Paul is called Jack's father because of the relation (real) of fatherhood. One must notice the same distinction between what it is to be a species (specificity) and that which is a species; also between what it is to be a specific difference and that which is a specific difference.

(3) Out of the preceding, one has a clear way of pointing out what logic is about. Logic considers questions like (a) what does it mean to be a genus, a species, a specific difference, and (b) what belongs to—i.e., what are the properties or more generally the *per se* accidents of—a genus as genus, a species as species, a specific difference as specific difference. Some science other than logic considers questions like (a) what is the genus animal—i.e., what does it mean to be an animal—and (b) what belongs to animal as animal (philosophy of nature); and questions like (a) what is the genus triangle—i.e., what does it mean to be a triangle—and (b) what belongs to triangle as triangle (mathematics); and questions like (a) what is the genus substance—i.e., what does it mean to be a substance—and (b) what belongs to substance as substance (metaphysics). An example of a simple proof in the logic of the first operation of the intellect, simple apprehension, will be of some help here:

To show: A category cannot have a specific difference.
Proof: A specific difference is what differentiates species in a same genus.
            Thus, whatever has a specific difference must have a genus. But a category is a genus which has no genus of itself. Therefore, a category cannot have a specific difference.

(4) It will be helpful to mention other examples of second intentions. Apropos of the first operation of the intellect: to be a universal, a predicable, a category, a definition. For the second operation of the intellect: to be a proposition, a subject,

a predicate, a copula, a contradictory, a contrary; to be true, false, implied. For the third operation of the intellect: to be a deduction, an induction, a syllogism, a necessary syllogism, a middle term, a major term, a minor term, a fallacy, the subject of a science.

From the preceding, one can understand that whenever a human knower confronts a knowable thing, the knowledge which is a result of this confrontation bears the stamp of the knower. The knowledge which is a result of this confrontation has characteristics deriving from the extramental things which are said to be known, but this knowledge also has characteristics deriving from our condition as beings who know extramental things in terms of a great number of different grasps or concepts or meanings. It is important, therefore, to be aware of what enters our knowledge from our condition as human knowers. This is important in order to avoid attributing to things what does not belong to them. And this is why St. Thomas considers the question of the relation of being and essence to logical intentions.

From the preceding, one can also understand what St. Thomas takes to be the difference between logic and metaphysics, indeed between logic and the whole of philosophy. Whereas the whole of philosophy is about real things, from different points of view, logic is about second intentions, which are not real things. Whereas logic and metaphysics can be said to be about all things (excluding God) as about a subject, metaphysics is about them as things, i.e., about those common features of things which are essential to and intrinsic to them, and which they have independently of our way of knowing them. But logic is about them as known, i.e., about those common features of things which are only incidental to them, which we come to attribute to them not as their own but precisely because of the way in which we know them, which we understand therefore to belong to what enters our knowledge from our condition as human knowers.

CHAPTER ONE

3. Since we ought to acquire knowledge of what is simple from what is composed, and come to what is prior from what is posterior, so that, beginning with what is easier, we may progress more suitably in learning; we ought to proceed from the meaning of the word "being" to that of the word "essence."

4. We should notice, therefore, that the word "being," taken without qualifiers, has two uses, as the Philosopher says in the fifth book of the *Metaphysics*. In one way, it is used apropos of what is divided into the ten genera; in another way, it is used to signify the truth of propositions. The difference between the two is that in the second way everything about which we can form an affirmative proposition can be called a being, even though it posits nothing in reality. It is in this way that privations and negations are called beings; for we say that affirmation is opposed to negation, and that blindness is in the eye. In the first way, however, only what posits something in reality can be called a being. In the first way, therefore, blindness and the like are not beings.

In (3) St. Thomas points out the order in which he will approach the first of the three tasks. He will treat the meanings of the word "being" before those of the word "essence"; for this is to proceed from what is composed to what is simple, from what is posterior to what is prior, from what is easier to what is more difficult.

In (4) he turns to part of the first task, to the meanings of the word "being"; beginning with (5) (see page 44), he turns to the second part of this task, to the meanings of the word "essence."

3

Apropos of what he does in (3), it will be helpful to consider, in a general way, how one can advance more suitably (perhaps most suitably) in the acquisition of knowledge. What comes immediately to mind is St. Thomas' distinction (but not his alone) between the order of determination (*ordo* or *processus in determinando*) and the order of demonstration (*processus in demonstrando*).[1]

The Order of Determination: From What Is Easier to What Is More Difficult

Very generally described, the order of determination is the order in which one takes up topics in his pursuit of knowledge, whether knowledge in general or in some particular domain, i.e., the order in which one makes determinations about (investigates) the topics he is pursuing. The order of demonstration (see page 27) refers to what one does when one does science about each of the topics set into order within the order of determination.

The general rule of the order of determination is this obvious one: begin with those matters which are for us the easiest and then pass on to the more difficult, except when the more difficult is necessary for what is to follow. For example, logic, both formal and material, is certainly not the easiest of disciplines, yet most men must study and master it before they can master the other sciences. No science can be mastered without a firm grasp of the ins and outs of valid and true and necessary reasoning, and not all men are naturally endowed with a grasp firm enough.

In applying this general rule, one looks to man's knowing equipment, his senses and his intellect, and to the relation between them; one also looks to the knowable objects themselves, especially to their accessibility to human investigation. Sense knowledge is easier than intellectual knowledge. Since intellectual knowledge takes its origin in sense knowledge, intellectual knowledge about sensibly perceivable things is easier than intellectual knowledge about things removed from sense observation. And this appears to be what St. Thomas has in mind when he writes in chapter two: "But because the essences of the simple substances are more hidden from us, we ought to begin with the essences of composed substances, so that we may progress more suitably in learning from what is easier" (see page 49, [13] in the text of the treatise). But God and the other simple substances are not the only knowable objects which can be described as things removed from sense observation. Concepts, or the meanings we attach to words, are also such objects. And there are other objects which, unlike God and the other simple substances and concepts, are in themselves sensible, but which can nonetheless be said to be removed from sense observation, either because they are too small to observe—e.g., subatomic particles—or because they are too far away, e.g., celestial bodies.

The application of this general rule—namely, to begin with what is easier and then pass on to the more difficult—can be summarized by two apparently opposed statements, on which St. Thomas comments in several places: [2]

(1) What is particular is easier than what is universal.

(2) What is more universal is easier than what is particular.

(1) takes into account all of man's knowing equipment, both the senses and the intellect; it is saying simply that sense knowledge, which is a grasp of particulars in the sense of individuals, is easier for us than intellectual knowledge, which is a grasp of universals; it is easier, for example, to look at and see a tree than to know what a tree is. (2) is a statement at the level of intellectual knowledge; it is saying that the more universal is easier for us than the particular in the sense of less universal; this is so because the more universal is the less detailed; for example, triangle is less detailed than right triangle, for the definition of right triangle includes that of triangle but adds a detail, namely, that of including an interior angle which is a right angle.

In his *Commentary on Aristotle's Metaphysics* [3] St. Thomas gives both (1) and (2) an interpretation at the level of intellectual knowledge. He does this in terms of a distinction between two sorts of universal: (a) universals which are, or can be used as, predicates; these are products of the intellect's first operation, simple apprehension (*universalia per praedicationem* or *secundum simplicem apprehensionem*); and (b) universals which are causes or explanatory factors in the real world (*universalia in causando*). Apropos of (a) he points out that we know the more universal in some way (*aliquo modo*, he writes) before we know the less universal. He gives the universal "being" as an example, from which one can conclude with some measure of certainty that by *aliquo modo* he means "in an implicit and unworded way" (see pages 4–5, 8). That is, whatever else we may know about sensible things when we first come to know anything at all about them, we know that they are something-there, at least implicitly; this, therefore, is what is easiest for us at the level of intellectual knowledge.

Apropos of learning to use a language, we must notice that the words first learned are very restricted in their applicability in proportion to one's restricted experience of the sensible world, e.g., the word "hot." Words with more universal meanings are learned later on. This is to say that the simply apprehended universals, especially being, which are implicitly grasped, but unworded, whenever anything at all is grasped about sensible things, become worded. However, though worded, they remain unanalyzed; that is, one knows how to use these words in different everyday situations or contexts, and knows how to use them accurately; but one is unable to give a precise formulation of their meanings, and this is so primarily because there is nothing in everyday situations which requires that a man reflect on them and give them precise formulations. It is not until one begins to bother about doing things like philosophy that he finds himself in a situation which requires such reflection and such attempts at precise formulation.

But the doing of philosophy does not end with reflection on, and analysis of, these simply apprehended universals. This is only its beginning point. Its goal is a knowledge of the real causes of real things, of all real things at all possible levels of universality, including the highest, and at all levels of our experience with them. That is, philosophy does not terminate in a precise formulation of the meanings of the word "being," for its goal is to understand the being of real things, of all real things; it does not terminate in a precise formulation of the meanings of the word "cause," for its goal is to come to an understanding of the causes of real things, of all the causes, both intrinsic and extrinsic, of all real things. And its goal is not only the causes appropriate to this and that given sort of thing (even if all the sorts of things were known)—i.e., not only particular causes—but also causes common to all the sorts of things, i.e., universal causes.

Since the investigation of the causes of real things cannot, obviously, be accomplished by simply analyzing the meanings of words, and since such an investigation requires careful observation of, or experience with, real things, it is clear that this investigation will grow only in proportion as our experience with the world grows, and that it will begin with those things which lend themselves most easily or readily to our careful observation. Such things are things which are sensibly observable. We will come to know the causes of things removed from sense observation, in all the senses of "things-removed-from-sense-observation" (see page 23), only later on, if at all, as our experience with the world broadens and reveals to us different sorts of things. And lastly, we will come to know the universal causes of all things only when our experience with things reveals to us that which they all have in common, and which is such that it requires universal causes. And this is why St. Thomas writes that the investigation of the causes (and of the properties) of things proceeds in an order which can be described as the opposite of that which is found in our simple apprehension of things:

Things which are more universal in simple apprehension are known first, for being is what first falls into the intellect, as Avicenna says, . . . But in the investigation of natural properties and causes, those which are less common are known first; because it is through particular causes, which are appropriate to some one genus or species, that we arrive at universal causes. Things which are universal in causing are posteriorly known by us (though priorly known according to nature), although things which are universal in predication are in some way known by us before things which are less universal (though not known before singular things). For knowledge of the senses which grasp singular things precedes in us intellectual knowledge which grasps universal things.[4]

What one does in pursuing the topics *within a given science*, as we have seen, is to begin with the more universal, the more universal being easier because it is less detailed, and proceed to what is progressively less and less universal, this being more difficult because more detailed (this is the *order of determination* within a given science). Now, what one does *in doing science* about each of the topics set into order within the order of determination (this is the *order of demonstration*) is somewhat different. First of all, the order of the movement *in the order of demonstration* is not from topic to topic; it is rather from the subject of the science to its definition, then to its properties, and lastly to its extrinsic causes (if it has any), and this movement *within the confines of a single given topic*. The mind moves with a view to formulating an acceptable and fruitful definition of the subject; that is, a definition which squares with the observed or introspected facts, and which will reveal necessary connections between the subject and its properties; a definition which can be used, further, to establish the existence and the characteristics of the extrinsic causes of the subject (in those cases in which it becomes clear that the subject must have extrinsic causes). Secondly, one is not moving from the more universal to the less universal; rather, one maintains the *same level* of universality. That is, in moving from the subject to its definition one does not produce a definition which is less universal than the subject. Such a definition would be, clearly, unacceptable. Nor does one proceed to properties and extrinsic causes which are less universal than the subject, for these, too, would be unacceptable. What one must do is to maintain the *same level* of universality, for this alone guarantees that the definition is *the* definition of the subject, and that the properties and extrinsic causes are *the* properties and *the* extrinsic causes of the subject. This is what is meant when it is often said that the subject, its definition, its properties, and its extrinsic causes must be *commensurately universal*.

From the Meaning of the Word "Being" to That of the Word "Essence"

St. Thomas' reason for clarifying the meaning of the word "being" before that of the word "essence" is but another application of the general rule of the order of determination, namely, "so that, beginning with what is easier, we may progress more suitably in learning. . . ." To proceed in this way is (1) to proceed from what is composed to what is simple, and (2) from what is posterior to what is prior, and (3) this is to proceed from what is easier to what is more difficult.

(1) From what is composed to what is simple. The meaning of the word "being" in relation to the meaning of the word "essence" is as what is composed to what is simple. What is simple is as something one in the relation in which it is simple. What is composed is as something multiple in the relation in which it is composed. For example, consider a rectangle which has been divided into two parts, each of which has been left undivided. The rectangle can now be described as composed of two parts, and so as something multiple in relation to these parts. But each of the parts, viewed precisely as a part, is actually undivided, and can therefore be described as something simple, that is, as not composed; and so as something one. Now divide the parts, which entails considering each of them as in its own turn a whole. Each part can now be described as itself composed of parts, and so as something multiple in relation to *its* parts. And so, a whole in relation to its parts is something composed, and so is something multiple; a part in relation to its whole is something simple, and so is something one. Applied to the words "being" and "essence," this is to say that the meanings of the word "being" are many (at least two, in the context here) in relation to the meaning of the word

"essence." It is also to say that the meaning of the word "essence" is one in relation to the many meanings of the word "being"; that is, it is to say that one of the many meanings of the word "being" is the meaning from which the meaning of the word "essence" is taken.

(2) From the posterior to the prior. Our grasp of the many meanings of the word "being" in relation to our grasp of what we later call by the name "essence" is as what is posterior to what is prior. The word "being" used apropos of being which has essence is analytically (and temporally) prior to all other meanings of the word "being"; and this is why our grasp of what we later call by the name "essence" is analytically prior to all meanings of the word "being" other than its first meaning.

We have pointed out that the meaning to which we later give the name "being" is grasped in the temporally first meaning which a child forms, but that it is implicit and that it is unworded; recall the example of hot. The same thing is to be pointed out about the meaning to which we later give the name essence; it, too, is grasped in the temporally first meaning which a child forms, but it is implicit and it is left unworded. The same thing is to be said about the meaning to which we later give the name "existence."

Any process of analysis is such that it begins with a given that is composed or multiple, and seeks to distinguish each of its many elements and their interrelations. The word "being" is a given with many elements, a word with many interrelated meanings. The elements of a composite are analytically prior to the composite. It is obviously easier to know a composed thing, in the sense of identifying it as a composed thing, than it is to know its simple components, for its simple components come to be known only after the effort and pain of analysis.

(3) From what is easier. Human knowledge can advance only when it begins with what is easier for us men to know. And clearly what is known by all men, or by most men, is to be

counted among the things which are easier for us to know. It is
a fact of experience that we, all of us (or better, most of us),
know in some way the many meanings of the word "being"; for
we use this multiplicity, and with great accuracy, in everyday
discourse. It is also a fact of experience that all of us do not
know this multiplicity precisely as analyzed, i.e., we have not
reflected on the ways in which we use the word "being" (or the
expressions "what is" and "it is"), or have we taken the trouble
to notice the precise differences among them and to formulate
or articulate these differences. For, although we know how to
use these many meanings, we are hard put to it to formulate
them in answer to questions of the form, "But what exactly did
you mean by the word 'being' when you just used it?" Clearly,
then, an unanalyzed knowledge of the many meanings of the
word "being" is to be counted among the things which are
easier for us to know. To know this multiplicity as analyzed
means, among other things, to know the meaning of the word
"essence" as analyzed.

It is important to notice that St. Thomas at this point is
concerned with the meanings of words, those of the word
"being" and those of the word "essence"; he is not at this point
concerned with the essences of real things. This is why it is not
acceptable to interpret St. Thomas' reason for proceeding from
the meaning of being to that of essence in terms of the
distinction between essence and existence, as some do,[5] following Cajetan. What they say is, or at least appears to be,
acceptable, in a different context, in a context in which one has
already established the distinction between essence and existence in real beings; or at least in a context in which one is
concerned with the difference between the question What is
it? and the question Is it? The context, at this point in *On
Being and Essence,* is one in which the meanings of the word
"being" are about to be looked at, meanings which in fact
extend in their use beyond the realm of real beings (where

alone the distinction between essence and existence applies)
into the realm of beings of the mind. All one needs at this point
is to be able to use the word "being," and/or its verb form "is,"
in everyday discourse.

4

TWO USES OF THE WORD "BEING": (1) APROPOS OF REAL THINGS AND (2) APROPOS OF THE TRUTH OF PROPOSITIONS

It was pointed out above that most of us know the many
meanings of the word "being"; for we use this multiplicity of
meanings, and with great accuracy, in everyday discourse. Yet
our knowledge of this multiplicity is an unanalyzed knowledge. This unanalyzed knowledge will readily lend itself to
analysis if we begin with a consideration of things with which
we are familiar. We are all familiar, to some extent at least,
with the things appearing in the following list:

(a) Jack
(b) Jack's height
(c) the missing button on Jack's shirt; Jack's blindness
(d) nothing
(e) centaurs, phoenixes, witches, goblins
(f) genera, species, differences
(g) human souls, angels, God

What follows is an attempt to come to some understanding of
three fundamental uses of the word "being": (a) real being,
(b) being of reason, and (c) being as true (or true being, or
propositional being). Though St. Thomas does not here discuss
being of reason, we shall touch on it as an aid to understanding
the distinction which he does discuss, namely, propositional
being as opposed to real being.[6]

Consider, now, whether we would in fact say, or at least be

willing to say, that any member of the above list of seven is a being, or a thing (the word "thing" is more usual than the word "being," and an equivalent of it); or be willing to say of it, "it is," which is the same thing. Or, perhaps better, consider whether we would in fact, or at least be willing to, call by the word "being" or by the word "thing" anything for which we already have a word, but a word other than the word "being" or the word "thing." And consider why, i.e., consider what we mean by the word "being" or by the word "thing" when we predicate it. We shall limit this consideration to the above list of seven.

We would certainly call Jack a being (by Jack I mean this man, the one I'm pointing to, here and now before me). Why, now, would we call Jack a being? Clearly, because *he is,* in the sense of *he exists.* Or (which is to ask the same question) what do we mean by the word "being" when we say, "Jack is a being"? Clearly, we mean *he is* in the sense of *he exists.* Anything of which we say, or of which we are willing to say, "it is," in the sense of *it exists,* we also say, or are willing to say, of it, "it is a being."

Perhaps this can be made clearer. If a thing (in this case Jack) *is there,* in the sense of being there at all rather than in the sense of being there and not here, we call it a being. Thus, to call Jack a being, or to say of him, "he is," is to say that he *is there* in the sense just described. This is what everybody understands by the word "being," that which is, i.e., that which is there. Perhaps this too can be made clearer. *That which is,* in the sense of that which is there, is first of all something present to, or given to, and grasped by the senses, something seen, heard, tasted, etc.; something experienced.

We would not in fact, it seems, call Jack's height a being. Or would we at first be willing. On reflection, however, and perhaps with some hesitation, we would not be unwilling to say that it is something which *is there* in part of the sense described above—i.e., *there* as opposed to *not there at all*—but not in the sense in which we say that Jack is there, i.e., simply or without qualification. We would want to make a qualification; we would say it is there *in* something which is there simply, in this case *in* Jack. The word "in" would mean *as a modification* or *characteristic of.*

We would not call the missing button on Jack's shirt a being. Yet we would without hesitation refer to it as something which *is there.* Consider a mother addressing her four-year-old, just returned home from an afternoon of rough outdoor play. "How many missing buttons *are there* on your shirt today?" "I think *there are* three of them, Mother." But we would immediately point out that we do not mean *is there* in the sense in which Jack is there, nor in the sense in which Jack's height is there. We mean simply to call attention to the fact of the absence or privation of what in other circumstances would very likely be there in the way in which a part of Jack, say Jack's hand, is there, namely, the button. A button, like Jack's hand, is there as something positive (in St. Thomas' words a button *posits* [hence our word *positive*] something in reality: "aliquid in re ponit"), rather than as the absence of something positive. From this point of view, then, we would just as readily say that the missing button is something which is *not* there (and this is why we would not call it a being) as that it is something which *is* there; the missing button, from this point of view, is something we can talk about rather than something which is there. Similarly, in referring to Jack's blindness as something which *is there,* we mean to call attention to the fact of the absence of sight, which in other circumstances was, or may have been, there in the eye in the way in which Jack's height is now in Jack.

Though we would not call nothing a being, we would nonetheless, in certain circumstances, say that nothing *is there* with as little hesitation as we say that the missing button is there. Consider being sent to the living room to get the dog, discovering on arrival that it is not there, and exclaiming, "*There is* nothing in the living room!" It is clear that "there is" is not used in the sense in which we use it when we say that Jack is there, or in the sense in which we would say that Jack's height is there, or, lastly, in exactly the sense in which we would say blindness is there. For the word "blindness" is used to call attention to the absence of sight, and sight is a characteristic of something; whereas the exclamation "There is nothing in the living room!" is used to call attention to the absence of the dog, and the dog is rather a something than a characteristic of something. Moreover, to speak of the dog's absence from the living room is to indicate that the dog is to be found elsewhere; to speak of Jack's blindness, of the absence of sight in his eyes, is not to indicate that his sight is to be found elsewhere.

In other circumstances we would deny that nothing is there. Consider being asked the question, "Does nothing exist?" A characteristic response would be to say, "Look out there, and you will see that many things exist; there are trees, dogs, etc." This response indicates that the question was taken to mean, "Is it true that there is nothing in existence?" Consider, now, the question, "Can nothing exist?" There are at least two possible characteristic responses, according to at least two possible interpretations of the sense of the question: (1) "Yes, nothing can exist" in the sense of "Yes, it is possible that there be nothing in existence, i.e., it is not necessary that any of these things which I see about me be in existence, though it is a fact that they do exist." (2) "No, nothing cannot exist" in the sense of "No, that which is an absence of all things which exist simply, i.e., in the way in which Jack exists, cannot exist." To use the word "nothing" in this last sense—i.e., in the sense of an absence of all things which exist simply—is not to indicate that these simply existing things are to be found elsewhere any more than to speak of the absence of sight in a blind man's eyes is to indicate that his sight is to be found elsewhere. Absence, here, is absence in a strong sense, in the sense of a negation; and negation, here, may be taken in at least two senses, which give us two strong senses of the word "nothing:" (1) what does not exist and (2) what neither is nor can be. We would not call nothing, in either of these senses, a being. Nor would we say that nothing, in either of these senses, is an absence which *is there;* though we would speak of privations, like blindness, as absences which are there. The word "blindness" is taken to refer to an absence *in a subject,* ultimately in something positive which is there simply, i.e., in the way in which Jack is there. It is because the subject of a privation is there that we say that the absence is there, meaning *in the subject which is there.* But if all simply existing things are negated, and this is what is intended by the word "nothing" in both its strong senses, we do not speak of an absence which is there. Such an absence is not an absence *in* a simply existing subject; it is the absence *of* simply existing subjects, of all of them. Privations have been called relative negations, i.e., negations *in* things; nothing has been called absolute negation, i.e., the negation *of* things, of all of them.

As regards centaurs, phoenixes, and such, and the logical intentions—genus, species, and difference—we would not say that any of these is a being, that any of these is there, in the sense described above (see page 32). We, would, however, say that they are beings *of* (i.e., produced by) and *in* (i.e., modifications or characteristics of) the mind (and of the imagination). Logical intentions are *of* the mind in the sense that they are relations which the mind discovers among its concepts. Witches, phoenixes, and such are *of* the mind in the sense that the mind invents or creates them.

Apropos of human souls, angels, and God, we would certainly say that each is a being, that each is something which is there; but in a sense partly like, and partly unlike, the sense in which we say Jack is there. Jack is there sensibly; they are not. We cannot see, feel, touch, or hear them. And not only can we not see them, but they are such in themselves that they are not sensibly perceivable. But each is something which is there simply, i.e., in the way in which Jack is there as opposed to the way in which Jack's height is there.

To summarize, now, and to clarify: of Jack and of Jack's height we would say that each is something which is there as something positive (*aliquid in re ponit*) and as something sensibly perceived. Of human souls, of angels, and of God, we would say that each is something which is there as something positive, but not as something sensibly perceived. What is important here is that we would say of each of them that it is something which is there as something positive. Of Jack's blindness, and of the missing button on his shirt, we would say that each is an absence which is there, but this is only to say that neither is something positive which is there. If we would say that each is there, but not as an absence, "there" would mean *in the mind;* and "in the mind" would mean in the mind *in knowledge,* i.e., as a known content. So, too, if we would say that nothing is there; or that centaurs, phoenixes, and such are there; or that logical intentions are there; "there" would mean in the mind. If therefore, we say of a thing "it is," in the sense of being there as something positive, it is a real being (or a categorical or predicamental being); if we say of a thing "it is," in the sense of being in the mind, it is a being of reason.

But there is a third way in which we say of a thing "it is." [7] Consider two men disputing the statement that a phoenix is a mythical bird. "It is not," says the one. "It is," replies the other. "It is not," emphasizes the first. "It is," insists the other. Notice that one of these men has said of the phoenix "it is." Is "it is" being used here in the sense of real being? Clearly not. First of all, the phoenix is an imaginary being, or a being of reason. Secondly, the context of the dispute indicates that "it is" said of the phoenix means, It *is* a mythical bird, in the sense of *It is true* that the phoenix is a mythical bird; or, in this sense, namely, the statement "the phoenix is a mythical bird" is a true statement. The "is" of "it is" is the copula, the predicate not being explicitly stated. Here, "to be" means *to be true*. Here, to say "it is" is to insist that phoenix is a suitable subject for the predicate, mythical bird. Thus, not only is "it is" not used here in the sense of real being, but it is also not used in the sense of being of reason. "It is" is here used simply in the sense of *it is true*.

It is to be noticed that of anything at all for which we have a word we can say "it is" in this third sense of "it is." That is, we can make true affirmative statements, or at least statements which we feel are true, about anything for which we have a word, whether it is a real being or a being of reason. Anything, therefore, which is the subject of a true affirmative proposition can be said to be a true being or a propositional being, i.e., a being in a third sense of the word. A true being or a propositional being is anything which has a true affirmative statement made about it, precisely as having that statement made about it.

Thus, whether a thing is something which is there (real being) or not (being of reason), it is in any case something one can make statements about. One can make statements about beings of reason as well as about real beings; and precisely as having statements made about them, they are all in the mind. This is why one can say that both beings of reason and propositional beings, as such, are only in the mind. Still one must not say that propositional beings are the same as beings of reason; for beings of reason are found among the products of all three of the intellect's operations, whereas propositional beings pertain to the intellect's second operation, composing and dividing. Moreover, beings of reason can exist only in the mind, whereas what has a statement made about it can be real.

The word "being" means *what is;* and "what is" means *what is there* (real being); but "what is" also means *what is true.* The proposition "it is" means *it is there,* but "it is" also means *it is true.* These are the two uses of the word "being" (and of the word "is") which St. Thomas appears to have in mind when he writes here: "the word 'being,' taken without qualifiers, has two uses."

OTHER USES OF THE WORD "BEING"

In his *Commentary on Aristotle's Metaphysics* St. Thomas discusses a number of uses of the word "being." In addition to its use apropos of real beings and the truth of propositions, there is its use (1) in an essential sense as opposed to an accidental sense, its use (2) apropos of substances and accidents, and its use (3) in a potential sense as opposed to an actual sense:

He [Aristotle] says therefore that the word "being" is sometimes used essentially, sometimes accidentally. And we must note that this division of the word "being" is not the same as its division into substance and accident . . .[8] Then he divides the word "being" into potency and act . . .[9]

(1) Essential (*secundum se* or *per se*) as opposed to accidental (*secundum accidens* or *per accidens*). When we talk about things, we talk about them in statements or propositions; and in propositions a predicate is said of a subject. Sometimes the predicate is, or at least belongs as a part to, what the subject is; e.g., man is an animal, man is a substance;

whiteness is a color, whiteness is an accident. Being an animal and being a substance belong as a part to what man is. Being a color and being an accident belong as a part to what whiteness is. The "is" in such propositions has the sense of *is essentially;* e.g., "man is an animal" has the sense of *man is essentially an animal.* Sometimes the predicate does not belong to what the subject is; e.g., man is white, man is thin; whiteness is round, whiteness is human. The "is" in such propositions does not have the sense of *is essentially;* rather it has the sense of *is accidentally,* the sense of *happens to be.*

This can be put in another way. Combining predicates with subjects, we get the following descriptions: (a) the animal man, (b) the substance man, (c) the color whiteness, (d) the accident whiteness; and each of the four is said to be a being in an essential sense. We also get the following descriptions: (e) the white man, (f) the thin man, (g) the round whiteness, (h) the human whiteness; and each of these is said to be a being in an accidental sense.

The preceding can perhaps be made clearer if it is put in this way. Would we call any of the combinations just listed a being; e.g., would we call *the animal man* a being? Since each is something which is there as something positive, we would readily say that each of the eight is a being, but not in the same sense. We would immediately notice a basic difference between the first four, on the one hand, and the last four, on the other. In (a), whereas *being an animal* does not include in its explicit meaning *being a man, being a man* does include *being an animal.* The same thing is to be noted about the two notions expressed in (b), (c), and (d); one of each set of two includes in its explicit meaning the other; the two are essentially connected. And this is why, when each combination is called a being, it is called a being in an essential sense. In the last four neither of the two notions includes the other; the two are only accidentally connected. And this is why, when each of these combinations is called a being, it is called a being in an accidental sense.

Thus, when a thing (whether it is there in the sense in which Jack is there, or in the sense in which Jack's height is there) is described in terms of one or more of those of its characteristics which pertain to what it is, it is called, so described, a being in an essential sense. When, on the other hand, it is described in terms of characteristics, one at least of which does not pertain to what it is, it is called, so described, a being in an accidental sense, if it is called a being at all.

(2) Substance and accidents. If we say that man is a substance, not only do we see that being a substance belongs to what man is but we also understand what being a substance means. Indeed, we must understand what it means before we can see that it belongs to what man is. To be a substance means to be *what is* or *what exists,* to be there simply and as something positive, in the sense in which Jack is there (see page 32). So, too, if we say that whiteness is an accident, not only do we see that being an accident belongs to what whiteness is but we also understand what being an accident means. To be an accident means to be *what exists in* something which is *what exists simply,* to be there as something positive in what is there simply, to be there in the sense in which Jack's height is there. An accident is such that it is dependent on a subject, ultimately a substance, in which to exist. A substance is such that it is independent of a subject in which to exist; there is no subject in which it exists, for *it* is the existing subject; this is what it means to say that substance is *what exists.* What exists is substance; what exists in substance is accident. And this is why we readily predicate the word "being" of things which are there in the way in which Jack is there, and, only after hesitating and reflecting, of things which are there in the way in which Jack's height is there.

It is to be noticed that to say that a substance is independent in its existence is to attribute to it but a relative independence. A substance is not absolutely independent; if it were, it would be God. Its independence is only an independence *of a subject in which* to exist; it may have any number of other sorts of dependencies. For example, Jack depends on food, air, sunlight, God, all the while being independent *of a subject*.

(3) Actual and potential. The word "being" (or the word "is") is used in an actual sense when it is used apropos of things which are there in the sense we have in mind when we say, "There is a man on the corner," when there in fact is a man on the corner; i.e., in the sense of *being there at all* as opposed to *being there rather than somewhere else*. It is used in a potential sense when it is used apropos of things which are not there in the sense in which there is a man on the corner, but things which can be there in that way; e.g., as when with an acorn in my hand I say, "There's an oak tree in my hand," or as when with a five-dollar bill in my hand, which I have marked for clever investment, I say, "There's a million dollars in my hand."

It is to be noted that things of which we use the word "being" in a potential sense are such that considered *per se* they actually are not, like nothing (in its strongest sense; see page 35); but unlike nothing, they are such *per se* that they can be there actually. Nothing *per se* neither is nor can be. One must also notice that although things of which we use the word "being" in a potential sense do not actually exist *per se*, they do actually exist; but they exist *per accidens*, where *per accidens* means by virtue of the actual existence of another; e.g., the oak tree exists *per accidens*, i.e., by virtue of the actual existence of the acorn which I hold in my hand. Nothing, on the contrary, exists neither *per se* nor *per accidens*.

We have seen four divisions of the uses of the word "being" (these are divisions as well of uses of the word "is"):

$$\text{I. "being" } \begin{cases} 1) & \text{real} \\ 2) & \text{of reason} \\ 3) & \text{true} \end{cases}$$

$$\text{II. "being" } \begin{cases} 4) & \text{essential } (per\ se) \\ 5) & \text{accidental } (per\ accidens) \end{cases}$$

$$\text{III. "being" } \begin{cases} 6) & \text{substance} \\ 7) & \text{accident} \end{cases}$$

$$\text{IV. "being" } \begin{cases} 8) & \text{actual} \\ 9) & \text{potential} \end{cases}$$

To summarize, now, and to clarifiy: (1) The main point of division I is to focus on two basic uses of the word "being" when this word is used by itself or simply, i.e., without expressed verbal qualifiers of any kind. This, namely without expressed verbal qualifiers, is what St. Thomas means by the expression *per se* when he writes, "ens per se dicitur dupliciter," which we have translated in (4) (see page 21) as: "the word 'being,' taken without qualifiers, has two uses." The word "being," used by itself or simply, means *what is;* and it is used first of all in the sense of *what is there;* it is used secondly in the sense of *what is true.* The proposition "it is" is used first of all in the sense of *it is there;* it refers first of all to real things. "It is" is used secondly in the sense of *it is true;* in this sense it is used to insist on the truth of propositions. We do not use the word "being" by itself or simply (or the word "is") apropos of beings of reason. We qualify it to make it say being *of reason,* or we qualify it to make it say *non-*being, where the being which is negated means *what is there.*

(2) Divisions II, III, and IV are divisions of uses of the word "being" apropos of real beings. Their main point is to focus on the fact that the word "being," by itself or simply (so, too, the word "is"), is used first of all apropos of substances (secondly, apropos of accidents), first of all apropos of substances desig-

nated or described in terms of characteristics pertaining to what they are (secondly, apropos of substances designated in terms of characteristics not pertaining to what they are), first of all apropos of substances which are there actually (secondly, apropos of those which are there potentially).

FURTHER REMARKS ON BEING AS FIRST CONCEIVED BY THE INTELLECT

In terms of a reference to the uses of being as real, of reason, true, actual, and potential, one can express the *content* of being as first conceived in this way: what is actually there. Recall that our first intellectual knowledge is a knowledge whose explicit content is rooted in a sense experience and whose implicit content is being (see page 4). This implicitly grasped content, that to which we referred before as *something-there,* can now be expressed as *real actual being,* i.e., what is there actually. It is not to be expressed as *what can be there* (potential being), for *what can be there* is conceivable only by reference to what is there actually. Nor is it to be expressed as *what is there as an absence* (being of reason), for this too is conceivable only by reference to what is there actually. Nor, lastly, is it to be expressed as *what is* in the sense of *what is true,* for to make a true statement about what is there obviously presupposes a grasp of what is there, since conception is analytically prior to judgment.

In terms of a reference to substance and accident, one can express *that of which we first predicate* the content of being as first conceived: *what is there actually* is first predicated of *substances.* It is clear that the word "substance" does not mean the same as the word "being"; the word "substance" includes, but adds to, the meaning of the word "being." But it is also clear that the meaning of the word "being" is first predicated of that of which we also predicate the word "substance." A sign of this is the easily observable fact that when we say of something that it is a being, we say this without hesitation only of that which is a substance. Only that which is a substance is a being without qualification, or simply; i.e., without the qualification of being *in another,* as is an accident. If it is not a substance, we hesitate to call it a being. We do not hesitate to call Jack a being, but we do hesitate, at first at least, to call Jack's height a being. Further, if we consider the word "being" used as *subject* of a sentence, we can easily observe that when we say something about a being, we say it about those things which are substances; for example, when we say all beings are God's effects, *all beings* refers to all substances.

5. So, the word "essence" is not taken from the word "being" used in the second way; for some things which do not have an essence are called beings in this way, as is clear in the case of privations. Rather, the word "essence" is taken from the word "being" used in the first way. It is for this reason that the Commentator says in the same place that the word "being" used in the first way is what signifies the essence of a real thing.

6. And because the word "being" used in this way is used apropos of what is divided into the ten genera, as we have said, the word "essence" must signify something common to all natures, by means of which (natures) diverse beings are placed into diverse genera and species; as, for example, humanity is the essence of man, and so with other things.

7. And because that by which a real thing is constituted in its proper genus or species is what is signified by the definition expressing what the real thing is, philoso-

phers sometimes use the word "quiddity" for the word "essence." This is what the Philosopher often calls *what something was to be,* i.e., that by which it belongs to something to be what it is.

8. It is also called form, in the sense in which the word "form" signifies the full determination of each real thing, as Avicenna says in the second book of his *Metaphysics.*

9. Further, it is given another name, nature, taking the word "nature" in the first of the four ways given by Boethius in his book *On the Two Natures.* In this way, whatever can in any way be grasped by the intellect is called a nature. For a real thing is not intelligible except through its definition and essence.

10. The Philosopher, too, says in the fifth book of the *Metaphysics* that every substance is a nature. But the word "nature" taken in this way appears to signify the essence of a real thing according as it has an ordering to the thing's proper operation; and no real thing lacks a proper operation.

11. The name "quiddity," however, is taken from the fact that what is signified by the definition is the essence. But it is called essence from the fact that through it and in it a real being has existence.

5–11

In (5) through (11) St. Thomas turns to the meanings of the word "essence." And whereas his concern with the word "being" was a concern with basic uses at the level of everyday discourse, his concern with the word "essence" is at the level of philosophical discourse. In (5) he formulates a meaning in terms of a reference to real being and to true being. In (6) through (11) he points out that the referent of the word "essence" has differently been described and named; he records a number of these names and descriptions.

Meanings of the Word "Essence"

Having noted that the word "being" (and the word "is") is used apropos of real beings and apropos of true beings (i.e., to signify the truth of propositions), St. Thomas points out in (5) that the meaning of the word "essence" is taken from the word "being" used in the first way, i.e., from its use apropos of real beings. This means that essence is that which *all that is real being* has. The meaning of the word "essence" can perhaps more clearly and precisely be formulated in terms of a reference to both of the uses of the word "being" distinguished in (4); thus, essence is that which *all that is real being* has and *all that is true being* has not. It can also be formulated in terms of a reference to beings of reason; thus, essence is that which real beings have, and beings of reason have not.

What follows in (6) through (11) can be taken as answers to the question which one naturally wants to ask apropos of the meaning of the word "essence" given in (5). The question is this, Well, what is it that all that is real being has, and all that is true being has not?

The answer proposed in (6) is this: something by virtue of which real beings can be differentiated from one another and can be placed into one or other of the ten categories which were discovered, apparently, by Aristotle's philosophical reflections on everyday discourse (in any case recorded by him) and which are easily recognized as present in everyday English. Placeability into a category is being taken here in the sense in which a genus or a species is placed into a category, as opposed to the sense in which a principle or a part is placed into a category; e.g., prime matter is placed into the category of substance as a principle of substance, not as a species or a genus of substance. This description of essence goes by the name "essence."

The answer given in (7) is this: something which can furnish the answer to the question "What is it?" This description goes by the name "quiddity." That by which a real being can be placed into a category is what is put into the definition which expresses *what* the thing is (hence the name "quiddity"). This is what St. Thomas, following Aristotle, often calls the *quod quid erat esse*, or *quod quid est esse*, or *quod quid est*, or simply *quid* (*rei*).[10] And it is to be distinguished from the *quid nominis* at least in this respect: to ask the question "What is it?" (the question about the quiddity of a real being) presupposes knowledge of the fact of the existence of the being; whereas the question "What does the word mean?" (the question of the *quid nominis*) is presupposed to asking the question "Is there such a thing?" (the question of *an est*).

In (8) we are told that essence is something which constitutes the total determination or identity of a real being, in the sense of the totality of the thing's shared characteristics. This description, Avicenna's, goes by the name "form," not in the sense of the form of the part (*forma partis*), which is nothing other than the substantial form [11] of a real being, and which is but part of its total identity, but in the sense of the form of the whole (*forma totius*), which is nothing other than what is expressed in the definition.

In (9) we are told essence is something by which real beings can be grasped by the intellect, i.e., by which they are intelligible. This description, Boethius', goes by the name "nature." A real being is intelligible only by virtue of its essence, which is expressed in its definition.

In (10) essence is something by which real beings are ordered to the performance of their proper operations or activities. This description, Aristotle's, goes by the name "nature." What a real thing does is determined by what it is.

In (11) essence is something by virtue of which real beings *are there* as something *positive*. This description goes by the name "essence." And it is to be taken as the most fundamental of the answers to the question "What is it that all that is real being has, and all that is true being has not?" For, first of all, their being there as something positive is that by which real beings can be differentiated from one another (the answer given in [6]); it is that which furnishes the content of their definition (the answer in [7]); it is that which constitutes their total identity (the answer in [8]); it is that by which they are graspable by the intellect (the answer in [9]); it is that whereby they are ordered to the performance of their proper activities (the answer in [10]). Secondly, beings of reason can be said to share with real beings, at least in some way, though not *per se*, the following: (a) placeability in a genus and in a species—e.g., the relation genus is placed in the genus "logical intentions of the intellect's first operation"—(of course, beings of reason are not placed in a genus within one or other of the ten categories recorded by Aristotle); (b) definability of some kind; (c) a total identity of some kind; (d) a graspability by the intellect of some kind; and (e) the fact that they do according to what they are, e.g., a centaur is thought to do according to what it is thought to be. What beings of reason lack (and this is what true being, considered precisely as true being, also lacks) is *being there* as *something positive;* what they lack is something by virtue of which *to be there.*

Essence, thus, is what all that is real being has, and all that is true being has not; and the name "essence" is taken from its fundamental character as that through which and in which a real being *is there:* "But it is called essence from the fact that through it and in it a real being has existence."

CHAPTER TWO

12. Because the word "being" is used absolutely and with priority of substances, and only posteriorly and with qualification of accidents, essence is in substances truly and properly, in accidents only in some way with qualification.

13. Further, some substances are simple and some are composed, and essence is in each. But essence is in simple substances in a truer and more noble way, according to which they also have a more noble existence; for they—at least that simple substance which is first, and which is God—are the cause of those which are composed. But because the essences of the simple substances are more hidden from us, we ought to begin with the essences of composed substances, so that we may progress more suitably in learning from what is easier.

12–13

In (12) and (13) St. Thomas does two things. (1) He points out the order in which he will approach the second of the three tasks set out in the introduction, the investigation of the being and essence of various sorts of real thing. He will examine

49

substances first, accidents last (accidents are done in chapter
seven); among substances, composed substances first, simple
substances last (simple substances are done in chapter five);
among simple substances, the human soul first, the intelligences and God last. (2) He gives a reason why (a) essence is
truly and properly in substances, whereas only in some
qualified way in accidents, and (b) why the being of the
simple substances is more noble than that of composed substances.

THE REASONS FOR THE ORDER IN APPROACHING THE SECOND TASK

Apropos of investigating substances before accidents, it is to be
noticed that St. Thomas does not suggest this order because it
is easier for us to come to know, and to define, the essence of a
substance than that of an accident. For some accidents are *per
se* sensible. Rather the reason is one of necessity. Accidents
depend on substances, as on a subject, for their being. Since a
statement of the essence of a thing should reveal the being of
the thing defined—i.e., its condition in the world—it is impossible to come to know, and to define, the essence of an accident
without a previous, or at least concomitant, effort to come to
know, and to define, the essence of the substance on which it
depends as on a subject. Since it is difficult, perhaps impossible, to come to know two things concomitantly, substance
should be investigated before accidents.

Apropos of investigating composed substances before simple
ones, it is to be said again (see page 23) that intellectual
knowledge about sensibly perceivable things is easier for us
than intellectual knowledge about things removed from sense
observation. And lastly, apropos of investigating the human
soul before the intelligences and God, it is to be noticed that
each man has an inner and immediate experience of the
thought and volitional activities of his soul; not so as regards

the thought and volitional activities of the intelligences and of God. Hence an investigation of the essence of the human soul is easier for us.

A POSSIBLE OBJECTION

The reason which St. Thomas appears to give here for claiming that essence is properly in substances, but only in some way in accidents, is the fact that the word "being" is said analogically of substances and accidents: "Because the word 'being' is used absolutely and with priority of substances, and only posteriorly and with qualification of accidents." If this is in fact his reason, one must object to it on the grounds that priority and posteriority in naming and predication is of itself no guarantee of a corresponding priority and posteriority in the reality of the things so named, as St. Thomas himself points out elsewhere.[1] We name things in the order in which we know them, and what we come to know first may well in reality have a posterior position; for example, we know and name creatures before we come to know and name God. But perhaps St. Thomas can be interpreted as saying here in (12) that *to say* absolutely and with priority that substances are beings—i.e., that there is nothing on which substances depend in the way in which accidents depend on substances—is equivalent to *saying* that essence is in them properly and truly. And this can be accepted, for the essence of a thing is indeed the source and the measure of its being. And then one can say either, as St. Thomas does here, (a) because being is said absolutely and with priority of substances, essence is in them properly and truly, or (b) because essence is in substances properly and truly, being is said of them absolutely and with priority. And the "because" will not be functioning as assigning a reason, but as indicating an equivalence. Or perhaps St. Thomas can be interpreted as understanding here that the word "being" *is said* absolutely and with priority of substances because substances *are* beings absolutely and with priority, in a way similar to the way in which we *say* that an apple is red because it *is* red. And *saying* that something is so because it *is* so is clearly acceptable. Then one can say that because being is said absolutely and with priority of substances (and this *is said* because substances *are* beings absolutely and with priority), essence is in them properly and truly. And the first "because" functions as indicating an equivalence; the second, as indicating that what *is said* is verified by what *is*. The second "because" allows one to say *say*, but to mean *is*.

His reason for maintaining that the being of simple substances is more noble than that of composed substances is not one of predication or naming. Their being is more noble because their essence is more noble; and their essence is more noble because they are the causes—or at least the first among them, God, is the cause—of composed substances. There is no quarrel with this reason since essence is indeed that according to which a thing has being. Similarly, the being of substances is more noble than that of accidents because their essence is more noble; and their essence is more noble because they are the causes of accidents (as will be explained below in chapter seven), at least as subjects in which accidents need to exist.

The Word "Being" Is an Analogical Word.

St. Thomas' reason (perhaps) here for maintaining that essence is properly in substances, but only in some way with qualification in accidents, invites one to ask the question, What is an analogical word? An analogical word is conveniently understood in reference to the univocal word and to the equivocal word.[2] A univocal word is a word said of many things with a meaning wholly the same; for example, the word "animal" said of John, Fido, and this horse is said of each with wholly the same meaning, namely, sensitive organism. An equivocal word is a word said of many things with meanings wholly diverse, for example, the word "pen" said of the writing instrument and of the enclosure for swine. An analogical word is a word said of many things with a meaning which is partly the same and partly different; different because each meaning includes a different relation; the same because each meaning includes a same meaning (which is for us humans, in some given context, the first meaning of the word) as a same point of reference. For example, the word "healthy" is said of many things in this way. Healthy said of animal is included in the meaning of healthy said of medicine; healthy said of medicine means cause of health in the animal. Further, healthy said of urine means sign of health in the animal; healthy said of climate means conservative of health in the animal. Healthy said of animal is the first meaning of the word "healthy," and it is included in all posterior meanings of the word "healthy."

The word "being" is an analogical word. Its first predication and meaning is apropos of real being which is actual substance (see page 40–42). The meaning of the word "being" so predicated is included in all posterior meanings of the word "being." For example, being said of accident means *that which exists in being* (the word "being" in the expression *that which exists in being* is being as said of substance) (for convenience, we shall use the word "substance" to stand for real being which is actual substance); being said of blindness, a privation, means *absence of sight,* and sight is an accident which is what exists in being (being, as said of substance); being said of nothing means *negation of being* (being, as said of substance).[3]

The extension of an analogical word from its first predication and meaning to its posterior predications and meanings indicates what is first in our knowledge and what is posterior in our knowledge. It also points to the fact that we name things according as we know them, so that we name first what we know first. It is to be noted again that what is first in our knowledge, in the context of analogical words, may or may not be what is first in the reality of the things of which the analogical word is said (see page 51). As regards the word "being," substance is prior to accident in our knowledge (intellectual) as well as in their reality. It is prior to accident in our knowledge in at least two senses: (1) in the sense that our temporally first knowledge (all our knowledge by intellect is via sense experience) is a knowledge whose explicit content is a sense experience (not an intellectual grasp) of a sensible accident and whose implicit content is an intellectual grasp of *something-there,* i.e., being without qualification (see pages 4–5); (2) in the sense that it is included in the definition of the essence of an accident (see page 50). It is prior to accident in their reality in the sense that substance is that on which accidents depend, at least as on a proper subject, for their existence. The word "substance" (as well as the word "being") is said of composed substances before it is said of simple substances, since composed substances are prior in our knowledge; in their reality, however, simple substances are prior to composed substances. The word "essence" is used first to designate the essence of substances, then that of accidents; the essence of material substances, then that of immaterial substances.

FURTHER REMARKS ON SECOND INTENTIONS

Having considered the character of the analogical word, by way of contrast with the univocal and the equivocal word, one can very conveniently expand, and thereby make clearer, the notion of a second intention.

The description of second intention given above (see pages 16–20) is but a *first* description, i.e., a description in terms of a reference to the first context in which one notices second intentions. This is the context of *first intentions,* of concepts about things in the real world.

As one pursues an investigation of second intentions in the study of logic, relations among second intentions themselves are very quickly noticed. For example, it is easy to notice the relation of genus between the second intention supposition, on the one hand, and its ordinarily distinguished types—namely, proper and improper supposition (metaphor)—on the other hand. The relation of genus is also noticed within proper supposition, between proper, on the one hand, and its types—namely, real, logical, and material—on the other hand. Such relations are clearly second intentions arising out of the plurality of our concepts, in this case a plurality of second intentions based immediately on a plurality of first intentions. At this point, one can give a second description of second intention, a description in terms of a reference to a second and broader context. Second intentions are certain sorts of relations among any sorts of concepts, whether first intentions or not.

There is a third context in which one can describe second intentions, a context conveniently exemplified by the analogical word. For a proper understanding of this context one must notice carefully that the human way of knowing (the human way of knowing is what gives rise to second intentions) involves not only (1) a *plurality* of concepts (we cannot know reality by but *one* concept) but also (2) the formation of this plurality with *dependence* on *referents* in the real world (our knowledge in this respect is quite unlike that of God) and (3) the use of *words*. In this context second intentions can be described as certain sorts of relations among anything and everything involved in the human way of knowing, so long as *at least one* of the relata is a *concept*. Thus the analogical word (so too the univocal word and the equivocal word) involves a triadic relation, a relation among three terms, *only one* of which is a *concept;* the other two are a *word* and the *referents*. In the case of the analogical word (as the word "healthy" previously discussed) the relation goes by the name of *anal-*

ogy, and is described as the relation which obtains among a word, concept, and referent when the same word is said of different referents with a concept or meaning which is partly the same and partly different (see page 53 for the exact sense of this partial sameness and partial difference).

It is clear that the three contexts and the three corresponding descriptions of second intention are so related that the second includes the first, and the third the second; hence the third also the first. Thus the third description of second intention is to be taken as the most inclusive one.

Apart from expanding, and thereby making clearer, the notion of a second intention, it is important to notice that it is in a sense misleading to say that logic is about second intentions as about a subject. For second intentions are *concepts* about certain sorts of relations among anything and everything involved in the human way of knowing. It is rather the noticed relations themselves which are the subject of logic. Here, as in any case in which the intellect is concerned to investigate something or other, it forms concepts about those things. But the concepts are the means by which the investigation is carried on, and not the things themselves which are investigated. Just as philosophy is not about first intentions, but rather about things in the real world by means of different sorts of first intentions; so too, logic is not about second intentions, but rather about the noticed relations themselves. And second intentions become the means by which the investigation is carried on. Most properly put, logic investigates *secunda intellecta* (see text on page 17), and not *secundas intentiones.*

SOME REMARKS ON BEING AS SUBJECT OF METAPHYSICS

There are at least two reasons at this point for saying some things about being as the subject of metaphysics: (1) what has been said so far in this interpretation, for some of what has been said is useful in the attempt to pinpoint what metaphysics investigates as a subject, and (2) what is yet to be said in this interpretation, for some of what is yet to be said has to do with investigating being as the subject of metaphysics. It is not uncommon to want to know what is to be investigated before the investigation begins, in at least the sense in which one knows that what is to be investigated is trees, if he can point to certain objects and identify them as trees.

The divisions apropos of the word "being" recorded above (pages 42–43) make possible a convenient identification, and one in terms of what everybody knows, of what the primary concern of metaphysics is: the acquisition of scientific knowledge about *per se* real being.

Metaphysics, or first philosophy, has been an inquiry into real or extramental being from its very beginning among the ancient Greeks. This is why true being (as well as beings of the mind like witches and goblins, and like logical intentions) does not belong to the primary concern of metaphysics; for true being, precisely as true, is only in the mind. This is not to say that true being is in no way a concern of metaphysics. Metaphysics *is* concerned with true being; metaphysics has its clarificatory function apropos of the meanings of the word "being" (see pages 11–16). Metaphysics is concerned with understanding what it means to be a true being, for such an understanding is indispensable to its primary work, namely, the work of investigating real being.

Metaphysics, or first philosophy, is scientific knowledge. This is why what is *per accidens* in real being cannot belong to the primary concern of metaphysics. (Still metaphysics is concerned with understanding what it means to be *per accidens;* this concern, like the concern with what it means to be a true being, falls to metaphysics in its clarificatory function apropos of the meanings of the word "being".) Every science has a subject which it attempts to investigate, and not in just any way, but in this determinate way: by elaborating a definition of this subject (or at least a notion or meaning, if a definition is impossible), and by using this notion to come to a knowledge of (1) the properties of the subject and of their necessary connection with the subject, and (2) of the extrinsic cause(s) of the subject (if it has any). Quite clearly, one can neither elaborate a notion of being, nor come to a knowledge of its properties, nor of its extrinsic causes, in terms of what is *per accidens* in relation to it. For what is *per accidens* is irrelevant or beside the point, and hence scientifically useless. For example, cheese is often sold in supermarkets in various triangular shapes; nonetheless one can learn nothing scientific about cheese as cheese in terms of the way it is shaped.

The distinction between what is first in our knowledge and what is first in reality (see pages 53–54) makes possible a clear and simple way of stating what metaphysics is primarily about: what is first in reality. Metaphysics is primarily about substance, as about a subject, and secondarily about accidents, since substance is prior to accident in their reality (not only in our knowledge). This means that metaphysics is primarily about substance as substance, the properties of substance, and the extrinsic cause(s) of substance. To be sure, since the Extrinsic Cause of substance is prior in reality to substance, metaphysics is primarily about this Extrinsic Cause, though not as about its subject. Thus, one way [4] of saying that being as being is the subject of metaphysics is to say that substance as substance is its subject. St. Thomas puts it in this way:

Then he [Aristotle] states that the principal consideration of this science [metaphysics] is about substances, though all beings fall into its consideration. And he gives the following reason. Any science about many things, which are said in reference to some one first thing, is properly and principally the science of that first thing, on which the others depend for existence, and for their name; and this is true in every case. But substance is this first thing

among all beings. The philosopher, therefore, who considers all
beings must, first of all and principally, have in his consideration
the principles and causes of substances; and consequently his consideration is first of all and principally about substances.[5]

14. In composed substances there are form and matter, for
    example, in man soul and body.
15. But we cannot say that either one of them alone may
    be said to be the essence. That matter alone is not the
    essence of a real thing is clear, since through its
    essence a real thing is knowable and assigned to a
    species or to a genus. But matter alone is neither a
    principle of knowlege, nor is it that by which some-
    thing is assigned to a genus or to a species; rather a
    thing is so assigned by reason of its being something
    actual.
16. Neither can the form alone of a composed substance
    be said to be its essence, although some try to assert
    this. For it is evident from what has been said that
    essence is what is signified by the definition of a real
    thing. And the definition of natural substances con-
    tains not only form, but matter as well; otherwise
    natural definitions and mathematical ones would not
    differ.

14–16

In (14) St. Thomas turns to part of the second task of this
treatise, to the investigation of the being and essence of
composed substances. In (14) he begins by noticing that
matter and form are found in composed substances. In (15) he
argues that matter alone cannot be the essence of a composed
substance; in (16) that form alone cannot be the essence.

To Investigate the Essence of a Thing Is to Investigate Its Being

The second of the three tasks of this treatise, as these three tasks are set down in the introduction (see page 1), is to show how *being and essence* are found in diverse things, in substances, both composed and simple, and in accidents. Yet the treatise pursues and completes this task by showing only how essence (not how both being and essence) is found in diverse things. At the beginning of chapter four we read: "Having seen what is signified by the word "essence" in composed substances [this is a reference to what was done in chapters two and three], we must see how a composed essence is related to the notion of the genus, of the species, and of the difference." (It is clear from chapter four that the third task, too, of this treatise is pursued and completed in terms of essence alone, rather than in terms of being and essence both.) Chapter five opens in this way: "It remains, now, for us to see in what way essence is in separated substances, namely in the soul, in the intelligences, and in the First Cause." As chapter six begins, St. Thomas writes: "Having seen the preceding, it is clear how essence is found in diverse things. For we find that substances have essence in three ways." The sentence which opens chapter seven reads: "What remains now is to see how essence is in accidents; how it is in all substances has been discussed." Is there a reason for this, i.e., for showing only how essence is found in diverse things, and not both being and essence? It seems that there is; and the reason appears quite clear and direct. The second task of this treatise is a task concerned with real being; it is not a task concerned with true being. And what is it that characterizes real being? Essence is what characterizes real being; that is, real being is what has essence. Clearly, then, to understand how diverse real things have essence is also to understand how they have being, for essence is that according to which real beings are beings.

It Is Useful for Doing Metaphysics to Have Done Some Natural Philosophy.

The goal of metaphysics, and of *On Being and Essence* as well, is to discover how essence is found in immaterial things. But one cannot begin to understand what it means to be immaterial if one does not first understand what it means to be material; such is the way with all expressions which contain a relation of negation. It is thus quite useful, in a sense even necessary, for doing metaphysics to have done some philosophy about natural or material things. One must therefore come to a clear understanding of what it means to say of a thing that it is a material thing, not only for the sake of the goal of metaphysics but also for the sake of a proper understanding of the reasons given in (15) by St. Thomas for maintaining that matter alone cannot be the essence of a composed substance.

What follows here is an attempt to walk the path whereby one comes by the knowledge that matter and form are found in sensible or natural substances; to walk this path is to come to understand why natural substances can be called *material* substances, and why they can be called *composed* substances. We call the substances about us by different names, and for different reasons; we call them *natural* substances when we have it in mind to contrast them with artificial substances; *sensible* substances when we focus on the fact that they are given to us in sense experience, perhaps in a context in which we want by a negative contrast to characterize God and the angels as nonsensible substances; *corporeal* substances when we focus on the fact that they are three-dimensional things. Thus natural substances, sensible substances, corporeal substances, and composed substances are the same reality (*idem secundum rem*), but diversely described (*different ratione*).

In order to come to understand why natural substances can be called *composed* substances, one must allow that natural substances exist, i.e., that there are such things as natural substances (their existence is given to us through sense experience). One must also allow that natural substances are things which undergo changes of two basic sorts, corresponding to the distinction of being into substance and accidents: (1) accidental change, which is such that the natural substance which undergoes it does not cease to be what it was or does not simply cease to be, e.g., a man becomes educated; (2) substantial change, which is such that the natural substance which undergoes it ceases to be what it was or simply ceases to be, e.g., a man dies. If one conducts an inductive analysis of change,[6] first of accidental change (since this is easier) and then of substantial change, one will notice a number of things. Consider the accidental change when marble becomes a statue, and notice these things:

(1) the change (marble becomes statue) can be described in at least one other way, namely, what is not statue becomes statue, so that both descriptions are descriptions of numerically one and the same change.

(2) there are two terms: the term from which the change proceeds—i.e., that which is there before the change begins, here the marble—and the term toward which the change tends, i.e., that which is there after the change has been completed, here the statue.

(3) the term from which is one in number, but at least two in description. The term from which here can be described as *marble* and as *what is not statue;* these are two descriptions of numerically one and the same term from which.

(4) something, a natural substance, survives in the term toward which which was in the term from which, here the marble.

(5) what survives, here the marble, is a natural substance such that it *can acquire and maintain* the form (here, the shape of the

statue) which appears in the term toward which. Not just any sort of natural substance can be made into a statue, e.g., water in its liquid state.

(6) we can define *form:* that in the term toward which by virtue of which the term toward which is differentiated from the term from which; here the shape of statue.

(7) we can define *matter:* what survives the change and has a potentiality (i.e., can acquire and maintain) for the form which appears in the term toward which, here the marble.

(8) we can define *privation:* an absence *in* the term from which *of* the form which appears in the term toward which; here what we described as *what is not statue.*

The accidental change of marble becoming statue is a change from the realm of art. Changes in this realm are easier for us to understand than changes in the natural realm, since it is we humans who make artefacts. Consider, now, the natural change (accidental) man becomes educated. This, too, can be described in at least one other way, namely, what is not educated becomes educated. Here, too, we have a term from which which is one in number but at least two in description, namely, *man* and *what is not educated;* we also have a term toward which, namely, educated. Here, too, something survives the change, namely, man, and man is a natural substance capable of acquiring and of maintaining education. Here the form is education; the matter is man, and the privation is what is not educated.

Consider, now, a substantial change: seed becomes animal. This can be described in at least one other way, namely, what is not animal becomes animal. What we describe as *seed* and what we describe as *what is not animal* is numerically one and the same thing, numerically one and the same term from which. Now, what can be said about what survives? Here is

where substantial change becomes more difficult to analyze
than accidental change. That something survives is clear;
otherwise substantial change would not be an instance of
change. Is what survives the *natural substance* which was the
term from which, as is the case in the change of marble
becoming statue, and in the change of man becoming educated? It cannot be the natural substance which is the term
from which, for that is seed, and seed does not survive, for
what we have in the term toward which is not seed but animal.
If seed survived, then the change of seed becoming animal
would obviously not be a substantial change. This much, at
least, can be said: whatever has survived is such that it can
acquire and maintain (has a potentiality for) the form of
animal, that in the term toward which whereby it differs from
the term from which. But the form of animal is clearly an
intrinsic part of the term toward which, namely, animal. From
this we can see that whatever has survived from the term from
which is also a part of animal, that part of animal which is
related to the other part—namely, to the form of animal—as
what can maintain that form. Thus, whereas in accidental
change what survives—i.e., the matter—is a *complete* natural
substance; in substantial change what survives is but a constituent of the newly generated natural substance. The matter in
substantial change can be defined as: that constituent of the
newly generated natural substance which has survived from
the term from which and which is related to the form of the
natural substance which is the term toward which as potentiality to actuality.

To make this clearer, one must notice that we have in fact
touched on two senses of the potentiality-actuality relation,
which we should now explicitly distinguish. In the first sense,
one is considering the matter in the state in which it was *before*
the change took place. Marble, before it became a statue, is
describable as something perfect*ible* in relation to a perfection

(the shape of the statue which appears after the change): as something which *can acquire* but *does not now possess* the form. Considered *after* the change, the marble can be described as something perfect*ed* (no longer simply perfect*ible* as before) in relation to a perfection, as something *now in possession* of the form. This is the second sense of the potentiality-actuality relation; and it must be properly understood. Though *now in possession* of the form, marble as marble has no claim on this form, does not require this form; otherwise it could never be found without it. This form is something over and above the nature of marble; it adds something to marble as marble, and what it adds can be called a perfection.

To summarize, now, and to add clarifications. In accidental change the form is an accidental form, or accident (accident is the same as accidental form, and accident is here taken as opposed to substance). Accidental form, though existing in substance, is not a part of substance. In substantial change the form is a substantial form; substantial form is the differentiating part of the natural substance which has come to be. Substantial form is that whereby a natural substance which has come to be first begins actually to exist and also that whereby the natural substance continues in existence. In accidental change the matter is a complete natural substance with a potentiality for the acquired accidental form; this is in accord with the definition of accidental change. In substantial change the matter is but part of the newly generated natural substance, that part related to substantial form as potentiality to actuality in the second sense described above; the matter in substantial change has come to be called *prime,* or *first, matter.* In accidental change the privation is privation of accidental form; in substantial change the privation is privation of substantial form. In accidental change there may but need not be, in the term from which, an accidental form in addition to the matter and the privation; e.g., in the accidental change of man becoming educated there is none, whereas in the accidental change of green apple becoming a red apple there is a form (green). In substantial change there must be a form in the term from which in addition to the matter and the privation, for if the term from which had no form (this is substantial form), it would be a nonexistent term. Substantial form is that in a natural substance which accounts for the fact of its existence.

What has just been said has been said apropos of the natural substance *which has come to be* in substantial change; that is, any natural substance which comes to be in substantial change is a substance intrinsically composed of prime matter and substantial form, which are related within the substance as potentiality to actuality in the second sense described above (page 63). But the same thing can be said about the substance which *ceases to be* in substantial change, the substance from which the substance which comes to be comes to be, the term from which. For the substance which is the term from which is an existing term, and it differs from the substance which is the term toward which; hence, it has a substantial form to account for this existence and for this difference. And that which survives in the term toward which was *before the change* in the term from which; hence, it was *then in possession* of the substantial form of the term from which. Which is to say that what survives was *before the change* related to the substantial form of the term from which as potentiality to actuality in the second sense described above, and at the same time was related to the substantial form of the term toward which as potentiality to actuality in the first sense described above. It could not of its own nature have had a claim on that prior substantial form, for if it did, it could not have survived without that prior substantial form.

Thus, for a thing to be a material substance is, in one way of putting it, for it to have prime matter as part of what it is; and prime matter is potentiality for substantial form in both the senses described above. For a substance to be immaterial is, in one way of putting it, for it *not* to have prime matter as part of what it is. Similarly, for a thing to be a composed substance is for it to have prime matter and substantial form as its intrinsic components, as the components of what it is. And for a thing to be a simple substance is for it *not* to have prime matter and substantial form as its intrinsic components.

Having begun here in (14) by noticing that matter and form are found in composed substances, St. Thomas uses man as an example: "for example, in man soul and body." It is clear that he intends *soul* to exemplify form, and *body* to exemplify matter. That the soul of man is a substantial form is clear, but that man's body is prime matter is not clear. The problem of the relation between man's body and prime matter will be considered below (see pages 95–100, especially page 96, [5]) in an appropriate context.

NEITHER MATTER ALONE, NOR FORM ALONE, CAN BE THE ESSENCE OF A COMPOSED SUBSTANCE.

To make clear why matter alone cannot be the essence of a composed substance, one must recall what the word "essence" means. Among other meanings, it has this one: that in real beings in virtue of which they can be grasped by the intellect, i.e., in virtue of which they are intelligible (see page 47). Essence is thus something in a real being which is *of itself* intelligible to the human intellect, as opposed to being intelligible by virtue of something else; in a way similar to the way in which colors are perceivable by sight by virtue of light, whereas light is perceivable by sight neither by color nor by something other than color, but simply by virtue of itself (light). But matter, prime matter, is not of itself intelligible, for of itself prime matter is potentiality for substantial form.

Thus, it is intelligible only by virtue of, or in terms of a reference to, substantial form. Potentialities, generally speaking, are intelligible only by virtue of the actualities to which they are related. Prime matter thus cannot be the essence of a composed substance because it cannot be a "principle of knowledge."

What has just been argued can perhaps be argued somewhat differently. Since prime matter of itself is potentiality for substantial form, it follows that substantial form is no part of what prime matter is of itself. This means that prime matter does not exist of itself. Hence it is not of itself intelligible, for only what exists of itself is intelligible of itself. Thus, prime matter alone cannot be the essence of a composed substance.

The word "essence" also has this meaning: that in real beings by virtue of which they can be differentiated from one another and can be placed into one or other of the ten categories (see page 46). But prime matter of itself is potentiality. Since, therefore, only that which is actuality can differentiate and categorize, prime matter alone cannot be the essence of a composed substance. Further, matter is what all natural substances have in common, and what is common to many cannot be the principle of their differentiation. Briefly, since prime matter of itself cannot fulfill the functions of essence, it cannot alone be the essence.

Why, now, is it that form alone cannot be the essence of a composed substance? The word "essence" also has this meaning: that which is placed in a definition expressing what a real thing is (see page 47). Now, the fact is that definitions of natural substances include not only form but matter as well. Thus, form alone cannot be the essence. Otherwise, explains St. Thomas, definitions of natural entities would not differ from definitions of mathematical entities. But this explanation appears to be without point, for though definitions of mathematical entities are in terms of form alone without matter, this is

form in the category "quantity"; the form of a natural substance, by contrast, is form in the category "substance," i.e., a
substantial form. But perhaps he means that whereas the form
in terms of which mathematical entities are defined can be
understood without understanding matter, though it cannot
exist except in matter, the form in terms of which natural
entities are defined cannot be understood without understanding the matter in which it must exist. So that if form alone
were the essence of a natural substance, the definitions of
natural entities and those of mathematical entities would have
this in common that they are expressed by a form which can be
understood without understanding the matter on which it
depends for existence.

To St. Thomas' arguments just above ([15] and [16]) one
can add the following. Essence (called by the name "form") is
the total or full identity or perfection of a real thing (see pages
47–48). But matter and form together constitute the total
perfection of a composed substance (see pages 61–67). Thus
neither matter alone nor form alone can be the essence of a
composed substance.

17. Neither can it be said that matter is placed in the
    definition of a natural substance as something added to
    its essence or as something outside its essence, because
    this mode of definition is proper to accidents, which do
    not have a perfect essence. This is why accidents
    must include in their definition a subject which is out-
    side their genus. It is clear therefore that essence in-
    cludes matter and form.

18. Further, neither can it be said that essence signifies
    some relation between matter and form or something
    added to them, because this would of necessity be
    an accident or something extraneous to the real
    thing, and the real thing would not be known through

it. And these are traits of essence. For through the form, which is the actuality of matter, matter becomes something actual and something individual. Whence what supervenes does not confer on matter actual existence simply, but such an actual existence; as accidents in fact do. Whiteness, for example, makes something actually white. Whence the acquisition of such a form is not called generation simply, but generation in a certain respect. It remains, therefore, that the word "essence" in composed substances signifies that which is composed of matter and form.

19. Boethius is in agreement with this in his commentary on the *Predicaments,* where he says that *ousia* signifies the composite. For *ousia* in Greek is the same as *essentia* in Latin, as he himself says in his book *On the Two Natures.* Avicenna, too, says that the quiddity of composed substances is the composition itself of form and matter. And the Commentator, likewise, in his considerations on the seventh book of the *Metaphysics,* says: "The nature which species have in generable things is something in between, i.e., composed of matter and form."

20. Reason, too, is in accord with this, because the existence of a composed substance is not the existence of the form alone nor of the matter alone, but of the composite itself; and essence is that according to which a real thing is said to be. Whence it is necessary that the essence, whereby a real thing is denominated a being, be neither the form alone nor the matter alone, but both, although the form alone in its own way is the cause of such existence.

21. We see the same in other things which are constituted of a plurality of principles, namely, that the real thing is not denominated from one of these principles alone,

but from what includes both, as is evident in the case of tastes. Sweetness, for example, is caused by the action of what is hot dispersing what is moist; and although heat in this way is the cause of sweetness, a body is not denominated sweet from heat, but from the taste which includes what is hot and what is moist.

17–21

In (17) through (21) St. Thomas argues in different ways that the essence of a composed substance includes both matter and form. In (17) and (18) he argues this by dispelling two possible misconceptions about the way in which matter and form are included in the essence. In (19) he argues it by appealing to the authority of Boethius, of Avicenna, and of Averroes. In (20) he argues it by appealing to the last meaning of the word "essence" which he formulated in chapter one (see pages 45 and 48). In (21) he exemplifies the argument put forward in (20). Although we no longer speak of sweetness as being caused "by the action of what is hot dispersing what is moist," but rather as being caused by some sort of chemical reaction between some substance in solution and the end organs of gustatory sensitivity, this is no way affects the point of St. Thomas' example. For if a thing is constituted of several principles or parts, it is clearly not proper to denominate it from only one of them. A book is *not* called a book *only* because of its cover.

THE ESSENCE OF A COMPOSED SUBSTANCE INCLUDES BOTH MATTER AND FORM.

Suppose one says that matter is indeed included in the definition of a natural substance, in order perhaps to have some way of differentiating natural definitions from mathematical ones (see page 68), but that it is included as an addition to, hence

as something really not pertaining to, the essence of the
substance; that the essence is only the form; that matter is not
of the essence, perhaps because it is simply potentiality,
whereas essence ought clearly to be some sort of actuality. This
view cannot be accepted, argues St. Thomas, because only
those things which have an imperfect or incomplete essence
must be defined in that way, i.e., by including in their definition something which is outside their essence; for example,
accidental forms, substantial forms, prime matter. Soul is a
substantial form, and must therefore include in its definition
something which is outside its essence, namely, its proportionate subject, physical body having life potentially; soul is
defined as the first actuality of a physical body having life
potentially. But a substance has a complete or perfect essence;
which is to say that a substance is something which exists in
itself as a subject. A substance is an ultimate existing subject; it
is an intrinsically (though not necessarily absolutely) complete
existent; or simply, a substance is what exists (period). This is
not to say that a substance is God (see page 41). Neither
accidental forms nor substantial forms are intrinsically
complete existents; each depends on an appropriate subject. It
is not necessary, therefore, that a substance be defined in the
way in which the soul must be defined. It is possible for a
substance to have a definition such that what is included in it
pertains to the essence of the substance. This will be a
definition by intrinsic causes; and it is clear from the inductive
analysis of change that these intrinsic causes are two, matter
and form (see pages 61–67). But it is also possible for a
substance to have a definition such that what is included in it
does not pertain to its essence; this will be a definition by
extrinsic causes, as when the human soul is defined as something created by God. One must insist, therefore, that a definition by matter and form includes nothing which does not
belong to the essence.

Suppose, now, that someone goes a step further and says that both matter and form are included in the definition of a natural substance, but that neither pertains to its essence; that the essence of a natural substance is something superadded to the matter and the form, perhaps some sort of relation between them. This view, too, cannot be accepted, argues St. Thomas, because it is clear from the inductive analysis of change that when matter acquires form, a natural substance comes to be and comes to be what it is. Hence, anything superadded to the substance would presuppose the substance as already constituted by its matter and its form; anything superadded would be *per accidens* or extraneous to what the substance is. Now, essence is that in a real thing in virtue of which one can know what the thing is (see page 47). It is clear that one cannot know what a thing is by virtue of what is *per accidens* or extraneous to what it is. Thus, one must conclude that it is not only the definition of a composed substance which includes matter and form but also the essence as well includes matter and form. One must conclude, further, that the essence of a composed substance includes only matter and form. So much apropos of (17) and (18).

In (20) we find a last argument for the claim that the essence of a composed substance includes both matter and form. Among the several meanings of the word "essence" distinguished above (see pages 45–48), we find this one: "it is called essence from the fact that through it and in it a real being has existence" (see page 45). Here in (20) this meaning of the word "essence" receives the following formulations: "essence is that according to which a real thing is said to be" and "essence [is that] whereby a real thing is denominated a being." (See pages 51–52 for a brief discussion of the use of the word "say" to mean *is*. What is the case with the word "say" is also the case with the word "denominated.") St. Thomas' last argument appeals to this meaning of the word "essence." Its point can be seen by asking the following question: Can matter alone be the essence of a composed substance, i.e., be that something intrinsic to a composed substance whereby the substance has existence in the real world? Clearly not, for this would be to say that a composed substance can exist without a substantial form, which is impossible. Neither can the form alone be the essence of a composed substance, for this would be to say that a composed substance can exist without matter, which again is impossible. Since, therefore, neither alone is, but both together are, that whereby a composed substance has existence (see the inductive analysis of change on pages 61–67), it follows that essence includes both matter and form.

Yet, the form alone can be said in a sense to be the cause of the existence of a composed substance, for the composed substance does not begin to be until the form has been introduced. This can perhaps be more fully explained. Matter is an ultimate subject, for matter is not in another; but it is also potentiality, and hence cannot be an actual ultimate subject. On the other hand, form is not an ultimate subject, since form is in another, namely, in matter; but form is actuality. It is because form is actuality that form, when introduced into matter, brings about a composed entity, matter plus form, which is an actual ultimate subject. The ultimate existing subject is a matter-form composite, its character as ultimate subject deriving from matter, its character as actual deriving from form.

22. But matter is the principle of individuation. From this it might perhaps appear to follow that an essence which includes in itself matter along with form is only particular and not universal. And from this it would follow that universals would not have a definition, if essence is that which is signified by a definition.

23. We should notice, therefore, that the principle of individuation is not matter taken in just any way whatever, but only designated matter. And I call that matter designated which is considered under determined dimensions. Such matter is not placed in the definition of man as man, but it would be placed in the definition of Socrates, if Socrates had a definition. Rather, it is nondesignated matter which is placed in the definition of man; for this bone and this flesh are not placed in the definition of man, but bone and flesh absolutely. These latter are man's nondesignated matter.

22–23

Having shown in (17) to (21) that the essence of a composed substance includes both matter and form, St. Thomas notices in (22) that the inclusion of matter may give rise to a difficulty. For essence is what is signified by the definition, and the definition is universal. How, then, can the definition, being universal, include matter, since matter is the principle of individuation? (To say that matter is the principle of individuation represents an attempt to account for the fact that there are many individuals of a same specific essence, e.g., the individuals Fido and Rover are of the same specific essence dog, the individuals Jack and Paul are of the same specific essence man.) He proposes a solution in (23).

DESIGNATED MATTER IS THE PRINCIPLE OF INDIVIDUATION

The difficulty just raised is easily dispelled if one considers that the matter which is the principle of individuation is not the matter which is included in the definition of a composed substance. The definition of a composed substance includes common sensible matter, which can also be described as

nondesignated matter; for example, bone and flesh without
qualification are placed in the definition of man as man, and
not this bone and this flesh, e.g., my bone and my flesh, or your
bone and your flesh. (To talk about common sensible matter
and about nondesignated matter is to talk about the same
thing, and at the same level of universality; but it is to say
something different about it; see pages 147–151). Individual
sensible matter, which can also be described as designated
matter—i.e., as matter considered under determined dimensions (see pages 147–151)—is the matter which is the principle
of individuation; for example, this bone and this flesh, not in
the sense of an ambiguous this, of an "any" this, but in the sense
of a *determinate this,* one to which one can point with his
finger. Designated matter would be included in the definition
of Socrates (taking Socrates as an example of a *determinate
this* man to whom one can point with his finger) if Socrates had
a definition, but this individual as a determinate "this" individual is indefinable because unique; or more properly, not
simply because it is unique, but because its uniqueness is
rooted in matter. This is not to say that individual is
indefinable, for all individuals have this in common that they
are individuals, and this common characteristic is definable.
This individual is a determinate "this" individual, and is
unique by reason of designated matter, by reason of matter
considered under determined dimensions. In the phrase "determined dimensions," the word "determined" means *circumscribed so as to be just so much,* and the word "dimensions"
means *three-directional quantification or spread-out-ness.* The
composed essence is numerically multipl*ied* into individuals of
a same species by reason of the division, i.e., the circumscription to so much, of quantified matter. The composed essence is
numerically multipl*iable* into individuals of a same species by
reason of the divisibility of matter. If the matter (matter,
recall, most universally described, is what survives in the *term*

toward which and which is such that it is related to the newly acquired substantial form as potentiality to actuality in the second sense; see pages 64–65) out of which natural substances are generated were not divisible, it would be impossible to have a plurality of them.

Although it is a fact, easily verified through sense observation, that the matter of natural substances is divisible into parts, it is nonetheless, we must note, not of itself, or *per se*, so divisible. This is clear from the fact that of itself matter is simply potentiality for substantial form. In every case in which there is something which is such-and-such but not *per se* (which is to say, *per accidens*) there must be something other which is such-and-such *per se*. In this case this other is obviously the three-dimensional quantity which we see natural substances have, for dimensive quantity is of itself divisible. In a word, matter is divisible, but not because it is matter, for of itself matter is simply potentiality for substantial form, hence of itself not the source of divisibility. Rather matter is divisible because it is three dimensionally quantified. It is a fact that matter is both quantified and divisible, but it is neither of itself. This appears to be what St. Thomas has in mind when he writes:

. . . since dimensive quantity alone possesses by its nature that whereby the multiplication of individuals in a same species can take place, the primary source of such multiplication appears to be rooted in dimension. For even in the genus of substance, multiplication takes place according to the division of matter; and the division of matter would be unintelligible unless matter were considered under dimensions; for, remove quantity, and all substance is indivisible, as is clear from what the Philosopher says in the first book of the *Physics* . . .[7]

It is to be noted that whether we speak of prime matter, or of nondesignated matter, or of designated matter, we are in all cases speaking of that matter which is a part of the intrinsic constitution of an individual composed substance, for only individual substances exist. The difference among the three is a difference of greater and lesser universality, or, to put this in another way, a difference of lesser and greater detail in intellectual grasp and expression. Thus, to speak of prime matter, or perhaps better of matter *as prime,* is to speak of what the matters of all individual composed substances have in common. To speak of nondesignated matter, or of matter *as nondesignated,* is to speak of what the matters of all individuals of a same species have in common. Lastly, to speak of designated matter, or of matter *as designated,* is to speak of what is proper to and distinctive of the matter of some determinate, individual, composed substance. Whether we speak of prime matter, or of nondesignated matter, or of designated matter, we are talking about the same thing (namely, about the matter of individual, composed substances); but in each case we are saying something different about it. The thing talked about is one in number, but three in description; much like the sense in which the *term from which* in change is one in number, but at least two in description (see page 62).

If someone should object that dimensive quantity cannot be a principle of the individuation of composed *substances* because it is an *accident,* and that therefore matter *alone* is the principle of individuation, it is to be granted that his claim is an acceptable one provided he makes clear what he understands by accounting for individuation. If he takes accounting for individuation to mean accounting for the irreceivable character of an individual composed substance, his claim is acceptable. For matter (prime matter) is of itself an absolutely irreceivable subject; that is, whereas accidental forms are related to a composed substance as inherents to a receptive subject, and substantial form is related to prime matter as inherent to a receptive subject, there is nothing to which prime matter is related as inherent to receptive subject. This absolutely irreceivable character of prime matter is what accounts for the irreceivable character of an individual composed substance. One of the differences between the individual nature and the specific nature is that the latter is communicable to others as to inferiors (namely, to individuals), whereas the former is not. But if accounting for individuation is taken to mean accounting for the possibility of numerical plurality and for the factual numerical plurality of natural substances of a same species, then matter alone cannot be the principle of individuation; for matter of itself, as has been seen, is not the source of divisibility.

From the immediately preceding it is clear that individuation can mean more than one thing, and that accounting for individuation can mean more than one thing. So, too, the problem of individuation can be more than one problem; that is, there can be several problems which go by the name of the problem of individuation, or there can be several questions which are asked in the context of a problem about individuation. Thus, too, there can be several principles of individuation, a different principle for each different problem. The problem, as stated by St. Thomas in (22), is this, How is it possible to define when what is defined includes matter, since matter is the principle of individuation and definitions are universal? This question leads naturally to the question about the difference(s) between the specific nature and the individual nature. And this leads, in turn, to the following questions: (1) what accounts for the possibility of the numerical plurality of natural substances of a same specific nature, the answer being, as we have seen, quantified matter, or matter as quantified; (2) what accounts for their factual numerical plurality, the answer being designated matter, or matter as designated (this is also, as St. Thomas indicates here in [23], the key to answering the question about individuation which he raises in [22]). We have touched all these questions in some way. There are at least two other questions about individuation which should be mentioned here, though we shall not treat them here: (1) what, intrinsic to individuals of a same species, is that in virtue of which we, human knowers, distinguish these individuals one from another and (2) what, intrinsic to individuals of a same species, accounts for the fact of the identity (over a span of time) of each individual?

CHAPTER THREE

24. It is clear, therefore, that the essence of man and the essence of Socrates do not differ, except as the non-designated from the designated. Whence the Commentator says in his considerations on the seventh book of the *Metaphysics* that "Socrates is nothing other than animality and rationality, which are his quiddity."

25. The essence of the genus and that of the species also differ in this way, i.e., as the nondesignated from the designated, although the mode of the designation differs in each case. Whereas the designation of the individual with respect to the species is through matter determined by dimensions, the designation of the species with respect to the genus is through the constitutive difference which is taken from the form of the thing.

26. This designation which is in the species with respect to the genus is not through something in the essence of the species which is in no way in the essence of the genus; rather, whatever is in the species is also in the genus, but as undetermined. For, if animal were not the whole that man is, but a part of man, it would not be predicated of man, since no integral part may be predicated of its whole.

27. We can see how this comes about if we examine how body taken as part of animal differs from body taken as genus; for body cannot be a genus in the same way in which body is an integral part.

28. The word "body" can be taken in many ways. Body according as it is in the genus substance is so called from the fact that it has a nature such that three dimensions can be designated in it; but the three designated dimensions themselves are a body according as body is in the genus quantity. Now, it happens in things that what has one perfection may also attain to further perfection. This is clear, for example, in man who has a sensitive nature, and further an intellectual nature. Similarly, another perfection, such as life or some other such perfection, can be added to the perfection of having a form such that three dimensions can be designated in it. The word "body," therefore, can signify some real thing which has a form from which follows the possibility of designating in it three dimensions, and signify this in an excluding way, i.e., in a way such that no further perfection may follow from that form; in a way such that if anything be added, it is outside the signification of body. Taken in this way, body will be an integral and material part of animal because soul will be outside what is signified by the word "body"; the soul will be something over and above the body, in a way such that animal is constituted out of these two as out of parts, i.e., out of soul and body.

29. The word "body" can also be taken in another way, namely, to signify a thing which has a form such that three dimensions can be designated in it, no matter what sort of form it is, whether some further perfection can come from it or not. And taken in this way, body

will be a genus of animal, because there is nothing in animal which is not implicitly contained in body. Soul is not a form other than the form through which three dimensions could be designated in that thing; thus, when we said that body is that which has a form such that because of it three dimensions can be designated in the body, form meant any form, whether animality or stoneness, or any other form. And so the form of animal is implicitly contained in the form of body, when body is its genus.

30. And such likewise is the relation of animal to man. For, if animal were to name only that thing which has a perfection such that it can sense and be moved by a principle within itself, and name this thing as excluding other perfection, then any further perfection would be related to animal as a part, and not as implicitly contained in the notion of animal; and so, animal would not be a genus. Animal is a genus according as it signifies a thing from whose form the senses and movement can come forth, no matter what sort of form it is, whether a sensible soul only or a soul which is both sensible and rational.

In chapter three, St. Thomas considers how the matter-form composition of natural substances affects our knowledge about them, how it affects the *way* in which we know them as well as the *content* of our knowledge about them. Apropos of the way in which we know them, St. Thomas considers a number of logical relations among our various intellectual grasps or expressions of what natural substances are; for example, the relation of the nondesignated to the designated, the relation of the unexpressed-but-unexcluded to the expressed, the difference between signifying with precision (or in an excluding way) and signifying without precision (or in a nonexcluding way). Apropos of the content of our knowledge about them, St. Thomas points out what in the essences of natural substances furnishes the content of those first intentions which can be denominated genera, and species, and specific differences. Some of the effort of chapter three is clearly a preparation for the task of chapter four, the task of coming to understand how the essence of a composed substance is related to the logical intentions, genus, species, and difference.

24-30

In terms of the solution proposed in (23), St. Thomas concludes in (24) that the specific essence—e.g., the essence of man—does not differ from the individual essence—e.g., the essence of Socrates—except as the nondesignated differs from the designated. Both include matter and form. But the matter of the specific essence, being common or nondesignated matter, thanks to intellectual abstraction, requires a correspondingly common or nondesignated form; whereas the matter of the individual essence, being a unique or designated matter, requires a correspondingly unique or designated form. Both man and Socrates can be said to be something composed of flesh and bones (matter) and soul (form); for the essence of each is the same essence. The difference between them is rooted in the designation of the matter which is found in the individual.

In (25) through (30) St. Thomas shows that the generic essence is related to the specific essence as the nondesignated to the designated in a manner similar to the way in which the specific essence is related to the individual essence. In (25) he points out how the designation of the species with respect to the genus differs from the designation of the individual with respect to the species. In (26) he makes clearer the source of the designation of the species with respect to the genus. In (27) through (29) he considers several meanings of the word "body" to clarify the point of (26). In (30) he concludes his explanation by applying what he has said about a relation between body and animal to the relation between animal and man.

THE GENERIC ESSENCE IS RELATED TO THE SPECIFIC ESSENCE AS THE NONDESIGNATED TO THE DESIGNATED.

The essences of things can be grasped and expressed by the intellect in different ways. Let us try to understand something about a certain relation between the generic expression and the specific expression of the essence of a composed substance.

We must here keep in mind what we said above (page 77) about matter, namely, "whether we speak of prime matter, or of nondesignated matter, or of designated matter, we are in all cases speaking of that matter which is part of the intrinsic constitution of an individual composed substance, for only individual substances exist." We must here keep this in mind and apply it to the *whole* composed substance itself; the generic expression and the specific expression are expressions of the individual composed substance, for only individual substances exist.

The genus is the whole that the species is; that is, the essence expressed generically ("animal") is the whole that the essence expressed specifically ("man") is. Otherwise animal, argues St. Thomas, would not be predicated of man, since an integral part may not be predicated of its whole; we cannot say that a whole is its part. This is not to say that the word "animal" and the word "man" mean the same thing; what each means—i.e., what each determinately or actually or explicitly expresses—is not the same. "Animal" means *sensitive organism;* man adds to the meaning of animal the designation *rational;* "man" means *rational animal.* Man adds a designation to animal much like Socrates adds a designation to man. But the designation which

Socrates adds to man is rooted in individual matter; the designation which man adds to animal is rooted in the difference *rational*, taken from man's soul considered as exercising its proper activity. (To say that the difference rational is taken from man's soul considered as exercising its proper activity is simply to notice that *rational* means *what has a thinking soul*.) [1] Animal does *not* determinately express all that man determinately expresses. Animal expresses just so much of what man expresses, but what it does not determinately express (i.e., rational) it does not exclude. Animal is said, therefore, to contain rational indeterminately or potentially or implicitly. If one takes into consideration both what animal determinately expresses (i.e., sensitive organism) and that in man which it does not determinately express but does not exclude (i.e., rational), animal is the whole that man is. And if one adds to this the consideration that what is unexpressed-but-unexcluded is what accounts, when expressed, for the multiplication of the genus into species, much as designated matter accounts for the multiplication of the species into individuals, one can begin to see what it means to say that the genus is to the species as the nondesignated to the designated.

This will become clearer if, following St. Thomas' suggestion, we consider another example, the meaning of the word "body" in relation to the meaning of the word "animal." Body in relation to animal can be taken in two ways. Body in relation to animal is in the genus of substance, and it means *something having three dimensions;* but this can be taken (1) either with precision—i.e., in an excluding way—or (2) without precision, i.e., in a nonexcluding way. Taken with precision, it means *something having three dimensions,* and nothing else; if anything be added, it is outside the meaning of body so taken. Taken in this way, body signifies an integral (and *material;* see page 112) part of animal, the other, and formal, part being soul; animal is constituted out of body and soul as out of two parts, and soul is outside the meaning of body. Taken with precision, body cannot be predicated (by direct predication—i.e., by a predication in terms of the verb *is*—as opposed to an indirect predication, i.e., one in terms of the verb *has*) of animal.

Taken without precision, body also means *something having three dimensions,* but *not* without something else. Its explicit meaning is exactly the same as that of body taken with precision. But the *way in which it signifies* differs. Whereas body with precision excludes *everything* in animal which is outside this meaning—namely, something having three dimensions—body without precision does *not* exclude *anything* in animal which is outside that meaning. Body is the whole that animal is, and hence can be predicated (by direct predication) of it. (Body can be taken in a third way, namely, the *three dimensions themselves;* but this is body in the genus quantity, and for this reason plays no part in the attempt here to make clearer the point of [26].)

If animal in relation to man is taken without precision, animal is a genus of man; animal expresses generically the essence which man expresses specifically. If animal in relation to man is taken with precision, animal is an integral and material part of man. When one finds himself saying, "That's the animal in me," he is using the word "animal" with precision; he is using the word "animal" to speak about an integral part of himself. It is quite usual to use the word "body" in conjunction with the possessive *my* to designate an integral part, as when one speaks of "my body" as opposed to "my soul"; it is also quite usual to use the word "body" (without the possessive *my*) to designate a genus, as when one says that "organism" means *living body.* This is clearly the case with the Latin word "corpus," too; and this is perhaps why St. Thomas chose the word "corpus" in order to clarify the point of (26). But it is not usual to use the word "animal" in conjunction with the possessive *my* to designate an integral part; it would be unusual, indeed, to speak of "my animal" in the sense in which one speaks of "my body."

Thus, the genus signifies all that the species signifies, part of this determinately, part of it indeterminately; and the genus is related to the species as the nondesignated to the designated.

31. The genus, thus, signifies indeterminately everything that is in the species; it does not signify the matter alone. Similarly, the difference, too, signifies everything in the species, and not the form alone; the definition, too, signifies the whole, and so does the species, but in diverse ways.

32. The genus signifies the whole as a name determining what is material in the real thing without the determination of the proper form. Whence the genus is taken from the matter, although it is not the matter. And from this it is clear that a body is called a body from the fact that it has a perfection such that three dimensions can be designated in the body, and that this perfection is related materially to further perfection.

33. The difference, on the contrary, is a name taken from a determinate form, and taken in a determinate way, i.e., as not including a determinate matter in its meaning. This is clear, for example, when we say *animated*, i.e., that which has a soul; for what it is, whether a body or something other, is not expressed. Whence Avicenna says that the genus is not understood in the difference as a part of its essence, but only as some-

thing outside its essence, as the subject also is understood in its properties. And this is why the genus is not predicated essentially of the difference, as the Philosopher says in the third book of the *Metaphysics* and in the fourth book of the *Topics*, but only in the way in which a subject is predicated of its property.

34. The definition, lastly, and the species include both, namely the determinate matter which the name of the genus designates, and the determinate form which the name of the difference designates.

31–34

In (31) St. Thomas points out that the genus, the specific difference, the species, and the definition, all four, signify the same essence, but each differently. In (32) he explains how the genus signifies it; in (33) how the specific difference signifies it; and this he does with a careful consideration of the relation between the genus and the specific difference. In (34) he explains how the definition and the species signify it.

THE GENUS, THE SPECIFIC DIFFERENCE, THE SPECIES, AND THE DEFINITION—ALL FOUR SIGNIFY THE SAME ESSENCE, BUT EACH DIFFERENTLY.

The genus, we have seen, signifies all that the species signifies, part of this determinately, part of it indeterminately. We have also seen that the genus is related to the species as the nondesignated to the designated. Lastly, we have seen that what the genus signifies indeterminately is what is unexpressed-but-unexcluded by it, that this is expressed by the species, and that it is that whereby the species is designated with respect to the genus. Having seen, therefore, something about the way in which the genus is related to the species, let us consider briefly, following St. Thomas, how the difference and the definition are related to the species.

If we focus, first of all, on what the genus signifies determinately, we will notice that this is related to what the genus signifies indeterminately as what is material to what is formal. In (28) (see page 82), in his reflections on the many uses of the word "body," St. Thomas pointed out that things having some one perfection may well have attained to a further perfection; for example, man has the perfection of being a sensitive organism, but beyond that the further perfection of an intellectual nature. Now, a word which signifies man in a way such that what it expresses is man's being a sensitive organism, without expressing but also without excluding man's intellectual nature, will express a genus of man. It is clear that man's being a sensitive organism is related to his intellectual nature as the less perfect to the more perfect, as that which is fulfilled by it. And this is what it means to say that the genus signifies the whole essence of the species, but as determinately expressing only that which is material in the species, without however excluding that which is formal in it. And to say that the genus is taken from [2] matter is simply another, and perhaps misleading, way of saying that the genus expresses determinately only that which is material in the species. One must be careful to notice that the matter from which a genus is taken is not prime matter, or can it be prime matter, for prime matter is not a principle of knowledge. It is always matter along with some form.[3] (The relation between matter-form definitions and genus-difference definitions will be considered on pages 96–100.)

The difference, now, signifies the essence signified by the genus, but as determinately expressing only what is formal in the essence, e.g., *rational* determinately expresses *something having reason,* which is as formal in relation to *sensitive organism.* Sensitive organism, though not determinately expressed, is not excluded. Thus, what the genus determinately expresses is unexpressed, but unexcluded, by the difference; and conversely, what the difference determinately expresses is unexpressed, but unexcluded, by the genus. Thus, if one takes into consideration *both* what each (i.e., the genus and the difference) determinately expresses *and* what each leaves unexpressed but unexcluded, each signifies the same whole, but differently, as has been said. What has just been said applies to the genus and to the difference as predicable of, or in relation to, the species; not, however, in relation to each other (see just below).

The species and the definition signify the essence signified by the genus and by the difference, but they are including *both* what is determinately expressed by the genus *and* what is determinately expressed by the difference. But the definition in its determinate expression explicitly differentiates the genus from the difference, whereas the species does not. To think *man* (the species), for example, is to think what is expressed by *rational animal* (the definition), but without explicitly focusing on and differentiating man's rationality and man's animality.

If one considers the genus and the difference *in relation to each other* (above we considered the genus and the difference in relation to the species), one must notice that what is determinately expressed by the genus, precisely as determinately expressed, is outside the meaning of the difference; e.g., when we say *rational*—something having reason—*animal* is not expressed; *rational* does not mean "*animal* having reason"; this is what *man* means. And conversely, what is determinately expressed by the difference, precisely as determinately expressed, is outside the meaning of the genus. This is what Avicenna has in mind, says St. Thomas, when he points out that "the genus is not understood in the difference as a part of its essence, but only as something outside its essence, as the subject also is understood in its properties" and, one might add, as the soul's proportionate body is understood in understanding what the soul is, for soul is the first actuality of a physical body having life potentiality. But such a body is outside the essence of the soul. This is why the genus is not predicated *per se* of the difference; we do not say that *rational is animal* because being an animal is not of the meaning of rational, although we can say that *whatever is rational is animal* in the way in which a proper subject can be predicated of its properties, as in "whatever is such that its exterior angle is equal to the sum of its opposite interior angles is a triangle." Similarly, we do not say that the soul is the body, although we do say that the soul is the actuality of the body and that whatever is a soul has a body in which it exists.

35. From this it is clear why the genus, the difference, and the species are related proportionately to the matter, to the form, and to the composite in the real world, although they are not identical with them.
36. The genus is not the matter, but taken from the matter as signifying the whole; nor is the difference the form, but taken from the form as signifying the whole.
37. Whence we say that man is a rational animal, and not that man is made up of animal and rational as we say that man is made up of soul and body. Man is said to be composed of soul and body as some third thing constituted of two other things, and which is neither of them. For man is neither soul nor body. But if man

may be said in some way to be composed of animal
and rational, it will not be as a third thing out of two
other things, but as a third concept out of two other
concepts. For the concept "animal" is without the determination of the form of the species, and it expresses
the nature of a thing from that which is material in
relation to the ultimate perfection. But the concept of
the difference "rational" consists in the determination
of the form of the species. And from these two concepts the concept of the species or of the definition is
constituted. And thus just as the constituents of a real
thing are not predicated of that real thing, so too the
concepts which are the constituents of another concept are not predicated of that concept; for we do not
say that the definition is the genus or the difference.

35–37

In (35) St. Thomas concludes from his discussion in (31) to
(34) that the relation of the genus to matter is like that of the
difference to form and that of the species to the composite of
matter and form, although the genus is not identical with
matter, or the difference with form, or the species with either
matter or form. In (36) he explains that the relation is that of
being taken from. That is, the genus is not the same as the
matter, but it is taken from the matter to signify the whole, i.e.,
the composite of matter and form. So, too, the difference is not
the same as the form, but it is taken from the form to signify the
whole. And, we can add, the species is not the same as either
the matter or the form, but it is taken from both, and to signify
the whole. In (37) St. Thomas exemplifies and clarifies the
point of (36), and in effect contrasts two sorts of definitions of
composed substances: (1) matter-form definitions and (2)
genus-difference definitions.

"Taken From"

It is important to understand clearly the sense of the words "taken from" in expressions such as "the genus is taken from the matter but as signifying the whole" and "the difference is taken from the form but as signifying the whole." A reflection on a certain ordinary use of "has" and "is" will be helpful here. Sometimes we express by using "is" what we also express by using "has," making of course certain appropriate changes. For example, we say, "This thing *is* a body," as well as saying, "This thing *has* three dimensions." And no difference in meaning is intended; *to be* a body means *to have* three dimensions. Or, we say, "This thing *is* a being," as well as, "This thing *has* existence." And again no difference in meaning is intended; *to be* a being means *to have* existence. The predicate used with "is" designates the whole which is the subject, for a part cannot be predicated of its whole in a direct predication (see page 85). Neither can something (though not a part) which belongs to something other, and is therefore not the same as the other, be predicated of the other in a direct predication; for example, existence belongs to a being, but one cannot directly predicate existence of it, i.e., one cannot say that the being *is* its existence. The predicate used with "has," on the other hand, does not designate the whole which is the subject, or something which is the same as the subject; it designates rather a part of the subject, or something which belongs to the subject. Whenever "is" and "has" function as just described, it can be said that the meaning of the word predicated by using "is" is *taken from* that in the subject to which the predicate used with "has" refers. This is to say that that to which the predicate used with "has" refers furnishes the meaning of the word, or the content of the concept we attach to the word, predicated by using "is." Thus, the expression "taken from" is used apropos of a word designating a whole, but in terms of, or as determinately expressing only, something which belongs to, and is therefore not the same as, the whole, whether a part or whatever. The difference *rational,* for example, is taken from *the thinking soul;* or the thinking soul furnishes the content of the concept we attach to the word "rational." Rational designates the whole which is man (for we say that man *is* rational), but in terms of, or as determinately expressing only, his thinking soul, which is something belonging to man and not identical with man (we do not say that man *is* a thinking soul but that man *has* a thinking soul).[4]

MATTER-FORM DEFINITIONS AND GENUS-DIFFERENCE DEFINITIONS

To each genus-difference definition of composed substances there corresponds a matter-form definition. For example, man can be defined as rational animal, and corresponding to this genus-difference definition is this matter-form definition, namely, something composed of human body and human (thinking) soul. Animal can be defined as sensitive organism, and corresponding to this genus-difference definition is this matter-form definition, namely, something composed of sensitive body and sensing soul. A number of things are to be noticed here:

(1) the genus of the genus-difference definition is not the matter of the corresponding matter-form definition. This is clear since the genus signifies the whole, and the matter signifies but part of the whole.

(2) the difference of the genus-difference definition is not the form of the corresponding matter-form definition. This is clear since

the difference signifies the whole, and the form signifies but part of the whole.

(3) from (1) and (2) it is clear that matter-form definitions are wholes composed of *parts*, whereas genus-difference definitions are wholes composed of *wholes*. And this is what underlies the clarifications which St. Thomas offers in (37).

(4) to say that the genus is taken from matter (or to say that matter furnishes the content of the concept of the genus) cannot mean from prime matter, as we said above (page 90), since prime matter is of itself unknowable, and the genus is a principle of knowledge. It means from matter considered under some *common form* which is open to further perfection. To say that the difference is taken from form (or to say that form furnishes the content of the concept of the difference) is to say that it is taken from this further perfection.

(5) in matter-form definitions the matter is named from the form. Although it is always prime matter which enters such definitions, it is prime matter named from the form it *now has*, i.e., named from the form from which the specific difference is taken. If one considers, for example, this definition of man—namely, something composed of human body and of human (thinking or rational) soul—the expression "human body" is naming prime matter, not from prime matter's own nature, but from the characteristics conferred on it by the human soul.

Although in genus-difference definitions the genus is taken from matter, it is not taken from matter as named from the form which it now has, i.e., not from the form from which the specific difference is taken. In other words, the genus of the genus-difference definition is not taken from the matter of the corresponding matter-form definition, even though the difference of the genus-difference definition is taken from the form of the corresponding matter-form definition. For example, the genus of man—namely, *animal*—is not taken from *human body*. It is taken from matter taken with a *common form*, from matter with the common form *sensing soul*, which is to say from *sensitive nature*, which is related to the form from which the specific difference is taken as something material to a further perfection.

The following chart and accompanying explanation will perhaps help to clarify the preceding:

I	Components of matter-form definitions		IV	Components of corresponding genus-difference definitions	
	II	III		V	VI
Definiendum	Form	Matter	Fused statement of m-f definitions	Difference	Genus
5. Substance which comes to be	10. substantial form	15. prime matter	20. composed nature	25. composed	30. substance
4. Body	9. corporeal form	14. body	19. bodily nature	24. three dimensional	29. substance
3. Organism	8. soul	13. natural organized body	18. living nature	23. living	28. body
2. Animal	7. sensing soul	12. sensitive body	17. sensitive nature	22. sensitive	27. organism
1. Man	6. human (thinking or rational) soul	11. human body	16. rational nature	21. rational	26. animal

Columns II and III contain the components of the matter-form definitions of the five definienda: (1) man, (2) animal, (3) organism, (4) body, and (5) substance which comes to be. In reading columns II and III one should supply the expression "something composed of"; e.g., man's definition is "something composed of rational soul and human body"; animal's definition is "something composed of sensing soul and sensitive body."

Column IV contains a statement of the matter-form definition which can be called a *fused* statement, i.e., one which does not explicitly differentiate and state the matter and the form. In reading column IV one should supply the expression: "something having"; e.g., man's fused matter-form definition is "something having rational nature"; animal's is "something having sensitive nature."

Columns V and VI contain the components of the corresponding genus-difference definitions. In reading columns V and VI, one need supply no additional expression; man's definition is simply "rational animal"; animal's, "sensitive organism."

Apropos of (4) (page 96) one must notice the following exceptions. (1) Although genera are taken from matter considered under some common form, this is not the case with the supreme genera. For example, man's genus, 26 in the chart, is taken from 7 and 12 in the chart; or 7 and 12 supply the content of the concept of man's genus, for *to be an animal* means *to be composed of a sensing soul and a sensitive body*. Sometimes St. Thomas uses what we have called the *fused* statement (column IV) to indicate what supplies the content of the genus; e.g., 17 supplies the content of 26, for *to be an animal* means *to have a sensitive nature*.[5] Similarly, the conceptual content of organism, 27, animal's genus, is supplied by 8 and 13; or by 18, to use the fused statement. Similarly, apropos of body, 28. But the conceptual content of a supreme genus is obviously supplied by the way in which things exist in the real world (see pages 261–263). *To exist* without qualification is the way proper to substance; *to exist in substance* is the way proper to accidents (see page 40).

(2) Apropos of the statement that the difference is taken from form, although it holds for 21 in relation to 6, for *to be rational* means *to have a thinking soul;* for 22 in relation to 7, for 23 in relation to 8, and for 24 in relation to 9; it does not hold for 25 in relation to 10. 25 is taken from 10 and 15, i.e., from *both* matter and form; for *to be composed* means *to be composed out of matter and form*. And this is exactly what one would expect; for composed substances have nothing in common with simple substances and thus must be differentiated

from them in terms of their *total* essence, rather than in terms
of some part of it.

It is easy, in terms of the observation made above (page 96,
[3])—namely, that matter-form definitions are wholes composed of parts, whereas genus-difference definitions are wholes
composed of wholes—to understand the claims which St.
Thomas makes in (37); and these claims make clearer the
sense of that observation. (1) We do not say that man is made
up of animal and rational as we say that man is made up of soul
and body. This is so because soul and body are parts of man,
whereas rational and animal are the whole that man is. This
reason can be put more clearly: "soul" and "body" express parts
of the whole which is man; neither, therefore, expresses the
whole which is man, and each excludes the other from its
meaning; "animal," on the other hand, and "rational" express,
though partially, the whole which is man; neither excludes the
other from its meaning, though of course neither expresses the
other. (2) There is, nonetheless, a sense in which we may say
that man is made up of animal and rational; we may say that
the *concept* of man is made up of the concept of animal and of
the concept of rational. That is, even though "animal" and
"rational" signify the same *whole* that "man" signifies, they are
parts of the definition of man. (3) Just as the parts of a real
thing are not predicated (directly) of that real thing (for we
do not say that man *is* his arm), and just as the matter and the
form which appear in the matter-form definition of a composed
substance are not predicated (directly) of the substance
defined (we do not say that man *is* his body, or his soul), so,
too, concepts which are parts of other concepts are not predicated of them. We do not say that the concept which is the
definition is the same as the concept which is the genus or as
the concept which is the difference; we do not say, for example,
that the concept *rational animal* is the concept *animal* or the
concept *rational*. Nonetheless, we do predicate the definition of

that of which we predicate the genus and the difference, for we do say that man is a rational animal and that man is an animal and that man is rational. And we do this because the definition, the genus, and the difference signify the same whole.

Thus, if one considers carefully the relations among the definition, the genus, and the difference, one can see that from one point of view they are *wholes,* though each differently. The genus and the difference are wholes in a way such that each leaves unexpressed but unexcluded what the other expresses; the definition is a whole which expresses what the genus and the difference both express. (The species, too, is a whole which expresses what the genus and the difference both express, but in a fused, rather than in a differentiated, way; see page 91). From another point of view, the definition, the genus, and the difference, all three, are not wholes. The genus and the difference are *parts* of the definition, and the definition is their *whole.* And this is perhaps a clearer way of stating what it means to say that the genus-difference definition is a whole composed of parts which are themselves wholes.

38. Although the genus signifies the whole essence of the species, it is not necessary that the diverse species in a same genus have one essence.

39. For the oneness of the genus proceeds from its very indetermination or indifference; not however in such a way that what is signified by the genus is some numerically one nature found in diverse species, and to which another thing supervenes, namely the difference, determining the genus as form determines matter which is numerically one. It is rather because the genus signifies some form, not determinately this form or that form, which the difference expresses

determinately, but which is not other than the form
which was indeterminately signified by the genus.

40. This is why the Commentator says in his considerations
on the eleventh book of the *Metaphysics* that prime
matter is said to be one by reason of the removal of all
forms, whereas the genus is said to be one by reason
of the commonness of the designated form.

41. Whence, it is clear that when one adds the difference
and removes that indetermination which was the cause
of the oneness of the genus, there remain species
which are diverse in essence.

38–41

In (38) St. Thomas disagrees with the possible objection that if
the genus signifies the whole essence of the species, then the
diverse species in the genus are not diverse at all, but rather
must have one essence. In (39) he gives the reason for his
disagreement, which amounts to pointing out that the source of
the oneness of the genus is not the same as the source of the
oneness of the species. The source of the oneness of the genus
lies in the fact that it leaves unexpressed (though unexcluded)
the distinctive or determinate forms which are expressed by
the differences of that genus. The source of the oneness of each
species in a genus lies in the distinctive form which is expressed by its proper difference. From which it clearly follows
that the oneness of the genus cannot be attributed to its
species, so as to say that the diverse species of the genus must
have one essence. Further, he in effect points out that the
source of the oneness of the genus is not the same as the source
of the oneness of a given individual. The source of the oneness
of the individual is designated matter.

From which it clearly follows that one cannot maintain that
"what is signified by the genus is some numerically one nature
found in diverse species, and to which another thing super-

venes, namely the difference, determining the genus as form
determines matter which is numerically one." This follows
because the oneness of the genus is not a numerical oneness,
but a oneness of indetermination or indifference, i.e., a oneness
rooted in the fact that the genus leaves unexpressed (though
unexcluded) the distinctive or determinate forms which are
expressed by the differences of that genus and which, when
added to the genus, give rise to plurality within it. In (40) he
notices that Averroes is in agreement with him on this point
when he writes that whereas prime matter is said to be one by
reason of being considered apart from all forms, the genus is
said to be one by reason of the common or indeterminate way
in which it signifies forms, the same forms which the differences signify determinately. In (41) he affirms again, and gives
a clearer statement of, his position in this matter. If one adds
differences to the genus, this removes its oneness; this gener-
ates a plurality of species, each with a distinctive essence
rooted in the distinctive form which is determinately expressed
by the added difference.

Genus Is to Difference as Matter Is to Form, but Not in All Respects.

Perhaps the point of (39) will be made clearer if one considers
the following. It is clearly the case that $\dfrac{genus}{difference} : \dfrac{matter}{form}$ if
we read in either direction; that is, just as matter has a
potentiality for, or an openness toward, form, so too does the
genus for the difference. And just as form fills the openness of
matter, so too does the difference fill the openness of the genus.
But one must notice carefully that relations between genus and
difference are logical relations, second intentions, whereas
relations between matter and form are relations in the real
world. From which it follows that it is not necessary, though it

may happen, that the genus be related to the difference as matter is to form *in all respects*. It is clear that features of relations in the real world cannot legitimately be proved from second intentional relations, or vice versa. For the former belong to things intrinsically and essentially, and independently of our way of knowing them, whereas the latter belong to things incidentally, not as their own, but as consequent upon the way in which we know them (see page 20).

Here in (39) St. Thomas is looking at matter and form in a way different from the way in which he was looking at them above. Whereas before (see page 81) he was concerned with the effect which matter, as that which designates, has on form, as that which is nondesignated (namely, to multiply it); here he is concerned with the effect which form, the nondesignated, has on the designated via its effect on the matter which designates. Its effect is to determine the designated. When a form is added to matters each of which is numerically one, it is not only the case (1) that the form is multiplied into individuals and (2) that each individual is determined—i.e., has a unique set of features—by reason of the designated matter; but it is also the case (3) that each individual is determined by—i.e., has a certain set of features which are rooted in—the form itself. For example, each individual man is not only an individual but he is also a man. Similarly, when differences are added to a genus, it is not only the case (1) that the genus is plurified into species and (2) that each resulting species is determined, or has a certain set of features, by reason of the added difference, but it is also the case (3) that each resulting species is determined, or has a certain set of features, by reason of the genus itself. For example, man is not only rational but he is also animal. Along with these similarities there are also differences, one of which St. Thomas is concerned to point out here. Whereas that which form determines—namely, matter—is numerically one because its oneness is rooted in

determined dimensions, that which the difference determines
—namely, the genus—cannot be numerically one since its oneness is rooted, not in determined dimensions, but in the indeterminate way in which it signifies the forms which are
determinately expressed by its differences.

From the immediately preceding, it is clear that not only
does this proportion hold—namely, $\dfrac{genus}{difference} : \dfrac{matter}{form}$ —but
this one as well: $\dfrac{genus}{difference} : \dfrac{form}{matter}$.

The Oneness of Prime Matter

The point of (40) will perhaps become clearer if one considers
what it means to say that the oneness of prime matter is rooted
in the removal of all forms. It will be helpful to notice first that
to say that something is one, in a most ordinary sense, is to say
that it is numerically one, i.e., one in the sense which follows on
the division of continuous quantity. For example, divide an
apple into four parts; then each part can be said to be *one* part,
numerically one part, i.e., one when you count it. Each part is
divided from the other parts, and each is undivided in itself,
though each is further divisible. It is clear that the oneness of
prime matter cannot be a numerical oneness, for such oneness
is consequent on the division of quantity, and prime matter *per
se* is not quantified. *Per se*, prime matter is simply potentiality
for substantial form.

There is another sense of "one," the sense in which a genus is
said to be one, one by reason of the fact that the distinctive
forms which are determinately expressed by its differences are
not expressed, though not excluded, by the genus. In other
words, the genus is said to be one by reason of the removal of
determinately expressed (by the differences) forms. The genus
nonetheless expresses these forms in a common way.

There is still another sense of "one." And prime matter is said to be one in this sense. Its oneness is rooted, not simply in the removal of determinately expressed forms, but in the removal of *all* forms. Whereas the genus expresses a form, though commonly, prime matter expresses no form at all. This is not, however, to say that substantial form does not enter the definition of prime matter. It does. Prime matter is defined as potentiality for substantial form. But the substantial form which enters the definition of prime matter is not this or that *sort* of substantial form. The substantial form is not expressed *as to its sort*, even in the most common way. The definition simply notes the *fact* that prime matter is potentiality for substantial form. Thus, whereas the genus expresses a substantial form *as to its sort*, though commonly, and derives its oneness from the commonness of this expression or from this removal of determinately expressed forms, prime matter expresses no substantial form at all *as to its sort* and derives its oneness from this nonexpression or from this removal of all forms. And just as the genus is diversified, thus losing its oneness, by the addition of differences, so too is prime matter diversified, thus losing its oneness, by the addition of substantial forms.

There is perhaps another way to get at the sense in which prime matter is said to be one. Things are said to be numerically one by reason of their dimensive quantity (most properly by reason of the fact that their dimensive quantity is circumscribed); that is, by reason of something which is other than themselves, and which is of itself the source of divisibility. Prime matter, on the other hand, is said to be one by reason of itself, for to remove all forms is to consider it of itself; and of itself it is not a source of divisibility or diversifiability of any sort. Prime matter is diversified by something other than itself, by substantial forms. To say that prime matter is of itself one, therefore, is to say that of itself it is undiversifiable, that of itself it cannot be made many. Whereas each of the four quantitative parts of the divided apple is one in the sense that each is quantitatively divided from the others—quantitatively undivided in itself, though further quantitatively divisible— prime matter is one in the sense that, possessing of itself nothing which is the source of any sort of divisibility, whether quantitative or not, it cannot of itself become in any sense many.

42. The nature of the species, as we have said, is indeterminate in relation to the individual, as the nature of the genus is indeterminate in relation to the species.

43. Because of this, just as that which is a genus, as predicated of the species, implies in its signification, though indistinctly, everything that is determinately in the species; so too that which is a species, according as it is predicated of the individual, must signify, though indistinctly, everything which is essentially in the individual.

44. And it is in this way that the essence of the species is signified by the word "man"; whence man is predicated of Socrates. But if the nature of the species is signified as excluding designated matter, which is the principle of individuation, it will be as a part; and in this way it is signified by the word "humanity," for humanity signifies that by which man is man; and it is not the case that man is man by reason of designated matter. And so designated matter is in no way included among the things by which man is man. Since, therefore, humanity includes in its concept only those things by which man is man, it is clear that designated matter is excluded from or is cut out of its signification. And because a part is not predicated of its whole, humanity

is not predicated of man, or is it predicated of Socrates.

45. Whence Avicenna says that the quiddity of a composite is not the composite itself whose quiddity it is, even though the quiddity too is composed. Humanity, for example, though composed, is not man; it must be received into something which is designated matter.

46. As we have said, the designation of the species with respect to the genus is through forms, whereas the designation of the individual with respect to the species is through matter. This is why the word which signifies that from which the nature of the genus is taken, and signifies it as excluding the determinate form which perfects the species, must signify a material part of the whole, as, for example, body is a material part of man. But the word which signifies that from which the nature of the species is taken, and signifies it as excluding designated matter, signifies a formal part.

47. And thus humanity is signified as a certain form, and it is said to be the form of the whole, not indeed as something added to the essential parts, namely to form and matter, as the form of a house is added to its integral parts; rather, it is a form which is a whole, that is, a form which includes both form and matter, but which excludes those things by reason of which matter can be designated.

48. It is clear, therefore, that the word "man" and the word "humanity" signify the essence of man, but diversely, as we have said; the word "man" signifies it as a whole, inasmuch as it does not exclude designation by matter, but contains it implicitly and indistinctly, as we have said before that the genus contains the difference. And this is why the word "man" is predicated of individuals. But the word "humanity" signifies it as a part, because it contains in its signification only what

belongs to man as man, and it excludes all designation by matter. Whence it is not predicated of individual men.

49. And this is why the word "essence" is sometimes found predicated of a real thing, for we say that Socrates is a certain essence; and sometimes it is denied, as when we say that the essence of Socrates is not Socrates.

42–49

In (42) St. Thomas points out again something he noted before, namely, that the species is indeterminate in relation to the individual just as the genus is indeterminate in relation to the species. From which it follows, notes St. Thomas in (43), that just as the genus, predicated of the species, signifies *all* that is in the species, part of this determinately, part of it indeterminately (see pages 86–88), so too the species, predicated of the individual, signifies *all* that is in the individual, part of this determinately, part of it indeterminately. The species and the genus express determinately *just so much,* indeterminately signifying all else in the individual and in the species, respectively. In (44) St. Thomas contrasts the way in which "man" and "humanity" signify man's essence. "Man" signifies it as a whole, and this is why what "man" signifies can be predicated of the individual. "Humanity" signifies it as a part, and this is why what "humanity" signifies cannot be predicated of the individual. In (45) he explains why Avicenna says that "the quiddity of a composite is not the composite itself whose quiddity it is, even though the quiddity too is composed." By "quiddity of a composite" Avicenna understands what is signified, for example, by "humanity" in the way in which "humanity" signifies it, i.e., *as a part.* The expression "composite itself" signifies more than is signified by the expression "quiddity of the composite," since the composite itself is the *whole.* In (46) St. Thomas explains why the word which signifies *in an excluding way or with precision* that from which the *genus* is taken must signify a material part of the whole; and why the word which signifies *with precision* that from which the *species* is taken must signify a formal part of the whole. In (47) he notices that that which in (46) he called a formal *part* of the whole is from another point of view a *whole* itself. What "humanity" signifies, for example, can be said to be a form, but not in the sense in which substantial form is called form, since this sense entails being *part* of a whole, the other part being matter. Rather, what "humanity" signifies includes both substantial form and matter; it includes *all* the essential parts of a composed individual, and is hence a sort of whole. And this is why it is called the *form of the whole* (*forma totius*),[6] a form which expresses *all*, or the *whole of*, the essential parts of the whole which is the composed individual. On the other hand, substantial form is called the *form of the part* (*forma partis*), i.e., a form which expresses but part of the composed individual, the other part being matter. To make this clearer, one should notice that matter and substantial form are *parts* of the *whole* which is the composite; what "humanity" signifies is a part of the whole which is the composed individual, the other part being designated matter. Yet what "humanity" signifies is itself a whole, including both matter and substantial form, excluding however designation by matter. And this makes clearer Avicenna's observation recorded by St. Thomas in (45). In (48) he summarizes the points of (43) and (44). "Man" and "humanity" signify the same essence, man's essence, but differently. The former signifies it as a whole, hence can be predicated of the individual; the latter, as a part, and hence cannot be predicated of the individual. In (49) he points out that because an essence is sometimes signified as a whole, as by "man," and sometimes as a part, as by "humanity," the word "essence" also functions sometimes like "man" and sometimes like "humanity." And this is why it is sometimes predicated of the individual, as in "Socrates is an essence of a certain sort," and sometimes denied, as in "The essence of Socrates is not Socrates."

THE RELATION OF THE INDETERMINATE TO THE DETERMINATE IS NOT THE SAME AS THE RELATION OF THE NONDESIGNATED TO THE DESIGNATED.

It must be said, apropos of (42), that a careful reading of what precedes in this chapter reveals that St. Thomas did not observe prior to this point that the species is indeterminate in relation to the individual just as the genus is indeterminate in relation to the species. What he did say is that the species is related to the individual as the nondesignated to the designated, and that the genus has this same relation to the species, although, of course, the source of the designation in each case differs (see page 81). He also said that the genus, predicated of the species, signifies *all* that is in the species, part of this determinately, part of it indeterminately; in other words, that the genus is indeterminate in relation to the species (see page 88). And, although it is clearly the case that both the $\frac{\text{species}}{\text{individual}}$ and the $\frac{\text{genus}}{\text{species}}$ are as the $\frac{\text{nondesignated}}{\text{designated}}$ (call this $\frac{A}{B}$) and also as

$$\frac{\text{something which signifies partly determinately and partly indeterminately}^{7}}{\text{all that is determinately signified by another}}$$

(call this $\frac{C}{D}$), it is not the case that the two relations are the same relation; i.e., it is not the case that the relation of $\frac{A}{B}$ is the same at the relation of $\frac{C}{D}$. This is clear from the fact that the $\frac{\text{specific difference : C,}}{\text{species}} \frac{}{D}$, but not as $\frac{A}{B}$.

What designates another not only determines the other but also causes plurality in that other; and a given species does not cause plurality in its proper specific difference. Although it is clearly not the case that first intentions which are related as $\frac{C}{D}$ are also related as $\frac{A}{B}$, it is nonetheless clear that first intentions related as $\frac{A}{B}$ are also related as $\frac{C}{D}$, for what designates *determines* as well as plurifies. And this appears to be what St. Thomas had in mind when he wrote in (42) that he has already said that the species is indeterminate in relation to the individual as the genus is indeterminate in relation to the species.

But perhaps it can also be said that St. Thomas intends $\frac{\text{"nondesignated"}}{\text{"designated"}}$ and $\frac{\text{"indeterminate"}}{\text{"determinate"}}$ to be used interchangeably. If this is accepted, one would nonetheless still have to insist that the relation of $\frac{A}{B}$ and that of $\frac{C}{D}$ are not the same relation, for the reason given above. One would have to say that $\frac{\text{species}}{\text{individual}}$ and $\frac{\text{genus}}{\text{species}}$ and $\frac{\text{specific difference}}{\text{species}}$, all three, are as $\frac{C}{D}$; but that only $\frac{\text{species}}{\text{individual}}$ and $\frac{\text{genus}}{\text{species}}$ are as $\frac{A}{B}$.

THE SPECIES TOO, LIKE THE GENUS, CAN BE SIGNIFIED AS A WHOLE OR AS A PART.

Apropos of (43) and (44), one must notice that just as "body"—i.e., "something having three dimensions"—can be taken (1) to signify without precision, and in this way be a genus—e.g., body in relation to animal—and (2) to signify with precision, and in this way name an integral and material [8] part—e.g., body, as opposed to soul, as part of animal [9]—so, too, the specific essence can be signified both without precision and with precision. For example, "man" signifies a specific essence without precision; this means that designated matter is not excluded. "Humanity" (or "manness"), on the other hand, signifies the same specific essence, but with precision; this means that designated matter is excluded. What "man" and "humanity" *mean* is exactly the same: that by which man is man. But *the way in which each signifies* what it means is different. "Man" signifies *as a whole*, which is to say that it signifies without excluding designated matter; although designated matter is not expressed, neither is it excluded. And this is why man is predicated of the individual (by direct predication): Socrates is a man. "Humanity" signifies *as a part*, which is to say that it signifies as excluding designated matter. And this is why humanity is not predicated of the individual (by direct predication); we do not say *Socrates is humanity*. Yet we can predicate humanity of the individual by indirect predication—e.g., Socrates has humanity—for a whole can be said *to have* a part.

We must notice this difference between the genus signified with precision and the species signified with precision. The word which expresses that from which a genus (whether proximate or remote) is taken, and which signifies this in an excluding way, must signify a *material* part of a whole (e.g., body as a material part of animal) because that which is excluded is what is formal in the whole (this is some determinate form expressed by some difference; e.g., body as a material part of animal excludes soul). But the word which expresses the specific essence, and which signifies this in an excluding way, must signify a *formal* part of a whole (e.g., humanity as a formal part of Socrates) because the determinate form which the difference expresses is included, and because that which is excluded is what is material in the whole (this is designated matter). As St. Thomas explains in (46), the reason for this difference lies in the difference in source of designation; whereas the designation of the species with respect to the genus is through forms, that of the individual with respect to the species is through matter. It is the source of designation which is excluded when the genus and the species are signified with precision.

We must notice, further, that the specific essence signified *as a part*—e.g., by the word "humanity"—is nonetheless composite. "Humanity" determinately expresses that by which man is man, and man is man by virtue of *flesh and bones,* as well as by virtue of soul. What "humanity" excludes is not just any matter, but only that matter which is a principle of individuation. "Humanity" does not exclude flesh and bones simply; it excludes *this* flesh and *these* bones. It is important to bear in mind that *what is determinately expressed* by "man" and "humanity" is exactly the same; what differs is the *way in which each signifies* what each determinately expresses: the former without precision, the latter with precision. Thus, since what "man" expresses is composed, so too is what "humanity" expresses composed. And so, as Avicenna says (in [45]), both the composite—e.g., man—and the quiddity of the composite —e.g., humanity—are composed, although the latter is in its mode of signification but a part of the former.

Looking Back and Looking Ahead

In chapter three we have seen, among other things, (1) that we come to know and express individual composed substances in terms of generic and specific concepts, i.e., in terms of concepts which are related as the indeterminate to the determinate or as the less determinate to the more determinate. The basic reason *in us* (as opposed to a reason *in things*) for this lesser and greater determinateness of expression is the fact that we, human knowers, move from potentiality to actuality in acquiring knowledge, and hence grasp what things are by a number of progressively more detailed concepts. The basic reason *in things* for the possibility of our knowing them by generic and specific concepts is their matter-form composition, and the fact that matter is diversely actuated in different sorts of things.[10]

(2) that we also come to know and express composed substances in terms of specific differences, i.e., not only in terms of generic and specific concepts but also in terms of the differential concepts which diversify a genus, i.e., in terms of concepts which are related to generic concepts as the determining to the indeterminate. The basic reason for this, both in us and in things, is the same as the reason for our knowing things by generic and specific concepts.

(3) that we *signify* both *with* and *without* precision what we express. We signify our expressions—whether generic, specific, differential, or definitional—sometimes as a whole or without precision, sometimes as a part or with precision. For example, "man" signifies the specific essence as a whole, "humanity" as a part; "rational" signifies it as a whole, "rationality" as a part; "animal" signifies it as a whole, "animality" as a part; "rational animal" signifies it as a whole, "rational animality" (or "animal rationality") signifies it as a part. The basic reason in things for the possibility of our signifying them both with precision and without precision is their matter-form composition; when what is signified with or without precision is the *specific essence*, the basic reason in things for the possibility of such signification is the designated matter of their matter-form composition. *In us* the basic reason is again the fact that we pass from potentiality to actuality in acquiring knowledge.

At this point, we can perhaps see why one can say that it is useful, even necessary, for doing metaphysics to have done some logic about the intellectual grasps or expressions derived from substances which are matter-form composites. For metaphysics is ultimately about substances which are not matter-form composites. Since we know that the matter-form composition of things, along with the fact that matter is diversely actuated in diverse sorts of things, is the basic reason *in the things themselves* for the possibility of signifying intellectual grasps either *as a whole* or *as a part,* we shall be in a position to understand whether (or how) intellectual grasps signified *as a whole* and those signified *as a part* can be predicated of immaterial things (see pages 158–159).

What "Being" Expresses Cannot Be a Genus.

Some first intentions are related to other first intentions as genera to species—e.g., organism to animal and to plant, animal to man and to brute—and some as genera to differences, e.g., organism to sensitive, animal to rational. A question naturally arises at this point about the relation of the first intention we attach to the word "being" to those other, and less universal, first intentions which are the categories: substance, quantity, quality, etc. The question is this, Is what "being" expresses related to the categories (or to the ultimate genera) as a genus to its species or as a genus to its differences? Or, is it related to them in some other way? It should be clear that what we say here applies to being as first conceived by the intellect—i.e., to the content of our analytically first concept, *something-there*—whether one takes this as "worded" or not; and if worded, whether one formulates it as *something-there,* or as *being,* or as *what exists,* or as *thing,* or in some other way.

What "being" expresses cannot be related to what "substance" and "accident" express as a genus to its species. The genus does not determinately express the *whole* essence which is expressed by the species; it expresses determinately but a *part* of it. Yet the genus does not exclude what it does not determinately express; this is simply left undetermined. What "being" expresses, on the contrary, is the *whole* of what is expressed by "substance" and by "accident." And although it can be said that it is expressed indeterminately, "indeterminately" does not mean in the way in which a genus expresses the essence expressed by the species. It means, rather, in the way in which the species expresses what is expressed by the definition. It can be said that what "substance" and "accident" express adds something to what "being" expresses in a way similar to the way in which the definition adds something to what is expressed by the species. It is a differentiating addition. *Man* (the species) and *rational animal* (the definition) have the same meaning. Nonetheless, the definition explicitly differentiates the genus and the specific difference, thereby explicitly differentiating a species within the genus; whereas the species expresses them in a fused or undifferentiated way. So, too, "being" and "substance" have the same meaning. Nonetheless, "substance" expresses this meaning as explicitly differentiated from the meaning of "accident," whereas "being" does not. It is after one has begun to predicate the word "being" of accidents that he sees the need for this explicit differentiation. Thus, when it is said that "being" leaves unexpressed what is expressed by "substance," the meaning is that "being" leaves unexpressed the *explicit differentiation* of the meaning of "substance" from that of "accident." One must not conclude from the preceding that an ultimate genus has a specific difference as a species has. The similarity noticed here is only apropos of the *fused* or *undifferentiated way* in which the species expresses what is expressed by the definition.

What "being" expresses cannot be related to what "substance" and "accident" express as a genus to its differences. The differences of being—i.e., the ultimate genera—are not of the sort which a genus has. The differences of a genus are differences which are outside the genus because they do not participate in the genus. But the differences of being cannot be outside being because they do participate in being. Only *nothing* is outside being, and nothing cannot be added to being so as to constitute an ultimate genus of being.

Why is it said that the difference of a genus does not participate in the genus? A difference, writes St. Thomas, does not participate in the genus because it is taken from form, whereas the genus is taken from matter. For example, *rational* is taken from intellectual nature, *animal* from sensitive nature. Now form is not actually included in what matter is, for matter is in potency to form; or is matter included in what the form is. Similarly, what the difference determinately expresses is not actually contained in what the genus determinately expresses; rather, the genus leaves the difference unexpressed but unexcluded. Nor is the generic expression actually contained in the differential expression. When I say *rational*, points out St. Thomas, I signify simply *something having reason;* nor does *being an animal* belong to the meaning of *being rational.* As another example, when we say *animated,* we mean simply *something having a soul;* but this does not determine what it is, whether a body or anything else (see page 91). Now what is participated is of the determinate expression of what participates in it. And this is why it is said that the difference does not participate in the genus.[11]

The differences of being—i.e., the ultimate genera—on the other hand, participate in being, for what "being" expresses is of the determinate expression of each of them. Nor does "being" express something which is outside the ultimate genera in the way in which a genus expresses something outside its differences. For there is nothing outside the ultimate genera which "being" could express. Thus, being cannot have differences of the sort which a genus has.

What the differences of a genus determinately express adds something to what the genus determinately expresses. Similarly, what each of the ultimate genera determinately expresses adds something to what "being" expresses, although the mode of the addition differs in each case, as is clear from what has been said. Because of the addition, we can say that what both "being" and the genus express *contains or includes* their differences, but contains them *indeterminately or potentially.* Because of the difference in the mode of the addition, we can say that what "being" expresses includes or contains its differences in a way in which the genus does not include its differences. It can be said that being contains its differences *actually,* although in a *fused or undifferentiated* way.

CHAPTER FOUR

50. Having seen what is signified by the word "essence" in composed substances, we must see how a composed essence is related to the notion of the genus, of the species, and of the difference.

51. Because that to which the notion of the genus, or of the species, or of the difference, belongs is predicated of this designated singular, it is impossible that the notion of a universal—e.g., of the genus or of the species—belong to an essence according as it is signified as a part, as by the word "humanity" or "animality." And this is why Avicenna says that rationality is not a difference, but the principle of a difference. And for the same reason humanity is not a species, and animality not a genus.

52. Similarly, it cannot be said that the notion of the genus, or of the species, belongs to an essence as to some real thing existing outside singular things, as the Platonists held, because in this way the genus and the species would not be predicated of this individual; for it cannot be said that Socrates is what is separated from him. Nor, further, would this separated something be of any use in knowing this singular.

53. Whence it remains that the notion of the genus, or of the species, belongs to an essence according as it is signified as a whole, as by the word "man" or "animal," according as it contains implicitly and indistinctly everything that is in the individual.

50–53

The last of the three tasks of the treatise *On Being and Essence,* as these tasks are set down in the introduction, is to show how being and essence are related to the logical intentions genus, species, and difference.[1] Here in chapter four, as he points out in (50), St. Thomas considers how the essence of a *composed substance* must be taken in order that it be called a genus, or a species, or a difference. The considerations pursued in this chapter will perhaps add some precisions to the considerations pursued above on pages 16–20.

It is useful to notice that to speak of *how* an essence *is related* to the logical intentions just named can be to speak of at least two things: (1) How the essence must be taken in order that it be called a genus, or a species, or a difference. This is what is done here in chapter four apropos of composed substances. (2) What in the essences of things furnishes the content of the first intentions, a content which can be related to other contents as genera, or species, or differences when taken as they must be taken. This was done in chapter three apropos of composed substances (see pages 92–100); this is asked apropos of God and the intelligences in chapter six; in chapter seven, apropos of the accidents.

In (51) St. Thomas argues that the essence signified as a part cannot be a genus, or a species, or a difference; and in (52) St. Thomas argues that this is also true of a Platonist essence. In (53) he draws a first conclusion as regards how a composed essence must be taken in order that it be called a genus, or a species, or a difference: it must be taken signified *as a whole*.

In Order to Be Called a Genus, or a Species, or a Difference, the Essence Must Be Signified as a Whole.

St. Thomas embarks on the task of chapter four in terms of a distinction made in chapter three, a distinction between signifying *as a whole* and signifying *as a part*. It is clear from what we saw above (see, for example, pages 111–113) why what "humanity" expresses cannot be a species, and why what "animality" expresses cannot be a genus, and why what "rationality" expresses cannot be a difference. For the genus and the species and the difference can be predicated (directly) of the individual, e.g., of Socrates. Humanity, animality, and rationality cannot be predicated (directly) of Socrates because each of them signifies *as a part*. On the other hand, man, animal, and rational can be predicated of Socrates because each of them signifies *as a whole*. It is clear, therefore, that man, animal, and rational rather than humanity, animality, and rationality are a species, a genus, and a difference, respectively. This is to say that the logical intentions genus, species, and difference belong to the essence signified as a whole, not as a part. But this is not to say that humanity, animality, and rationality have nothing to do with the species, the genus, and the difference. They are their respective sources, or principles, as Avicenna says (see 51); that is, that to which "rationality" refers is that from which the difference rational is taken (see pages 94–95), although the word "rationality" is taken from the word "rational." When it is said that "rational" means "something having a thinking soul," one is expressing its meaning in terms of an explicit mention of that from which the difference rational is taken, namely, the thinking soul. But "rational" can also be said to mean "something having rationality." And when this is said, it must be noticed that the thinking soul is that to which "rationality" refers, although without explicit mention; and this is what it means to say that rationality is the principle of the difference rational.

Neither can the Platonist *man in himself* or *man as such,* if interpreted as an extramental idea or essence existing apart from individual sensible things, be a species; nor can the Platonist *animal in itself* or *animal as such,* so interpreted, be a genus. For, again, the genus and the species can be predicated of the individual. And neither *man in himself* nor *animal in itself* can be predicated of the individual, for the individual cannot be said to be *what exists separately from it.* Furthermore, knowledge about what exists separately from the individual contributes nothing to our knowledge about the individual itself, and the genus and the species are principles of such knowledge. Thus it is that St. Thomas concludes in (53) that "the notion of the genus, or of the species, belongs to an essence according as it is signified as a whole, as by the word "man" or "animal," according as it contains implicitly and indistinctly everything that is in the individual."

54. Now, a nature or essence signified as a whole can be considered in two ways. In one way it can be considered according to its proper content, and this is an absolute consideration of it. And in this way nothing is true of it except what belongs to it as such; whence if anything else is attributed to it, the attribution is false. For example, to man as man belong rational and animal, and whatever else falls in his definition. But white or black, or anything of this sort, which is not of the content of humanity, does not belong to man as man. Whence, if one should ask whether the nature so considered can be said to be one or many, neither should be allowed, because each is outside the content of humanity and either can be added to it. For if plurality were of its content, it could never be one, as it is in Socrates. Similarly, if oneness were of its content, then the nature of Socrates and Plato would be one and the same, and it could not be plurified into many individuals.

55. In the other way an essence is considered according to the existence it has in this or that. When the essence is so considered, something is predicated of it accidentally, by reason of that in which it is; for example, it is said that man is white because Socrates is white, although to be white does not belong to man as man.

56. This nature has a twofold existence, one in singular things, the other in the soul; and accidents follow upon the nature according to either existence. In singular things it has a multiple existence in accord with the diversity of these singular things; yet the existence of none of these things belongs to the nature considered in itself, i.e., absolutely. For it is false to say that the nature of man, as such, has existence in this singular thing; because if existence in this singular thing belonged to man as man, man would never exist outside this singular thing. Similarly, if it belonged to man as man not to exist in this singular thing, man would never exist in it. But it *is* true to say that it does not belong to man as man to exist in this or that singular thing, or in the soul. It is clear, therefore, that the nature of man, absolutely considered, abstracts from any of these existences, but in a way such that it excludes no one of them.

57. And it is the nature so considered which is predicated

of all individuals. Yet it cannot be said that the notion of a universal belongs to the nature so considered, because oneness and commonness are of the notion of a universal. Neither of these belongs to human nature considered absolutely, for if commonness were of the content of man, commonness would be found in whatever thing humanity is found. And this is false, because in Socrates there is no commonness, but whatever is in him is individuated.

58. Similarly, it cannot be said that the notion of the genus or of the species attaches to human nature according as it has existence in individuals, because human nature is not found in individuals with a oneness such that it would be some one thing belonging to all, which the notion of a universal requires.

59. It remains, therefore, that the notion of the species attaches to human nature according to the existence it has in the intellect.

60. For human nature exists in the intellect in abstraction from all that individuates; and this is why it has a content which is the same in relation to all individual men outside the soul; it is equally the likeness of all of them, and leads to a knowledge of all insofar as they are men. And it is from the fact that the nature has such a relation to all individuals that the intellect discovers and attributes the notion of the species to it. Whence the Commentator says in his considerations on the first book of *On the Soul* that "it is the intellect which causes universality in things." Avicenna, too, says this in his *Metaphysics*.

61. And although the intellectually grasped nature has the character of a universal according as it is compared to things outside the soul, because it is one likeness of all of them; still according as it exists in this intellect or in that one, it is something particular —a particular species grasped by a particular intellect. From this one can see the weakness of what the Commentator says in his considerations of the third book of *On the Soul;* from the universality of the intellectually grasped form he wanted to conclude that there is one intellect in all men. This falls short of the truth because the intellectually grasped form has its universality not according to the existence which it has in an intellect, but according as it is related to real things as a likeness of them.

62. What is true here is like what would be true of a corporeal statue representing many men: the image or form of the statue would have its own and individual existence according as it exists in this matter, and it would have the character of commonness according as it is the common representation of many.

63. Further, because it belongs to human nature absolutely considered to be predicated of Socrates, and because the notion of the species does not belong to it absolutely considered but is among the accidents which follow upon it according to the existence it has in the intellect, one can see why the word "species" is not predicated of Socrates, i.e., why it is not said that "Socrates is a species." This would of necessity be said if the notion of the species belonged to man according to the existence which man has in Socrates; or, if the notion of the species belonged to man absolutely considered, i.e., to man as man, for whatever belongs to man as man is predicated of Socrates.

64. Still, to be predicated belongs to the genus in virtue of what it is, since this is placed in its definition. For predication is something which is achieved by the combining and dividing activity of the intellect, and

which has for its foundation in the real thing the union of those things, one of which is said of another. Whence the notion of predicability can be included in the notion of that intention which is the genus, which (intention) is similarly achieved by the activity of the intellect. Nonetheless, that to which the intellect, combining one thing with another, attributes the intention of predicability is not the intention of the genus itself; rather it is that to which the intellect attributes the intention of the genus, for example, that which is signified by the word "animal."

65. It is clear, therefore, how an essence or nature is related to the notion of the species. The notion of the species is not among the things which belong to the nature absolutely considered, nor is it among the accidents which follow upon the nature according to the existence it has outside the soul, as whiteness or blackness. Rather the notion of the species is among the accidents which follow upon the nature according to the existence it has in the intellect; and it is in this way, too, that the notion of the genus and of the difference belong to it.

54–65

We said above (page 120) that in (53) St. Thomas draws a first conclusion as regards how a composed essence must be taken in order that it be called a genus, or a species, or a difference: it must be taken signified *as a whole.* There are more conclusions to be drawn in this matter; he draws them in (54) to (65). To this end he makes a number of distinctions.

In (54) to (55) he makes this distinction. An essence signified as a whole may be considered in two ways:

(1) absolutely or (2) in relation to the existence which it has in something. He lists some things which do not belong to the essence considered absolutely. In (56) he makes a second distinction: an essence considered in relation to the existence it has in something can be considered (1) according to the existence it has in individual things "out there," and (2) according to the existence it has in the soul, i.e., in the intellect in knowledge. He points out more things which do not belong to the essence considered absolutely. In (57) he argues that the notion of a universal, whether of the genus or of the species or of the difference, cannot belong to the nature absolutely considered, although the nature so considered is predicated of the individual. In (58) he argues that the notion of a universal cannot belong to an essence considered according to the existence it has in individuals. By elimination it follows (59) that the notion of a universal belongs to an essence considered according to the existence it has in the intellect in knowledge. Not only is this so by elimination but there is also the fact that the intellect knows by abstracting from all that individuates, and it is from this mode of knowing, argues St. Thomas in (60), that one can see why the notion of a universal belongs to an essence considered according to the existence it has in knowledge. In (61) St. Thomas makes a last distinction. An essence which exists in the intellect in knowledge can be taken either (1) in relation to the individuals of which it is the common likeness or (2) in relation to the individual intellect in which it exists in knowledge. He uses this distinction to point out the weakness of the argument which lead Averroes to claim that there is one intellect in all men. In (62) St. Thomas exemplifies the point of the distinction made in (61). In (63) he explains why the names of the logical intentions are not predicated of the real individual; for example, why it is not said that "Socrates is a species." In (64) he notices that

although the logical intention of predicability can be included
in the definition of the logical intention of the genus, as when
we say that the genus is a predicable, this is not to say that
what is predicable is the intention of the genus. Rather, what is
predicable is that to which the intellect attaches the intention
of the genus, e.g., what is meant by the word "animal." To say
that *the genus is a predicable* is to say that *that which is a
genus* is what is predicable (see pages 18–19). We do not say
that *Socrates is a predicable,* just as we do not say that *Socrates
is a genus;* we say *Socrates is an animal.* The same thing is to be
said about the logical intention of the species and that which is
a species. And similarly apropos of the difference: we do not
say that *Socrates is a specific difference;* we say *Socrates is a
rational animal.* In (65) he summarizes the conclusions argued
in (54) to (64).

THE ESSENCE SIGNIFIED AS A WHOLE MUST BE TAKEN ACCORDING TO THE EXISTENCE IT HAS IN KNOWLEDGE, AND AS RELATED TO THE INDIVIDUALS OF WHICH IT IS THE COMMON LIKENESS.

If an essence is considered absolutely, only that which belongs
to it *per se*—i.e., as such (this is the first mode of *per se*)—can
be attributed to it. For example, to man considered
absolutely—i.e., to man as man—belong only those things
which are included in man's definition: *rational* and *animal;* or,
from another viewpoint, *flesh* and *bones* and *soul.* Being
grammatical or artistic (though these belong *per se,* this is the
second mode of *per se*),[2] being black or white, and other things
of this sort, do not belong to man as man; that is, these do not
fall in man's definition. Clearly, then, being a universal (i.e.,
the logical intention of a universal), here being a species, can-

not belong to man's essence considered absolutely; for it is not included in the definition of man. This is clear by a simple inspection of man's definition. For the same reason, being a genus cannot belong to animal as animal; or being a difference, to rational as rational.

Further, neither existence in this given individual substance out there, say Socrates, nor in that one, say Plato, belongs to an essence considered absolutely, say to man as man, or to animal as animal; that is, being *Socrates* does not belong to man as man, or to animal as animal. If it did, the essence would be found only in that given individual and never in any other. And thus an essence considered absolutely cannot be said to be one (numerically); or can it be said to be many. Nor does nonexistence in this given individual belong to the essence considered absolutely; if it did, the essence would never be found in this given individual. Further, neither existence *out there* (in individual things) nor existence *in the mind in knowledge* belongs to the essence considered absolutely, for neither falls in the definition. If either did, the essence would not be found both out there and in the mind in knowledge. Further still, neither nonexistence out there nor nonexistence in the mind belongs to the essence considered absolutely, for neither falls in the definition. If either did, the essence would either not be found in the mind in knowledge or not be found out there. Thus, neither to be nor not to be—whether in this or that given individual substance, or out there at all, or in the mind in knowledge—belongs to the essence considered absolutely.

Perhaps we can get at the above in another way. Essence is at once that in a real being in virtue of which the real being exists out there [3] and that in the real being in virtue of which it is knowable.[4] Essence, thus, given the fact of the existence of things and the fact of human knowledge about them, is at once what is *out there* and what is *in knowledge*. From this it is easy

to see that it belongs to an essence considered absolutely
neither to be out there nor to be in knowledge, neither not to be
out there nor not to be in knowledge. All of these are *per
accidens* in relation to the essence, but the essence is open to all
of them. And this is what St. Thomas means when he writes in
(56): "But it *is* true to say that it does not belong to man as
man to exist in this or that singular thing, or in the soul. It is
clear, therefore, that the nature of man, absolutely considered,
abstracts from any of these existences, but in a way such that it
excludes no one of them."

If the essence is considered according to the existence it has,
whether according to the existence it has "out there" in individual things or according to the existence it has in the mind in
knowledge, many things can be predicated of it which do not
belong to it *per se;* these things can be predicated of it *per
accidens,* or accidentally, by reason of that in which it has
existence. For example, we can say that *man is white* because
Socrates, the individual, is white, although being white does
not belong to man as man; or we can say that *man exists*
because Socrates exists, although *existence out there* does not
belong to man as man. Thus, if universality is to be said of
human nature at all, it will have to be said of human nature
accidentally (i.e., not absolutely considered), according to
some existence which it has, either the existence it has out
there in individual things or that which it has in the mind in
knowledge. Universality cannot be said of human nature
according to the existence human nature has in individuals
because human nature is not found in an individual with a
oneness such that it is at the same time common to all
individual men; and this is what is required by universality. It
remains, therefore, by elimination, that the notion of a universal (species, in this case) attaches to human nature according
to the existence it has in the intellect in knowledge. But not

only is this so by elimination, for "human nature exists in the intellect in abstraction from all that individuates; and this is why it has a content which is the same in relation to all individual men outside the soul; it is equally the likeness of all of them, . . ." (see [60], page 124). It is the intellect which notices this uniform relation to all individuals and, because of this relation, attributes the notion of the species to human nature. This is why, notes St. Thomas, both Avicenna and Averroes remark that it is the *intellect* which causes universality in things. It is to be noted, however, that although universality belongs to human nature accidentally, according to the existence it has in the intellect inasmuch as it is seen by the intellect to be a common representation of all individual men precisely as men, nonetheless, inasmuch as human nature exists in knowledge in *this* intellect or in *that* one, it is something individual, an individual bit of knowledge in an individual intellect.

Thus, universality, whether generic or specific or differential, belongs neither to the essence considered absolutely nor to the essence according as it is found in individuals. Universality is among the accidents which follow upon the essence according to the existence it has in the intellect in knowledge, provided it is taken as related to the individuals of which it is the common likeness.

We must notice that in predications like "Socrates is a man" or "Socrates is an animal," what is predicated of the individual is the nature considered absolutely. That this is so becomes clear if we consider what it is we intend to communicate by the proposition "Socrates is a man." What we intend to communicate is simply that in Socrates we find all that belongs to man as man. This is nothing other than to predicate the content of the nature absolutely considered. Since this is so, we can see why arguments like the following are not proper:

(1) Socrates is a man.   (2) Man is an animal.
    Man is a species.   *Animal is a genus.*
    Therefore, Socrates is a   Therefore, man is a genus.
    species.

We can also see why it is that although what "predicable" means can be said to be of the definition of the genus, of the species, and of the difference, it is not the logical intention of the genus or the species or the difference which is predicable of Socrates, but *that which is a genus,* that which is a species, that which is a difference, e.g., animal, man, and rational, respectively. And that is why it is that what "predicable" means is not predicated of Socrates.

It is of interest to notice that to begin to pursue the *subject of a science* is to attempt to grasp and to be concerned with an *essence absolutely considered* [5] in those cases in which there can be a definition of the subject. In those cases in which there cannot be a definition of the subject, as is the case with the subject of metaphysics, to begin to pursue the subject is to attempt to grasp and to be concerned with a *notion or meaning absolutely considered.* This is not to say that what metaphysics investigates as its subject is but a set of notions or meanings; what it investigates as its subject is all real things other than God, but *via* notions or meanings absolutely considered. Every genuine investigation of real things proceeds via notions absolutely considered.

Perhaps one can see a difficulty of sorts arising out of the following consideration. In (51) St. Thomas pointed out that that to which the notion of the genus, or of the species, or of the difference belongs is predicated of the individual. And in (57) he pointed out that it is the nature absolutely considered which is predicated of the individual; he repeats this in (63). One may want to conclude from these two remarks that the notion of the universal belongs to the nature absolutely considered, and this appears to be unacceptable.

This difficulty is easily dispelled if one considers that "belongs" can have more than one meaning. It can be used to refer to the *per se* (first mode) contents of an essence. Taken in this way, "belongs" cannot, it is clear, be used to say that the notion of the genus belongs to the essence. But "belongs" can also be used to refer to anything at all which can be attributed to an essence, and for any reason at all. And taken in this sense, "belongs" can be used to say that the notion of the genus belongs to the essence; the reason here is the *way* in which the human intellect knows what it comes to know. This, too, is to be said. When A is predicated of *a, b, c, d,* etc. because A is their common likeness, it is clear that whatever else is being predicated, the fact that A is their common likeness is *not* being predicated, or is it being predicated that A is being predicated, or is it being predicated that A is predicable. These facts are genuine *accompaniments* of the contents of A, genuine accompaniments because of the human mode of knowing, but they are not *among* the contents of A.

In (61) St. Thomas speaks of "a particular species grasped by a particular intellect." It should be clear that the word "species" is not being used here to designate the logical intention which goes by that name. The fact is that in the usage of St. Thomas the word "species" has more than one meaning. It is used not only in a logical context but also in the context of knowledge as a fact in the real world. In this latter context the word "species" is used at the level of sense knowledge to designate what is produced in a sense in an act of sensation, and which is the means whereby the external object is sensed. This is called the sensible species. At the level of intellectual knowledge it designates what the intellect produces within itself as the means by which it knows things. This is called the intelligible species. It is clear that each individual human intellect is in possession of the species whereby it knows things, and it is to this that St. Thomas calls attention in (61).

SUMMARY OF THE POINT OF CHAPTER FOUR

The point of chapter four can be summarized with the help of the following:

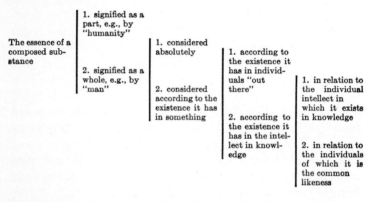

Each division has two members. If one takes the second member from each division, one can state exactly how the essence of a composed substance must be taken in order that it be a universal (whether a genus, or a species, or a difference): it must be taken signified as a whole, considered according to the existence it has in something—namely, in the intellect in knowledge—and related to the individuals of which it is the common likeness.

CHAPTER FIVE

66. It remains, now, for us to see in what way essence is in separated substances, namely, in the soul, in the intelligences, and in the First Cause.

67. Although everyone admits the simplicity of the First Cause, some try to introduce a composition of matter and form in the intelligences and in souls. The originator of this position appears to have been Avicebron, author of the book *Fountain of Life*.

68. But this is not in agreement with what philosophers commonly say, because they call them substances separated from matter, and prove them to be without all matter. The strongest demonstration of this is from the power of understanding which is in them. For we see that forms are not actually intelligible except according as they are separated from matter and from its conditions; nor are they made actually intelligible except by the power of a substance understanding them, according as they are received into, and are affected by, that substance.

69. Whence it is necessary that there be in any intelligent substance a total freedom from matter, such that the substance does not have matter as a part of itself, such

135

too that the substance is not a form impressed on matter, as is the case with material forms.

70. Nor can it be said that it is only corporeal matter that impedes intelligibility, and not any matter whatsoever. For if this were so by reason of corporeal matter alone, then it would have to be that matter impedes intelligibility by reason of the corporeal form, since matter is called corporeal only according as it is found under the corporeal form. But this cannot be—namely, that matter impedes intelligibility by reason of the corporeal form—because the corporeal form itself, just as other forms, is actually intelligible according as it is abstracted from matter. Whence there is in no way a composition of matter and form in the soul or in an intelligence if matter in them is taken in the sense in which matter is taken in corporeal substances.

71. But there is in them a composition of form and existence. Whence it is said, in the commentary on the ninth proposition of the *Book on Causes*, that "an intelligence is something having form and existence," and form is taken there for the simple quiddity or nature itself.

72. It is easy to see how this may be so. Whatever things are so related to one another that one is a cause of the other's existence, the one which is the cause can have existence without the other, but not conversely. Now the relation of matter and form is such that form gives existence to matter. It is impossible, therefore, that matter exist without some form. But it is not impossible that some form exist without matter, for form, to the extent that it is form, does not depend on matter. But if some forms are found which cannot exist except in matter, this happens to them because of their distance from the first principle, which is first

and pure act. Whence those forms which are nearest to the first principle are forms subsisting of themselves, that is without matter. For not every sort of form needs matter, as has been said; and the intelligences are forms of this sort. And therefore it is not necessary that the essences or quiddities of these substances be other than form itself.

73. Thus the essence of a composed substance and that of a simple substance differ in this: the essence of a composed substance is not form alone, but includes form and matter; the essence of a simple substance is form alone.

74. And from this follow two other differences. One difference is that the essence of a composed substance can be signified as a whole or as a part. This happens on account of the designation of matter, as has been said. And therefore the essence of a composed thing is not predicated of the composed thing itself in just any way, for it cannot be said that man is his quiddity. But the essence of a simple thing, which (essence) is its form, cannot be signified except as a whole, since nothing is there besides the form as receiving the form. Thus, no matter what way the essence of a simple substance is taken, it is predicated of the simple substance. Whence Avicenna says that the quiddity of a simple thing is the simple thing itself, because there is nothing other receiving the quiddity.

75. The second difference is that the essences of composed things, because they are received into designated matter, are multiplied according to its division. And this is why it happens that certain things are the same in species and diverse in number. But since the essence of a simple thing is not received into matter, such a multiplication is impossible here. And this is why, of

necessity, many individuals of a same species are not found among these substances; rather, as Avicenna expressly says, there are among them as many species as there are individuals.

66–75

Chapter five, as St. Thomas indicates in (66), is a continuation of the second of the three tasks set down in the introduction; it shows how essence is found in the separated substances: in the human soul; in the intelligences, which can be taken to designate what one ordinarily designates as an *angel* in religious language; and in the First Cause, God. In (67) St. Thomas notices that everyone agrees that the First Cause is simple, but that some, following Avicebron, hold the view that human souls and the intelligences are composed of matter and form. In (68) to (69) St. Thomas argues that human souls and the intelligences are entirely immaterial; that is, that they are totally free of matter, so that matter is not a component of their essence, nor are they in any way dependent on matter. He argues this from their power of understanding. In (70) he argues against the objection that it is not just any sort of matter which impedes intelligibility, but only corporeal matter. If this objection were accepted, then one could allow, it appears, that *incorporeal* matter is a component of the essence of an intelligent substance without undesirable consequences apropos of its functioning as intelligent or apropos of its being actually intelligible. St. Thomas argues against this objection by pointing out that the forms by reason of which matter is corporeal are actually intelligible, just as are other forms, by virtue of being abstracted from matter. From which it follows that it is not corporeal matter which impedes intelligibility, for if it were, then it would do this by virtue of the forms which render it corporeal. Thus, if "matter" is taken in the sense in which it is used apropos of physical substances (see pages 61–68), it cannot be said that matter is found in the essence of an intelligent substance, even though it be dubbed *incorporeal*. In (71) St. Thomas makes the claim that although the intelligent substances are not composed of matter and form, there is nonetheless a composition of form and existence in them. Most of what follows in this chapter is ordered toward making clear and establishing this claim. In (72) St. Thomas argues that it is not necessary that the essence of an intelligent substance be other than form alone; that is, that it is not necessary that an intelligent substance be composed of matter and form. He appears to argue this from the relation between matter and form. In (73) to (75) he points out two differences between a simple substance and a composed substance which follow from the fact that the essence of the latter includes both matter and form, whereas the essence of the former is simply form.

The Sort of Matter Which Is Found in Physical Substances Cannot Be Found in Spiritual Substances.

At first glance it does not seem unreasonable to hold that like physical substances, spiritual substances—namely, the intelligences and human souls—are composed of matter and form. For if one maintains that all things other than the First Cause are composed of matter and form, one has accounted in some way for the distinction between things not God, on the one hand, and God, on the other hand. God is simple; all things not God are composed. Nor does it seem, at first glance, unreasonable to maintain that the matter of physical things is a *corporeal or quantified* matter, whereas the matter of intellectual things is *incorporeal or nonquantified*. For in this way one can account in some way for the distinction between physical things on the one hand and the intelligences and human souls on the other. Thus, all things not God would have this in common that they would have matter as part of their essence, and in this way they would differ from God. Physical things would differ from spiritual things in that the matter of the former would be quantified and the matter of the latter would be nonquantified.

But if one considers this beyond a first glance, it is easy to see that it is impossible for spiritual and corporeal things to have matter in common as part of their essence, for matter of itself is indivisible. Consider that it would not be possible for the form of a spiritual substance and for the form of a corporeal substance to be received into the same part of matter; in such a case one and the same thing would be both corporeal and spiritual. Clearly, then, the form of the corporeal thing would have to be received into one part of matter; the form of the spiritual thing into another part of matter. But matter cannot be divided into parts unless it is quantified, for matter *of itself* is indivisible. Thus, the matter of spiritual things (if corporeal things and spiritual things have matter in common as part of their essence) would be a quantified matter, and not a nonquantified matter.[1]

Further, if one wants something of a same nature (or more simply, a same nature) to be found in more than one thing, it is clear that *formal division* is precluded. For one would not have a same nature in both these things. Formal division means precisely *difference in nature*. Thus, if prime matter, one and the same in nature, is to be found in more than one thing, a formal division is precluded. There must therefore be a quantitative division, so that if prime matter is found in more than one thing, it must be found in each as quantified.

Further, assume that prime matter *is* found in the realm of the intelligences. Then, (1) since potencies are understood in reference to their corresponding actualities, prime matter would be of an essentially different sort, for the *form* here is not the form of a thing which can come to be and cease to be (in change); and (2) there could be only *one* intelligence, *one* thing composed of prime matter and form, for there would be no quantity to permit a division. If one says that there can be many forms in the same prime matter (taking it as non-quantified), he has said that it is possible for a thing of one sort to be simultaneously of many different sorts.

One must notice, nonetheless, that matter of a different sort could without inconsistency be posited in the intelligences, so long as it is different from prime matter, and of a different sort for each individual intelligence.

The Human Soul Is Completely Immaterial

We have seen that the intelligences and human souls cannot have nonquantified matter as a component of their essences, for matter of itself is indivisible. If the intelligences and human souls had matter, they could have it only on condition that it were quantified. Thus, whatever has matter has quantified matter. And the quantified matter of whatever has it—i.e., the quantified matter of an individual composed substance, considered precisely as an *individual* substance—is not only quantified but also designated, i.e., circumscribed to being just so much (for the relation between matter *as quantified* and matter *as designated* see pages 147–150).

We shall now consider some evidence for the claim that human souls and the intelligences are entirely or completely immaterial. But first some preliminary considerations (1) apropos of the meaning of "completely immaterial" and (2) apropos of physical changes.

For a thing to be completely immaterial is for the thing to be such that matter is not a part of what it is *and* at the same time such that the thing is independent of matter for its existence and activity. To make this clear, one must consider that a thing can be said to be immaterial if it is such that matter is not a part of what it is, but such a thing may well be dependent on matter for its existence and activity; e.g., substantial forms, the accidental forms quantity and quality. A composed substance has matter as part of what it is, and hence it depends on matter for its existence and activity; this is why a composed substance can be said to be *completely material.* Any form found in a composed substance, whether it is a substantial form or an accidental form, is such that matter is not a part of what the form is; yet any such form depends on matter for its existence. This is why such a form can be said to be a *material form,* but no form is completely material. Only a composed substance can be said to be completely material.

In the context of physical changes, whether substantial or accidental, the forms received are *individual* forms because the recipient is *individual* matter. By "individual form" we mean a form which is *one, countably one,* of several of a same type. For example, consider the *type* whiteness, and consider the whiteness of this page of this book. The whiteness of this page is an individual whiteness, the whiteness of page 143 is another individual whiteness, and so on for each page of the book. Or consider the *type* manness, and consider Jack, Joe, and Paul; Jack is an *individual* man, so too Joe, and so too Paul. Consider, now, what it is that makes it possible that there be many (2 or more) individual whitenesses; what makes it possible that there be many individual men; what makes it possible that there be many individual chairs? The type man, considered as such, is neither *one* (countably one) nor *more than one;* so too the type whiteness, and the type chair. Man can be many only if man is found in something which is divisible in such a way that is actually being divided yields a numerical, i.e., countable, plurality; in the physical universe this is clearly three-dimensional extendedness. It is because the matter of the physical universe is three-dimensionally extended that it *can be divided* into diverse parts, each part of which *can be counted as one* (this is what is meant by "designated matter"), and into each of which, if subjected to an appropriate process, a form of a same type can be introduced.

We must notice that wherever matter is found, it is found as three-dimensionally quantified; and not only is it quantified, but it is circumscribed to being just so much (i.e., *actually divided* into diverse parts), just so much as is found in some given thing which we call an individual thing. If matter were not quantified *and* actually divided into diverse parts, the *forms* in the physical universe could not be numerically multiplied. There would be *no individuals* in the physical universe, which is to say that there would be no physical universe. Or there would be at most *one* thing in a nonquantified material universe, and this thing would not be countably one, but one in the sense in which something absolutely considered can be said to be one.

Thus, in the context of physical changes, whether substantial or accidental, the forms received are *individual* forms because the recipient is *individual matter*. The same thing is to noticed in the context of sensitive activity. The sensible form or species received into the sense is received into a bodily organ, like the eye, an organ which is three-dimensionally quantified and circumscribed to being just so much; and this is why the form received is an *individual* form. Thus, we can see that, universally speaking, if the recipient of a form is *individual matter*, the form received is an individual form. Thus, if we can discover in an examination of the contents of our diverse knowing experiences a form which is not an individual form, it will follow that there is in us a power which is not a power of some bodily organ.

Matter cannot be a part of what a human soul is, for the human soul performs the activity of understanding. To understand is to receive the forms (essences) of things absolutely, i.e., as separated from, or as abstracted from, individuality. For example, to understand *man* is to have grasped *something composed of flesh and bones and soul*, absolutely, or without qualification. It is true that existing men are *individual* men; each man is something composed of *this* flesh and *these* bones and *this* soul. It is the presence in the individual of *quantified matter circumscribed to being just so much*—i.e., designated matter—which accounts for its being an individual. But our intellectual knowledge of that to which we attach the word "man" is simply "something composed of *flesh* and *bones* and *soul*," i.e., the qualifiers *this* and *these* are not included.

Even though each human soul is an *individual soul*, it cannot be that it has matter (the matter of an individual is designated matter) as part of what it is. For it is clear that whatever is received into something must be received according to the mode (or capacity or nature) of the recipient. Since the human soul, *in knowing what things are*, receives the forms (essences) of things absolutely—i.e., since its mode of reception in intellectual knowledge is absolute—the human soul must be such that it is an absolute form. This is to say that matter cannot be part of what a human soul is.[2]

If the human soul were composed of matter and form, what would follow? It would follow that the forms of things received in knowledge would be received into it as individuals. This is what takes place with the senses which receive the sensible forms of things in a *bodily* and *material* organ; it is the matter (designated) of the sense organ which individualizes the forms received. This is also what takes place in the generation of a substance; it is the matter (designated) which survives from the term from which which individualizes the form received. The same thing would follow if the intellectual soul were held to operate through some bodily organ—e.g., the brain—in the way in which the power of sight operates through the bodily organ which is the eye. The matter (designated) of the organ would individualize the form received.

Thus, the human soul has a total freedom from matter such that it does not have matter as part of it, such too that it is not a form impressed on matter, i.e., a form which exists and operates with a dependence on matter.

It is to be noticed that St. Thomas adds this to what we have just said, "It remains, therefore, that the intellectual soul, *and every intellectual substance which knows forms absolutely,* is without matter-form composition" (*S.T.*, I, q.75, a.5, c.); nor is it a form impressed on matter. Thus, matter cannot be a part of the essence of an angel, or does the angel depend on matter for its existence and activity. For what is true of the human soul *qua* possessing the power of understanding by virtue of which it knows forms absolutely is true of everything which possesses the power of understanding. Angels, therefore, are substances which are not composed of matter and form. They are substances which are simply forms; they are completely immaterial substances. Thus, one can conclude with St. Thomas that "there is in no way a composition of matter and form in the soul or in an intelligence if matter in them is taken in the sense in which it is taken in corporeal substances" (70).

We must notice this difference between the human soul and an intelligence. Whereas an intelligence is a substance, the human soul is *part* of a substance, *part* of man's essence, the other part being the human body. It is not man's essence which is completely immaterial; only a *part* of man's essence is completely immaterial; only man's soul is completely immaterial. We must notice, further, that what we have just called the *complete immateriality* of man's soul must be properly understood; it can be described as a complete immateriality which is at the same time *partial*. When we say *partial*, we mean man's soul is the substantial form of man's body. As the form of a living body, man's soul is the originative source of vegetative and sensitive activities, which take place with a dependence on matter, on the matter which is man's body. Thus, man's soul has activities, hence *powers* or *parts,* which are material in the sense of *dependent on matter.* Thus, man's soul is in some of its powers or *parts* dependent on the body. In its intellectual power or part it is independent of the body. This is what is meant by describing the *complete immateriality* of the human soul as a *partial* one.

Suppose someone points out that certain sorts of brain damage result in impaired thought, and sometimes in the total cessation of thought. From this one may want to conclude that the human soul operates with a dependence on the matter of the body, and is therefore not completely immaterial. It is clear that the human intellect is an intellect which functions through the senses, both external and internal, and that damage to certain crucial bodily organs, including the brain, can affect thought. But to say that the intellect functions through the senses is to say that it depends on them for its contact with the things it knows, for an object to think about. It is not to say that the intellect depends on them as on an instrument through which it performs its proper activity, in the way in which the power of sight depends on the bodily organ which is the eye. For, if this were so, the forms received into it in knowledge would be individual and not absolute, as has been said. The bodily organs of the sense powers (both external and internal) are that by which the intellect is offered an object to think about, but the thinking itself is the intellect's own and proper activity.

We know by human knowing powers, unaided by Revelation, that human souls exist and that they exist as they were described just above. That is, each man, by introspection, knows this about his own soul. What is distinctive of human knowledge, among the features of the things which exist in the physical universe, is that it is knowledge of forms absolutely. Absolute knowledge of forms is an indisputable element of man's knowing experience. It is from this element in our knowing experience that the existence of the human soul as a simple form—i.e., as something completely immaterial—is drawn.

As regards our natural knowledge of the existence of angels, we can perhaps accept the traditional proof for the existence of God *from physical motion* (see St. Thomas, *S.T.*, I, q.2, a.3, c.). This proof (I am speaking of its explicit formulation in *S.T.*, I, q.2, a.3, c.) appears to conclude to the existence of a *pure form,* an immaterial thing, but this need not be God. It may, therefore, be taken to be an angel. Or, at any rate, it appears difficult to see why it must be God, for the middle term, *something in physical motion,* from which this proof proceeds does not appear to be adequately universal to rise to the existence of God. If God is taken as what is first among *all things,* then the middle term of a proof for God's existence must apply to *all things not God,* and physical things are not all things not God. Further, it is not necessary that what is immaterial be God, for what is immaterial need not be pure act (see pages 162 and 183–184), although it *is* necessary that God, the first among all things, be immaterial, for God is absolutely independent, and hence cannot be composed of matter and form. We must note that if this proof (or any other) is not accepted as having shown the existence of an angel, it is still acceptable to proceed hypothetically, i.e., to say that *if* an angel exists, it cannot be composed of matter and form, since we consider an angel to have the power of understanding.

FURTHER REMARKS ON MATTER

It seems useful at this point to add to the remarks made above about matter in the context of discussing matter as individuating principle (see pages 75–79). When we speak about *quantified* matter, as we have been in the two preceding sections (pages 139–147), we are not talking about anything other than that matter which is part of the intrinsic constitution of an *individual* composed substance, that matter which can also be described as *prime,* as *designated,* and as *nondesignated* (see pages 77–78). Thus, to talk about prime matter, quantified matter, nondesignated matter, and designated matter is to talk about the same thing, but to say *four different* things about it, to describe it in four different ways. To speak of quantified matter, or perhaps better of matter *as quantified,* is to speak of what the matters of *all* individual composed substances have in common, namely, that in their matters which accounts for the possibility of their matter's being divided from the matters of other individual substances; it is to speak of that which makes it possible for individual composed substances to have matter in common as part of their essence. Matter *as designated* presupposes, and *adds to,* matter as quantified; and what it adds is *actual circumscription so as to be just so much.* To say that matter is *quantified* is to say that it is three-dimensionally spread out, and nothing else. To say that matter is *designated* is to say that it is three-dimensionally spread out *and circumscribed to be just so much,* just so much as is in Jack or Paul or any given individual composed substance.

We wrote above (page 76): "The composed essence is numerically multipl*ied* into individuals of a same species by reason of the division—i.e., the circumscription to so much—of designated matter. The composed essence is numerically multipl*iable* into individuals of a same species by reason of the divisibility of matter." The divisibility of matter belongs to matter *as quantified;* the source of the multipliability of individuals of a same species lies in matter's being quantified, i.e., three-dimensionally spread out. The *fact of the multiplication* of individuals of a same species presupposes, but needs more than, the divisibility of matter which is rooted in matter's being quantified; the more which it needs is what we described as *designated* matter, matter's factual division and circumscription to being just so much.

The matter which is part of the intrinsic constitution of an individual composed substance can also be described as *common sensible matter* and *individual sensible matter*. These descriptions of matter are taken from and expressed in terms of the *sensibly perceivable qualities* of the matter of composed substances, e.g., firmness, warmth, color, rigidity, etc. The expression *common sensible matter* refers to a description of the matters of individuals of a same *species* or *genus,* a description in terms of the sensibly perceivable qualities found commonly in all of them, e.g., the expression *flesh and bones* is an attempt to characterize or describe the human body in terms of sensible qualities perceivable in the bodies of all individual men. The expression *individual sensible matter* refers to a description of the matter of a given individual, say Socrates, in terms of the sensible qualities which are proper to or distinctive of Socrates; the expression *these bones and this flesh* is an attempt at this.

Perhaps the preceding can be made clearer and fuller. Consider the following two columns containing six different descriptions of the matter which is part of the intrinsic constitution of an individual composed substance:

I	II
(a) Prime matter (matter as prime)	(d) Quantified matter (matter as quantified)
(b) Nondesignated matter (matter as nondesignated)	(e) Common sensible matter (matter as sensible and common)
(c) Designated matter (matter as designated)	(f) Individual sensible matter (matter as sensible and individual)

We must notice that description (d) includes, but adds to, description (a). Description (c) includes, but adds to, description (d); what it adds is *circumscription to being just so much*. Description (b) includes, but adds to, description (c) (hence also includes description [d]); what it adds is a relation of negation; what it adds is a denial of circumscription to being just so much as is, say, in Socrates; what it adds can be expressed as circumscription to being just so much, *but within the limits of variation* found in a given species or genus. Description (e) includes, but adds to, description (b); what it adds is the sensible qualities commonly found in the individuals of a species or genus, e.g., *flesh and bones* without qualification. Description (f) includes, but adds to, description (c); what it adds is the sensible qualities proper to and distinctive of some given individual, say Socrates, e.g., *this flesh and these bones*. Description (b) includes descriptions (c), (d), and (a); it does not include descriptions (f) and (e). Description (f) includes descriptions (c), (e), (b), (d), and (a).

We must also notice that the first description in each of the two columns is at a same level of universality, i.e., (a) and (d) describe something which is common to the matters of all individual composed substances. The second in each column—i.e., (b) and (e)—is at a same level of universality, and describes something which is common to the matters of all individuals of a same species or of a same genus. The last in each column—i.e., (c) and (f)—is at a same level, that of the individual, and describes something which is distinctive of the individual.

We must notice, too, that to describe the meaning of "individual sensible matter" is not the same as describing the individual sensible matter of some thing, and to describe the meaning of "common sensible matter" is not the same as to describe the common sensible matter of some genus or species. Also, to describe the meaning of "designated matter" is not the same as describing the designated matter of some individual thing, and to describe the meaning of "nondesignated matter" is not the same as describing the nondesignated matter of some genus or species.

We must notice, lastly, that each of the six descriptions are descriptions of matter in terms of something other than matter itself. This happens with any description of matter, for matter of itself, as we have seen above (page 68) is not intelligible.

THE HUMAN SOUL IS INCORRUPTIBLE.

We saw above (pages 141–146) that the human soul is a *subsistent form*—i.e., that it operates and therefore exists independently of matter as of a subject—although we did not use the expression *subsistent form*. Matter is the proper subject for a substantial form, i.e., a substantial form can exist only in matter as in a subject; there is no subject but matter in which it could exist. Thus, if the human soul in its existence is independent of matter as of a subject, the human soul is an ultimate existing subject; the human soul exists in the way proper to a *substance*. Of course, the human soul is subsistent only *partially*, i.e., only to the extent of its intellectual power or part (see page 145). From its immateriality—i.e., from its subsistent character—follows the incorruptibility of the human soul, argues St. Thomas.

There are two ways in which something can be corrupted: (1) *per se* or (2) *per accidens*. For a thing to be corrupted *per accidens* is for it to go out of existence in change because of, or at, the going out of existence of something other. Either this other can be that on which the first depends as on a subject, which (subject) is such that it is an ultimate existing subject *and* is such that it is composed of matter and form. Or this other can be a whole of which the first is a part. For a thing to be corrupted *per se* is for *it* to go out of existence in change without dependence, i.e., not because of a dependence which it has on another as on a subject which is composed of matter and form, for it itself is such an ultimate existing subject; nor because of a dependence which it has on another as a part on a whole, for *it* is the whole. Now, only that can be corrupted *per accidens* which exists *per accidens;* e.g., with dependence on another as on a subject—as an accident on substance, or a material form on matter—or with dependence on another as a part on a whole, as a substantial form on the composite. And only that can be corrupted *per se* which exists *per se*, and only ultimate existing subjects exist *per se.* This is so because corruption (and generation) belongs to a thing in the same way that existence, which is lost by corruption (and acquired by generation), belongs to it. If a thing cannot exist *per se*, it is clear that it cannot come to be *per se;* either can it cease to be *per se.*

Since the human soul is a *subsistent* form, it cannot be corrupted *per accidens*, i.e., by the corruption of the individual composed substance, say Socrates. (We are not saying that Socrates is not, or cannot be, corrupted; every man is subject to death, and to die is to be corrupted, or to go out of existence in change.) If the human soul is to be corrupted at all, it will have to be corrupted *per se.* But it cannot be corrupted *per se,* for corruption is the separation of a thing's substantial form from the thing itself. But the human soul *is* a substantial form, and a substantial form cannot be separated from itself; nothing can be separated from itself. Thus, it is impossible that a subsistent form be corrupted. The human soul is incorruptible.[3]

We must notice carefully *precisely what it is* that has been shown just above. It has *not* been shown that the human soul

cannot go out of existence absolutely. What has been shown
has been shown in a determinate context, in the context of
change. What has been shown is that a human soul cannot go
out of existence in change (substantial change). There is
nothing in the nature of the human soul to prevent its going out
of existence in some way other than the way of change. It has
not been shown, therefore, that the human soul cannot be
annihilated.

HAS THE ABOVE SHOWN THAT THE HUMAN SOUL IS INCORRUPTIBLE?

If the human intellect needs the bodily organs of the senses
(both of the external senses and of the internal senses, especially of the internal) as the means by which it is offered an
object to think about, even though the actual thinking is its
own proper activity,[4] then the human soul in separation from
the body is an entity without a function; that is, it is something
which cannot think. This appears to be to say that the human
soul has not been shown to be incorruptible, for a thing
without a function is an impossibility. If for the soul to be is for
the soul to think, then for it not to think is for it not to be.

This is to be said in reply. Since the human soul is to an
extent a subsistent form (see pages 141–146), it is to that
extent incorruptible; that is, to that extent it cannot, and
therefore does not, cease to be at the death of a man. Nonetheless, it must, and therefore does, cease to think at the death of
the man; and this is the case precisely because there is no
possibility of its confronting an object to think about; the
human intellect is an intellect which functions on objects
offered to it via the body.

Thus, the objection is in part acceptable, in part not. It
cannot be accepted as demonstrating that the human soul has

not been shown by the above to be incorruptible. But it can be accepted as having brought out an important feature of the condition of the separated human soul. The separated human soul cannot be said to be an entity without a function, as the objection has it, if this is taken to mean that it is a thinking thing which *cannot think,* although it is the case that it is a thinking thing which *does not* think. But if one can accept saying that the separated human soul is a thing without a function, that is a thinking thing which *cannot think,* this is not to be interpreted as pointing to some intrinsic change which the soul has undergone at the death of the man, as a result of which it is intrinsically no longer capable of thinking. Nor is this to be interpreted as saying that there are no knowable objects. The separated soul *is* intrinsically capable of thinking, and there *are* knowable objects, but its separation from the body makes these knowable objects unavailable to it. It is, in this respect, in a state much like the state of a man in a dreamless sleep: he is intrinsically capable of thinking, and there are knowable objects, but they are unavailable to him. From this it is clear that one cannot conclude, as the objection does, that the separated soul does not exist because it does not think. For the being of the soul is not identical with its thinking, or does its being depend on its thinking.

One must note that there appears to be no reason why objects which are of themselves actually intelligible, because actually separated from matter, could not be available to the thinking activity of the separated human soul. For even in the body the human soul knows by making actually intelligible, by abstraction from matter, that which is only potentially intelligible, namely, physical things. If this be accepted, then the separated human soul can be said to know, and know immediately on its separation from the body, at least itself. For in this state of separation from matter it is clearly something actually intelligible.

It Is Not Necessary That the Essence of an Intelligent Substance Be Other Than Form Alone.

Having put forth in (71) the claim that although human souls and the intelligences are forms without matter—i.e., although there is in them no matter-form composition—there is nonetheless a form-existence composition in them, St. Thomas pursues two arguments apropos of this form-existence composition. The first argument, given in (72), concludes that *it is not impossible* that some form exist without matter, and also that *it is not necessary* that the essence of a human soul or that of an intelligence be other than *form alone*. The second argument, given below in (76) to (81), shows that the form-existence composition of human souls and of the intelligences is a potency-act composition, and that although they are pure forms—i.e., forms without matter—human souls and the intelligences are not pure act.

If one considers the four causes according as they are related among themselves, it is clear that the final cause is the cause of causes.[5] The final cause causes the other causes (efficient, formal, and material) to function as causes, and in the order listed. That is, the final cause causes the efficient cause to function as an efficient cause, i.e., to cause efficiently (and not to be the thing that it is); the efficient cause causes the formal cause to cause formally; the formal cause causes the material cause to cause materially. And, it is to be noted, the material cause, too, causes the formal cause to cause formally. That is, it is not the efficient cause alone (drawn by the final cause) which causes the causality of the form; rather, it is the *active* causality of the agent along with the *receptive or subjective* causality of matter. For the form brought forth by the active causality of the agent is not brought forth except in some matter such by nature that it is capable (passively) of acquiring and maintaining the form. From this it follows, as St. Thomas argues in (72), that it is impossible that matter exist without some form. For, when two things are so related that one is a cause of the other, the one which is the cause can exist without the other, but not vice versa. Matter cannot exist without some form because form is a cause of matter's existence.

But it also follows from the causal relations between matter and form that form cannot exist except in some matter, since matter is a cause of form's existence. St. Thomas does not here draw this conclusion; he simply does not call attention to matter's causality in relation to form. Therefore, he appears, at least at first glance, to want to argue in this way. Since form is a cause of matter, and since a cause can exist without that of which it is the cause, but not vice versa, it follows that form can exist without matter, but that matter cannot exist without form. This would follow only if matter were in no way a cause of form. That is, the general statement "Whatever things are so related to one another that one is a cause of the other's existence, the one which is the cause can have existence without the other, but not conversely" is acceptable only if interpreted in this way: If two things, A and B, are so related that A is a cause of B, *and B is in no sense a cause of A*, then A can exist without B, but not vice versa.

A more careful consideration of (72) reveals that it contains two separate arguments. One argument establishes that it is impossible that matter exist without some form. The argument is this. Form is a cause of matter. Something which depends on a cause cannot exist without that cause. Therefore, ... And although his formulation of the argument includes pointing out that the cause can exist without that of which it is the cause, St. Thomas does not on this ground, and rightly does not, conclude that some form can exist without matter. His premises may therefore be said to contain this as a superfluous, and to some extent misleading, element. He offers a second and separate argument to show both (1) that it is not impossible that some form exist without matter and (2) that it is not necessary that the essence of a human soul and that of an intelligence be other than form alone. St. Thomas says, "form, to the extent that it is form, does not depend on matter." To make this argument clear, one must notice that one can ask, "How does one know that form as form does not depend on matter?" so that the *whole* reason is not explicitly stated. The whole reason is as follows: form, to the extent that it is form, does not depend on matter because some forms as a matter of fact (as has been shown from their power of understanding) exist independently of matter. His argument is of this sort: if something is a fact, it is not impossible, and its opposite is not necessary. It is a fact that some forms exist independently of matter; therefore, it is not impossible that they exist independently of matter, and it is not necessary that they be composed of matter and form.

One might wonder why St. Thomas makes it a point to *state explicitly* the conclusion (1) of the nonimpossibility of some forms' existing without matter and (2) of the non-necessity of a matter-form composition in intelligent substances. For is it not immediately clear that if something is a fact, it is not impossible, and that its opposite is not necessary? The reason appears to be a desire to counter *explicitly* the view that it is impossible for a thing to be simply a form without being God, and that it is necessary for a thing which is not God to be composed of matter and form. If everyone admits the simplicity of the First Cause, as St. Thomas points out in (67), then it is necessary that in everything other than God there be a composition. But if there is a thing other than God in which there is no matter-form composition, then that thing is simple; and so one might want to say that it must be identical with God. St. Thomas has offered a successful argument for the claim that intelligent substances are pure forms. But he sees the need for maintaining that they are not identical with God. There must, therefore, be some sort of composition in them which is not found in God. This composition is the form-existence composition. His argument for this claim is given below in (76) to (81).

Some Conclusions About the Simple Substances

If one does not allow that we know with a certainty based on our natural knowing equipment, our senses and our intellect, *that there are* such things (that there is at least one such thing) as those about which we are about to prove something, the bit of metaphysical science which one produces will be a disappointing, an improper and hypothetical, bit (see pages 146–147). Philosophical science is properly done about something only if one knows with a certainty based on our natural knowing equipment that there is such a thing. The primary question of philosophical science is, *What* is it?, but this question is not a properly scientific question until the question Is there such a thing? has been affirmatively answered.

One can draw some conclusions about the intelligences at this point. First of all, *if* (hence hypothetical) the intelligences exist, then they are incorruptible, for any subsistent form is incorruptible (see pages 151–153).

Secondly, one can draw the conclusions which St. Thomas draws in (74) to (75) apropos of the differences between composed substances and simple substances. The first of these differences bears on *us as knowers;* the second difference bears on the *intelligences themselves;* both differences are rooted in the absence of matter in simple substances. The first difference is this. Whereas the essence (specific) of a composed substance can be signified *as a whole* or *as a part* because of designated matter, the essence of a simple substance, which is simply a form, cannot be signified except as a whole, since there is no designated matter. Thus, whereas the essence (specific) of a composed substance can be predicated of it only if signified *as a whole* (we cannot say Socrates is humanity), the essence of a simple substance can be predicated of it, whether we use a word form which when applied in the context of composed substances signifies as a whole or as a part (we can say Gabriel [angel] is Gabrielity).

The second difference is this. The essences of composed substances are multiplied *in a same species* by reason of the division of designated matter. But there is no designated matter in the intelligences. Therefore, there cannot be a plurality of intelligences of a same specific nature. Each individual in the realm of the intelligences is as a species in the physical realm. This is why, notes St. Thomas, Avicenna can say, "there are among them [namely, the intelligences] as many species as there are individuals." Thus, *if* there exist substances which are simple forms, it is a property of each individual among them to be as a species in the physical world.

76. Although substances of this sort are forms alone without matter, they are not utterly simple so as to be pure act. They have an admixture of potency, which becomes clear in the following consideration.

77. Whatever is not of the understood content of an essence or quiddity is something which comes from without and makes a composition with the essence, because no essence can be understood without the things which are parts of it. Now, every essence or quiddity can be understood without anything being understood about its existence. For I can understand what a man is, or what a phoenix is, and yet not know

whether they have existence in the real world. It is clear, therefore, that existence is other than essence or quiddity, unless perhaps there exists a thing whose quiddity is its existence.

78. And there can be but one such thing, the First Thing, because it is impossible to plurify a thing except: (1) by the addition of some difference, as the nature of the genus is multiplied in its species, or (2) by the reception of a form into diverse matters, as the nature of the species is multiplied in diverse individuals, or (3) by this: that one is absolute and the other is received into something; for example, if there were a separated heat, it would by virtue of its very separation be other than heat which is not separated. Now, if we posit a thing which is existence alone, such that this existence is subsistent, this existence will not receive the addition of a difference because it would no longer be existence alone, but existence plus some form. And much less will it receive the addition of matter because it would no longer be a subsistent existence, but a material existence. Whence it remains that such a thing, which is its own existence, cannot be but one.

79. Whence it is necessary that in every thing other than this one its existence be other than its quiddity, or its nature, or its form. Whence it is necessary that existence in the intelligences be something besides the form, and this is why it was said that an intelligence is form and existence.

80. Now, whatever belongs to a thing is either caused by the principles of its nature, as the ability to laugh in man, or comes to it from some extrinsic principle, as light in the air from the influence of the sun. But it cannot be that the existence of a thing is caused by the form or quiddity of that thing—I say caused as by an

efficient cause—because then something would be its own cause, and would bring itself into existence, which is impossible. It is therefore necessary that every such thing, the existence of which is other than its nature, have its existence from some other thing. And because every thing which exists by virtue of another is led back, as to its first cause, to that which exists by virtue of itself, it is necessary that there be some thing which is the cause of the existence of all things because it is existence alone. Otherwise, there would be an infinite regress among causes, since every thing which is not existence alone has a cause of its existence, as has been said. It is clear, therefore, that an intelligence is form and existence, and that it has existence from the First Being, which is existence alone. And this is the First Cause, which is God.

81. Now everything which receives something from another is in potency with respect to what it receives, and what is received into it is its act. It is necessary therefore that the quiddity itself or the form, which is the intelligence, be in potency with respect to the existence which it receives from God; and this existence is received as an act. It is in this way that potency and act are found in the intelligences, but not form and matter, unless equivocally.

82. Whence, *to suffer,* and *to receive,* and *to be a subject,* and all things of this sort, which are observed to belong to things by reason of matter, also belong equivocally to intellectual and to corporeal substances, as the Commentator says in his considerations on the third book of *On The Soul.*

83. And because the quiddity of an intelligence is, as has been said, the intelligence itself, its quiddity or essence is identically that which it itself is; and its existence

received from God is that whereby it subsists in reality. And this is why substances of this sort are said by some to be composed of "that by which it is" and "that which is," or as Boethius says, of "that which is" and "existtence."

76–83

Having shown from their power of understanding that intelligent substances cannot be composed of matter and form, and having asserted that there is in them a form-existence composition, St. Thomas begins here an argument which establishes (1) the fact of the form-existence composition in them and (2) the fact that form in them is related to existence as potency to act. From which latter it becomes clear that although intelligent substances are simple with respect to matter-form composition—i.e., are pure forms—they are nonetheless not absolutely simple and hence not pure act, since there is potency in them. In (76) St. Thomas sets himself the task of showing this to be the case. And he does a number of things by way of pursuing this task. In (77) he shows, first of all, that in natural substances existence is other than essence. Then in (78) he argues that *if* there exists a thing in which existence and essence are identical, then there can be but one such thing. In (79) he draws two conclusions from the conclusion of (78). The first conclusion is that in everything other than the one thing in which existence and essence are identical, its existence must be other than its essence. The second conclusion, which is but a particularization of the first, is that the existence of an intelligence must be other than its form, which is its essence. It is obvious that this is the case with human souls as well. In (80) he establishes the existence of God, under the name of Subsistent or Pure Existence, as the First Cause of all things in which existence is other than essence. Then in (81) he shows that the form or essence of an intelligence, which is identical with the intelligence itself, is related to existence as potency to act; and thus he completes the task which he had set for himself in (76). In (82) he points out that expressions like *suffering, receiving,* and *being a subject* are predicated equivocally of intelligent and of corporeal substances, since these features belong to things by reason of matter. In (83) he explains why some refer to an intelligence as being composed of "that by which it is" and "that which is," or of "that which is" and "existence."

IN NATURAL SUBSTANCES EXISTENCE IS OTHER THAN ESSENCE.

The conclusion established in (77)—namely, that in natural substances existence is other than essence—is often put in other ways: (1) the existence of natural substances is not included in their essence, (2) their existence is an addition to the essence, (3) their existence is distinct from the essence, (4) their existence is composed with their essence, or there is in them an essence-existence composition, (5) their existence is *per accidens* in relation to the essence. All these expressions are expressions describing one and the same condition in natural substances.

The argument of St. Thomas begins by recalling, in effect, two of the meanings of the word "essence" recorded above in chapter one: (1) essence is that in a real thing in virtue of which it can be grasped by the intellect, i.e., in virtue of which it is intelligible (see page 47); (2) essence, designated by the name "quiddity," is that in a real thing which furnishes the answer to the question "What is it?," i.e., which furnishes what is included in the thing's definition (see page 47). In the terminology of chapter four what is included in a real thing's definition, and only that, is what belongs to the thing's essence or nature signified as a whole and considered absolutely. Clearly, knowing the definition of a natural substance, as knowing *what a man is,* does *not* include knowing *that a man actually exists in the real world.* The definition of man is rational animal, or something composed of flesh and bones and rational soul; to know this is not, *in and by that very knowing,* to know that a man exists out there. This must not be misunderstood. It is not being said that the one who knows *what a man is* does not know that men exist in the real world. What is being said is that the one who knows *what a man is* does not *in and by that very knowing* know that men exist, although he most certainly does know it *in another way,* namely, by means of sense observation. Indeed, since our knowledge of what man is is derived, at least in part, from our sense experience of individual existing men, it is clear that we know in some way that men exist even before we come to know *what a man is.* The above can be summarized in this way: whatever one knows in knowing what a man is, he does not know that men exist. And this, it appears, is what St. Thomas means when he says, "every essence or quiddity can be understood without anything being understood about its existence. For I can understand what a man is, . . . , and yet not know whether [he has] existence in the real world." We wrote above (page 129), "Thus, neither to be nor not to be, whether in this or that given individual substance, or out there at all, or in the mind in knowledge, belongs to the essence considered absolutely."

Having given an example, man, from our experience with real things, St. Thomas adds another example, an example not of our experience with real things, the phoenix. And he does this, it appears, in order to make clear that it makes no difference whether we consider the essence of a thing for which it is possible to be in the real world or the essence [6] of a thing for which it is impossible to be in the real world. For it would appear that one would grant rather easily that *existence out there* does not belong to a phoenix, and for this reason: it does not because it cannot. St. Thomas is here suggesting that *what a man is* and *what a phoenix is* are in a very important respect exactly alike. Or, to put this in another way, St. Thomas is suggesting that there is another reason—a reason other than it does not because it cannot—for allowing that existence out there does not belong to a phoenix, and that this reason is exactly the same as the reason for claiming that existence out there does not belong to man. That a phoenix cannot exist in the real world is not part of what it is to be a phoenix. It is something consequent upon, or deducible from, what it is to be a phoenix. For what is a phoenix? A phoenix is a bird with the miraculous power of consuming itself in fire by its own act and of rising in youthful freshness from its own ashes. Clearly, knowing *what a phoenix is* does not include knowing either (1) that it cannot exist in the real world, or (2) that it does not, or, for that matter, (3) that it does. And this in a way similar to the way in which knowing *what a man is* does not include knowing either (1) that men actually exist in the real world, or (2) that they can, or, for that matter, (3) that they do not.

We can add further examples: knowing *what anything is* (anything means anything in the ten categories) does not, in the very knowing, include knowing that it actually exists out there, although this may well be known in some way other than in knowing *what it is*. This is true not only of definitions but also of meanings which are not definitions, even of the meaning of the word "being." Clearly, to know that "being" means *what exists* does not, in the very knowing, include knowing that something actually exists, although one may be tempted to say that it does on the basis of the fact that *exists* appears in *what exists*.

It follows, therefore, that *being out there* is one thing and that *what a being is* is another thing; that existence is *per accidens* in relation to the essence of a thing, unless perhaps there exists a thing whose essence *is* existence—i.e., a thing such that *what it is* is *existence*—or unless there is a thing whose essence is being, i.e., a thing such that *what it is* is *being*.

To clarify the immediately preceding, we must notice the following things:

(1) Although existence belongs *per accidens* to the essence of a natural substance (as a matter of fact, to the essence of every substance which is not God, as will become clear below; see page 172) in the sense that it is no part of *what the thing is*, nonetheless there is a sense in which existence can be said to belong *per se* to essence, in the sense that essence is the *proper subject* of existence. Only that has existence which has essence, so that if a thing has no essence, neither does it have existence nor can it; thus neither beings of the imagination, nor the logical intentions, nor true beings, considered precisely as true beings, have existence. Existence can be said to be related to that which has essence in the way in which motion is related to the mobile.[7]

(2) To say that existence is other than essence is to say that *existence out there* is neither a *part* of, nor the *whole* of, what a composed substance is. This is clear by simple inspection of the meaning of the expression "composed substance." This expression simply means something composed of matter and form. And not only is this clear by simple inspection—i.e., by looking to the nature absolutely considered—it is also clear from the facts of generation and corruption. If existence were *part* or *whole* of what a composed substance is, then an individual composed substance, say Socrates, could neither ever come to be nor cease to be.

(3) One may ask here, Why does St. Thomas at this point in his argument suggest assuming the existence of a thing whose essence is identical with existence—i.e., a thing such that the *whole* of what it is is existence—rather than a thing such that existence is *part* of what it is? If one speaks of a thing such that

existence is *part* of its essence, one has to inquire about the character of the other part or parts. Whether one or more than one, the other part(s) will necessarily have the character of nonexistence; otherwise they will not be distinguishable from existence. Clearly, nonexistence cannot be part of what a thing is. Thus, to say that existence is *part* of what a thing is entails saying that existence is the *whole* of what that thing is. And in this, one has another way of making clear the point made just above in (2) apropos of the essence of a composed substance. For to say that existence is part of what a man is would entail saying that existence is the whole of what a man is. But what a man is is simply something composed of flesh and bones and rational soul.

It is sometimes asked whether the otherness which St. Thomas' *man-and-phoenix argument* claims to have established between essence and existence is an ontological otherness; that is, whether the otherness established is an otherness *in the real world*. For the argument appears to be saying that *such-and-such is so* because *I understand it to be so:* "I can understand what a man is, or what a phoenix is, and yet not know whether they have existence in the real world. It is clear therefore that existence is other than essence or quiddity." The argument appears to show a conclusion about the real world from something which occurs in knowledge.

Now, the argument proceeds in terms of a certain relation of identity between what is in the real world and our knowledge about what is in the real world. For it proceeds (1) in terms of the clearly defined meanings given to the word "essence" in chapter one and (2) in terms of fastening on the nature of a natural substance absolutely considered. The word "essence," recall, designates what is at once that in a real thing by which the thing exists independently of human knowledge about it, and that in the real thing by which the thing is intelligible. It designates that which is at once both a principle of independent existence and a principle of intelligibility. It designates that by which the real world is related to the intellect, that by which the real world has an impact on the intellect. It is true, of course, that the essence as found in individuals in the physical world is one thing, and that as expressed within an intellect which has grasped it, it is quite another thing. That is, in the physical world it is some individual substance, or, perhaps better, many individual substances, whereas in the intellect which knows it, it is some individual accident. But it is also true, and this is what is of importance here, that what the intellect expresses to itself in knowing what a physical substance is is something which is in the physical substance. This expressed content is what belongs to the nature or essence absolutely considered. And it is the essence so considered which is that wherein the real world and our knowledge about it are identical. Thus, if that by which a thing exists in the real world is intelligible in such a way that its existence in the real world is not included in its intelligibility, it follows that the otherness of its essence and its existence is an otherness in the real world. The proper understanding of the man and phoenix argument, therefore, lies in focusing one's attention on the twofold character of essence recalled just above, and on the fact that the nature or essence absolutely considered is that wherein human thought and reality are identical. Thus, in this context *for something to be understood to be so* is also *for it to be so.*

It is often said that the essence and the existence of a natural substance (for that matter, of any thing which is not God) are *really distinct.* Indeed, it has been said that there are four things in a material substance which are really distinct: matter, form, the essence composed of matter and form, and existence.[8] How is the expression *really distinct* to be taken in such locutions? In ordinary usage things are said to be really distinct if they are distinct in the way in which two material and bodily supposits, i.e., individual substances, are distinct. For example, in the way in which Socrates and Plato are distinct or, to move out of the natural realm into the artificial realm, in the way in which two books are distinct, or two lamps are distinct. A real distinction, thus, is the sort of distinction which obtains between two individuated material and bodily things. It is helpful to notice that the Latin word for things is *res,* and that the adjective *realis* is derived from the noun *res.* Thus, to have two *res* is to have two things which are *really distinct.*

It is clear that if the four things listed above are to be said to be really distinct, "really distinct" cannot be taken in the ordinary sense, for neither of the four is a supposit. But each of the four is related to the supposit. Matter is *part* of the essence of a supposit; so too is form. Matter and form together constitute the *whole* essence of the supposit, and it is the supposit with an essence which has existence, i.e., what has essence is the *proper subject* of existence. Since each of the four is related to the *essence* of the supposit, and since it is by its essence that a supposit both is and is called a *res*—i.e., something out there—it is not difficult to see how one might want to extend "really distinct" to apply to the four. Applied to matter in relation to form or to form in relation to matter, "really distinct" would mean "distinct as part of essence from other part of essence." Applied to matter in relation to the essence (so too, applied to form in relation to the essence), "really distinct" would mean "distinct as part of essence from the whole of the essence." Applied to existence in relation to essence, "really distinct" would mean "distinct from essence as what is not a part of it." It is to be noticed that this extended use of "really distinct" does not require that all the *distincta* be real things—i.e., supposits with an essence—or does it require that all of them be an essence or some part of an essence. For existence is said to be really distinct from essence. What is required is that *at least one* of them be a supposit, or an essence, or part of an essence. Otherwise there would be no reason to call the distinction a *real* distinction, for without essence there is nothing which is real.

It is to be noticed that there is a sense in which it can be said that essence and existence are *really the same*. The Latin expressions *idem re* or *idem secundum rem* are often used to convey this sense. It is the sense in which the term from which of a change can be described as being *idem re* but at least *duo ratione,* where *idem re* is taken to mean *idem subjecto*. Thus, John's essence and his existence are really the same, *idem subjecto*—i.e., the *same* John who has an essence also has existence—yet his essence and his existence are also really distinct in the sense that his existence is not included in his essence.

There Can Be but One Thing in Which Existence Is Identical with Essence.

If there is a thing in which existence is identical with essence, there can be but one such thing. Two things are to be noticed about this claim of St. Thomas. The first is that he does not assert that there *is* such a thing; he asserts, in effect: *if* there is such a thing. He is proceeding hypothetically, and his purpose is to show that there can be only one such thing, and this will offer grounds for the conclusion he draws in (79), a conclusion relating to all things which are not God. The second thing to be noticed is that a thing in which existence is identical with essence is often described by St. Thomas as a thing which is pure existence, or separated existence, or absolute existence ("pure" or "separated" or "absolute" in the sense of "nothing but"), or subsistent existence (so that what exists is existence). His argument is as follows. There are three possible ways of multiplying or plurifying something: (1) by adding differences to it, as a genus is multiplied in its species; (2) by having it received into diverse parts (quantitative) of matter, as a species is multiplied in its individuals; and (3) by having it in one instance in an absolute or separated state, in another instance (or instances) in a received state. In which of these three ways, if any, can something which is existence alone, something which is pure and subsistent existence, be multiplied? If one adds differences to it (this is the first way of multiplying), one will indeed generate a plurality of existences, but not a plurality of pure existences. Each member of the plurality will be *existence plus some differentiating form*, and thus no longer pure existence, just as each member of a plurified genus is the *genus plus a difference*, i.e., a species, and not simply the genus. If it is received into diverse parts of matter (this is the second way of multiplying), it will be plurified by the plurality of the parts of matter. But each member of the plurality will not be a subsistent existence; each will be a material existence. If one considers the third way of multiplying something, one will easily see that only *one* member of the plurality can be a pure and subsistent existence; the other member (or each of the other members) will be a received existence, an existence in a subject. Thus, *if* there is a thing such that what it is is existence, there can be but one.

To the possible objection that St. Thomas has not shown that the three ways of multiplying exhaust all possibilities, this is to be said. Whatever be the number of ways which one might be able to devise for multiplying something, if *what is being multiplied* is to be found among the members of the resulting plurality, it must be taken in a pure or unmixed state; this is why it can never be more than one. All other members of the plurality must be taken with some addition; otherwise they will not be distinguishable from each other or from *what is being plurified*. Consider assuming that there is more than one pure existence, say two. Then because they are two, they must differ. We must therefore be able to discover that whereby they differ. But this difference is in principle undiscoverable. For the only possible difference in this context is nonexistence, and nonexistence is clearly not a difference. Or, if one of the two assumed pure existences differs from the other, it will have the self-contradictory status of being a nonexisting existence.

THERE EXISTS A THING WHICH IS EXISTENCE ALONE, AND WHICH IS THE CAUSE OF THE EXISTENCE OF ALL OTHER THINGS.

The argument of (77) to (79) establishes in effect a middle term which is adequately universal [9] for rising to a knowledge of God's existence. All things not God are describable as things in which existence is other than essence. It is interesting to notice the method of its establishment. St. Thomas begins in (77) with natural substances—i.e., with substances with which we are in immediate cognitive contact via sense experience —and shows that they can be described as things in which existence is other than essence. In (78) he argues that *if* (the *if* is to be noticed) there is a thing in which existence is identical with essence—i.e., if there is a God—there can be but one such thing. From this it follows that anything and everything besides this one thing must be such that its existence is other than its essence. This includes therefore all those things which are not given, or are giveable, to us in sense observation, things like human souls and angels. Thus, the establishment of this middle term involves an argument which begins with sense perceivable things, moves to an assumed God which can be but one, and concludes with things which are not God and which are not sense perceivable.

Having established an adequately universal middle term, St. Thomas begins the argument for the existence of God. If there is in a thing a feature which is no part of what the thing is, either this feature is caused by the principles of the essence of that thing, as the ability to laugh in man, or it is caused by something other than, something extrinsic to, the essence of that thing, as light in the air is caused by the sun. There are no other possibilities. To make the point of this clear, one should consider that one does not ask why a thing is *what it is*. That is, the question *why* is not asked about the definition of a thing or about any element of the definition unless the question is taken to be the equivalent of, What evidence have you for claiming that the thing is properly defined? And in this case the question being asked is really not Why is it what it is? but Why do you say it is what it is? For example, one does not ask, Why is man man, i.e., a rational animal? or Why is man an animal? or Why is man rational? unless, of course, he means, What evidence have you for claiming that man is properly defined when man is said to be a rational animal? But one does ask the question *why* about features of things which are not included in their definition. The presence of such features needs to be explained, whereas a definition does not, with the exception noted above. And there are only two possible sources of explanation: (1) an intrinsic source, i.e., the elements in the definition which expresses the principles of the essence of the thing, and (2) an extrinsic source, i.e., some really distinct thing. For example, consider a triangle which I have drawn on a blackboard with white chalk. One can ask, Why is the triangle white? after he noticed that being white does not appear in the definition of triangle. Clearly, not because it is a triangle, i.e., not because of an intrinsic source. Therefore, since there is no other possibility, it is white because of some extrinsic source, i.e., because of some thing which is really distinct from the white triangle. In this case what explains the fact that the triangle is white is I and the piece of white chalk I used in the drawing of it. It is clear that I and the white chalk are related to the whiteness of the white triangle in the way in which, in St. Thomas' example, the sun is related to the light in illuminated air. Consider, further, the question, Why is a triangle a figure with exterior angle equal to the sum of the opposite interior angles? The feature expressed by the words "a figure with exterior angle equal to the sum of the opposite interior angles" is a feature which does not appear in the definition of triangle. It is, nonetheless, a feature which is easily seen to belong to triangle because of triangle's definition, i.e., because of an intrinsic source. It is clear that the essence of triangle is related to this feature of triangle in the way in which, in St. Thomas' example, the essence of man is related to his ability to laugh.

Now, can the existence of a thing such that existence does not appear among the principles of its essence be caused—as by an efficient cause, specifies St. Thomas—by the thing's essence? Clearly not, for if it were, then the thing would be its own cause. And this is impossible, for nothing can be both cause and effect in the same relation, since this is to say that the thing depends on itself and at the same time that it does not depend on itself. Clearly, then, it must be that the existence of such a thing is caused by something other, by some extrinsic source. And what about this extrinsic thing? It must be something which exists by virtue of itself, i.e., it must be something in which existence is not other than essence. And this is so because whatever has some feature by virtue of something other than itself must be led back as to a first cause to something which has this feature by virtue of itself. (For example, matter is divisible into parts, not by virtue of itself, but rather by virtue of something other, for of itself matter is pure potentiality. This other must be something which is divisible by virtue of itself; this other is clearly the three dimensional quantity of the matter of the physical universe.) If this extrinsic thing is not something which exists by virtue of itself, then it must be, like the first thing, such that existence is an addition to its essence. If this extrinsic thing is such, then *its* existence, too, must be caused by something other, by some extrinsic source. And this other, is it too such that existence is other than its essence? It is clear, thus, that there must exist something which is the cause of the existence of all things which exist *and* in which existence is other than their essence, and that this thing must be such that it is existence alone, that it is pure and subsistent and unmixed existence. If this is not the case, there would be an infinite regress of efficient causes, since, as has been said, everything such that existence is other than its essence must have an extrinsic cause as the source of its existence. Thus, we know that God, pure and subsistent and unmixed existence, must exist because we know that things exist in which existence is not pure and subsistent and unmixed. Not only is it the case, therefore, that the existence of an intelligence is other than its form which is its essence (this was established in [77] to [79]) but, concludes St. Thomas toward the end of [80], it is also the case that God is the extrinsic source of this existence.

DIFFICULTIES

There are at least two assertions in the proof for God's existence given in [80] which may cause some concern. The first is an assertion which is included as part of the following argument of St. Thomas: "because every thing which exists by virtue of another is led back, as to its first cause, to that which exists by virtue of itself, it is necessary that there be some thing which is the cause of the existence of all things because it is existence alone." The assertion which is of concern may be formulated in this way: If something exists *per aliud*, then it is necessary that something exist which exists *per se*. (Call this assertion I.) This assertion is clearly put forth by St. Thomas as a necessary proposition. But it causes difficulty. For although it is clear that the *per aliud* necessarily implies something other than itself, it is not immediately clear that this other must be something *per se*. It is clear therefore that this assertion needs some sort of elucidation or justification.

The second assertion is this one: "Otherwise, there would be an infinite regress among causes, . . ." (Call this assertion II.) What is the point of this assertion? That is, what is the exact role of this concern with an infinite regress of caused causes? Specifically, does the argument of (80) conclude that God exists because an infinite regress of caused causes is impossible? And if so, on what grounds is the infinite regress shown to be impossible? Or, does the argument of (80) conclude that an infinite regress of caused causes is impossible because God exists? If the latter alternative is the case, then this concern with an infinite regress appears to be irrelevant to the proof of God's existence. If the former alternative is the case, then it appears that the existence of God has not been established here.

To make this last point clear, consider the following argumentation:

(1) There exists a thing, A, such that its existence is other than its essence.

(2) Every such thing must have its existence caused by another, and hence this other must exist. Therefore A has its existence caused by another, B.

(3) Either B is such that its existence is other than its essence or it is not. If not, then B is Subsistent Existence, God. If B is assumed to be such that its existence is other than its essence, then it has its existence caused by still another.

(4) Let us assume that there exists no caused cause except B; i.e., let us assume that there exists but *one* caused cause. Then it is necessary that there exist an uncaused cause, Subsistent Existence.

(5) Let us assume that there exist caused causes in addition to B, and in causal series with it and A, but that their number is

finite. Then it is necessary that there exist an uncaused cause, Subsistent Existence.

(6) Let us assume that there exist caused causes in addition to B, and in causal series with it and A, and that their number is *infinite* except that there is a *last* caused cause in this series, like $1 \leqq x \leqq 2$. Then it is necessary that there exist an uncaused cause, Subsistent Existence.

(7) Let us assume, now, an infinite number of caused causes, in causal series with B and A, but a series such that there is *no last* caused cause in it.

Here, in step 7, we have a case in which it appears difficult, perhaps impossible, to conclude that God exists. For no matter which caused cause you take, it appears to be able to explain the existence of all prior caused causes, and thereby the existence of A. And to the objection that no matter which caused cause you take, there must be an explanation in turn for *its* existence, since it is a *caused* cause, one can apparently reply that there is always a posterior caused cause to which to appeal, since the series being assumed is not only infinite but such that there is *no last* caused cause in it.

Apropos of assertion I this is to be said. The *per aliud* in this context is a *per aliud* with respect to *existence*. This means that the *per aliud* is *completely dependent* on an extrinsic source. To make this clear, consider the following. First of all, a thing cannot be dependent on its essence for its existence as on an efficient cause, as was explained above. Secondly, if in depending on an extrinsic source for its existence a thing were not completely dependent on that other thing, then it would depend on that thing for more than its existence. But what is there besides its existence? Only its nonexistence. Clearly, then, a thing cannot depend on an extrinsic source for more than its existence. Thus, it is completely dependent on that other thing. And it is to be noticed that "completely dependent on an extrinsic source" means not only that the *per aliud* cannot depend on the extrinsic source for more than its existence, as was explained above, but also that the extrinsic source is *all* that the *per aliud* depends on. This other thing must be such, therefore, that of itself it can account for the existence of the first thing; otherwise, the first thing could not be said to be completely dependent on it. But if it, too, like the first thing, is a *per aliud*, it in turn is completely dependent on another. But to say that some A is completely dependent on some B, and that B in turn is completely dependent on some C, is self-contradictory. For it is to say both that A is completely dependent on B, and that it cannot be completely dependent on B.

But one may say that it is possible for A not to be completely dependent on B and still to have its existence adequately accounted for, and without self-contradiction, so long as there is an infinite series of caused causes such that there is no last member in the series. Here we confront again assertion II, in the aspect focused on in step 7 above. This suggestion can be made clearer in this way. A would depend in a serial way on B, C, D, etc. *ad infinitum* in such a way that it would depend to some extent (i.e., not completely) on B, to some other extent on C via B, to still other extent on each member of the series via predecessors in the series. That is, though A would not be completely dependent on any one member in the series, it would be completely dependent on the series as a whole.

This suggestion cannot be accepted because an infinite series (whether there is a last member or not) of things each of which is completely dependent on something other than itself is a series which cannot exist. It is to be pointed out, first of all, that the only existence which the series has is the existence of each of its members. That is, if the members do not exist, either does the series exist. That the members of such a series cannot exist is clear from the fact that no matter which member you

choose, it is a member which is completely dependent on
something other than itself. No matter which one you choose,
you can choose only something which is *completely dependent*
on something other than itself. Thus an infinite series produces
an infinite number of self-contradictions: A is completely
dependent on B, and cannot be completely dependent on B; A
and B together are completely dependent on C, and cannot be
completely dependent on C; A is completely dependent on B
and C, and cannot be completely dependent on B and C; A, B,
and C together are completely dependent on D, and cannot be
completely dependent on D; etc. *ad infinitum.*

The preceding may be summarized in the following way. If
A *depends completely* on some extrinsic source, B, it makes no
difference whether there is but one B in existence, or more than
one. Nor does it matter whether the number of B's is finite or
infinite; and if infinite, it doesn't matter whether there is a last
member or not. In any of these cases B must of itself be capable
of accounting for the existence of A. The reason for this point
must be stressed, for it is a justification for, or rather an
elucidation of, the proposition, If something exists *per aliud,*
then it is necessary that something exist which exists *per se.* B
must of itself be capable of accounting for the existence of A,
both because A is completely dependent on an extrinsic source
and because B is here being assumed to be the only thing in
existence other than A. This is to say not only that what exists
per aliud necessarily implies the existence of another but also
that this other must be something which exists *per se.* If B is,
like A, something *completely dependent* on another, then it is
self-contradictory to assert that A *depends completely* on B.
And to suggest that there may be an infinite series of B's
without a last member is but to suggest an infinite number of
self-contradictions.

It may be helpful to notice that the dependence of A on B is
being conceived as a dependence *right now.* It is not the sort of

dependence which a son has on his parents; he does not cease to be at their ceasing to be. It is rather the sort of dependence which a man, or any living thing as a living thing, has *right now* on the sun; or the sort of dependence which light in the air has *right now* on the sun. It is not a dependence for *coming into existence;* it is rather a dependence for *continuing in existence.* Thus whether B is one, or more than one, or finite or infinite in number; and, if infinite in number, whether there is a last member or not, B exists *right now.* So that all that exists right now is either A or B, i.e., either A or that on which A has a complete dependence. Thus B must be capable of itself of accounting for the existence of A because A is right now completely dependent on some extrinsic source and B is all that exists right now besides A.

Apropos of the question, What is the exact role of St. Thomas' concern with the infinite regress of caused causes? this is to be said. It is a fact that St. Thomas makes no *explicit* inference from it, as re does in the *Summa of Theology.*[10] Nonetheless, the position of assertion II in the argument of (80) and the use of the word "otherwise" appear to indicate that St. Thomas intends saying at least that, on the assumption of an infinite regress of caused causes, the existence of A which needs accounting for is left unaccounted for. If this can be accepted, then it appears that the role of the infinite regress of caused causes here in (80) is, *implicitly,* that of a case to be considered in the elucidation of assertion I.

In order to make this clear, one should consider the following:

(1) If one looks to the way in which the infinite regress of caused causes functions in the *Summa of Theology,* and assumes that it has the same function in *On Being and Essence,* then St. Thomas is here pointing out that the assumption of an infinite regress of caused causes is the logical equivalent of a denial of the existence of what exists *per se.* And a denial of the

existence of what exists *per se* implies, by *tollendo tollens* (on the assumption that the proposition "if something exists *per aliud*, it is necessary that something exist which exists *per se*" has been justified), a denial of the existence of the *per aliud*. This is patently opposed to what was established in the man and phoenix argument. The conclusion at this point would be that an infinite regress of caused causes is impossible. And the reason for this conclusion would be the prior conclusion that God exists. But if this is so, then one would have to ask about the ground on which the conclusion of God's existence was established. In *On Being and Essence* this ground is clearly the proposition that if something exists *per aliud*, then it is necessary that something exist which exists *per se*.

(2) Nonetheless, still on the assumption that the infinite regress of caused causes has the same function in *On Being and Essence* as it has in the *Summa of Theology*, it is more proper to say that *both* the existence of God *and* the impossibility of the infinite regress of caused causes are shown from the proposition that if something exists *per aliud*, it is necessary that something exist which exists *per se*. God's existence follows from this proposition by the simple addition of this *quid nominis* of God, namely, Subsistent Existence. The impossibility of the infinite regress follows from it by *tollendo tollens*. Thus, although it can be claimed, on this assumption, that assertion II is irrelevant to the proof of God's existence in the sense that it does not function as a premiss, it can nonetheless be claimed to be relevant to the proof of God's existence in the sense that it serves to point out something which does not in fact have the function of a premiss, although there are some who think it does.

(3) It is to be noticed that the infinite regress of caused causes was in fact taken, in the preceding pages, as a case to be considered in the justification of assertion I (see pages 178–180). But it is most important to notice that it was

considered in order to infer the infinite number of self-contradictions mentioned above, and that the *source* of the inference is the *complete dependence* of A on an extrinsic source and not the infinite regress itself. It is also most important to notice the intent of the expression ". . . taken as a case to be considered in the justification of assertion I. . . ." It does not mean that assertion I is justified separately for each case. It means that it makes no difference what cases were brought forth as possibilities for the description of B, for the *complete dependence* of A on an extrinsic source, and the assumption that B is all that exists besides A, requires that B of itself be capable of accounting for the existence of A, and without self-contradiction. But this is impossible without self-contradiction, as has been shown.

However one wants to interpret the role of assertion II in the argument of (80), it is most important to notice the two uses to which the infinite regress of caused causes has been put in the preceding pages: (1) to infer that the *per aliud* does not exist (patterning its function after that which it has in the *Summa of Theology*) and (2) to infer the infinite number of self-contradictions (in the context of justifying assertion I); otherwise *petitio principii* can easily become a charge.[11]

Once one has seen that it is necessary that Subsistent Existence exists, it is not difficult to see that there may well be an infinite series of caused causes, so long as there is a *first* and a *last* member in the series in order to allow for the serial communication of causality. We do not say infinite *regress*, but infinite *series*, for "regress" is used in a context in which one is denying, for the purposes of the argument, the existence of Subsistent Existence. "Series," on the other hand, does not connote this denial; it appears to be a word with an openness both to the assertion of, and to the denial of, the existence of Subsistent Existence.

ALTHOUGH INTELLIGENT SUBSTANCES ARE PURE FORMS, THEY
ARE NOT PURE ACT.

Since everything not God is such that its existence is other than
its essence, it is clear that intelligent substances, like everything
else not God, receive their existence from God. And since every
recipient is related to what is received as potentiality to
actuality, it is clear that the form or essence of an intelligence
must be in potency with respect to its existence which it has
from God, and that its existence is therefore its actuality. It is in
this way that potency and act are found in the intelligences,
even though matter and form are not. An intelligence is pure
form, but not pure act, for there is potency in it. Subsistent
Existence alone is Pure Act, for it alone is related to nothing as
recipient to received.

"Potency" apropos of the intelligences must be properly
understood. In the context (page 64) of attempting to determine the character of what survives in substantial change, we
explicitly distinguished two senses of the potentiality-actuality
relation. "Potency," or "potentiality," as used just above is not
to be identified with either of those two senses. It is being used
here in a third and distinct sense, which can be made clear by
differentiating it from the second sense. This third sense is like
the second sense in two respects. (1) It is to be described as
something perfect*ed* (second sense) (as opposed to something
perfect*ible* [first sense]) in relation to a perfection. For the
existing intelligence is *in possession* of the perfection which is
existence, and it could not be otherwise without self-
contradiction, for it would then be described as an existing
intelligence which is not in possession of existence, i.e., as an
existing intelligence which does not exist. (2) Though *in
possession* of existence, the intelligence as intelligence has no

claim on it, does not of itself require it. Existence is something over and above the intelligence; it adds something to the intelligence as intelligence, and anything added can be called a perfection. But this third sense differs from the second sense (and from the first sense as well) in this respect: it eliminates all reference to *change*, hence also to *before and after change*. The intelligences, not being composed of matter and form, neither come to be nor cease to be in change. For a thing to be in potency in this third sense, therefore, is simply for it to possess something on which it of itself has no claim, something it does not of itself require.

Thus, if one wants to say that matter and form are found in the intelligences, one cannot use these words to mean exactly what they mean when used apropos of natural substances. One will be using them to express the third sense of the potentiality-actuality relation explained just above. One will, thus, be using these words equivocally, i.e., in a sense which is not exactly the same, as St. Thomas indicates in (81). And although there is no absolute reason not to use the words *matter* and *form*, as long as one specifies that what he means by them is the third sense of the potency-act relation, there is a historical reason for not using them. There would be a tendency to overlook, or to forget, the specification made, since there have been men in the history of philosophy, Avicebron and others following him (see pages 138–141), who claimed that all things not God are composed of matter and form, and that the matter of all things is the same in its nature as the matter of natural things. What is true of "matter" and of "form" if predicated of the intelligences as well as of natural substances is also true, as St. Thomas notices in (82), of "suffer," "receive," "being a subject," and all other terms referring to characteristics which belong to natural substances because of matter.

As regards describing the intelligences as being composed of form (essence) and existence, or of "that which is" and "that by which it is," or of "that which is" and "existence" (see [83]), it is clear that this composition is of a different sort from that of matter and form. For the composition of matter and form is a composition which constitutes an essence, a composition of principles *intrinsic* to an essence; whereas that of essence and existence is not. For existence is precisely an actuality over and above, and therefore added to, an essence. And this is so whether the essence is intrinsically composed, as is the case with natural substances, or whether it is intrinsically simple, as is the case with the intelligences. So that one should say that in a natural substance there is a composition *out of* matter and form, the words "out of" indicating that the composition is *within* the essence; and that in all things not God, including the intelligences, there is a composition of essence *with* existence, the word "with" indicating that the composition is *not* within the essence, that existence is an *addition* to the essence.

84. And because there is potency in the intelligences as well as act, it will not be difficult to find a multitude of intelligences, which would be impossible if there were no potency in them. Whence the Commentator says, in his considerations on the third book of *On The Soul*, that if the nature of the possible intellect were not known, we would not be able to find multitude among the separated substances. The separated substances, therefore, are distinct from one another according to their grade of potency and act, in such a way that a superior intelligence which is nearer to the First Being has more act and less potency, and so with the others.

85. This grading has its termination in the human soul, which holds the lowest grade among intellectual substances. Whence its possible intellect is related to

intelligible forms in the way in which prime matter, which holds the lowest grade in sensible existence, is related to sensible forms, as the Commentator remarks in his considerations on the third book of *On The Soul*. And this is why the Philosopher compares it to a blank tablet on which nothing has been written.

86. And because it has more potency than other intelligible substances, the human soul is so close to material things that a material thing is drawn to it to share its existence, but in such a way that from soul and body results one existence in one composed thing; and yet this existence is not dependent on the body inasmuch as it is the soul's existence.

87. And posterior to this form which is the soul are found other forms which have more potency, and which are still closer to matter, so close that they do not exist without matter. Among these forms, too, is found an order and a grading, down to the first forms of the elements, which are the closest to matter. These last are so close to matter that they operate only according to the active and passive qualities, and the other sorts of things, which are required as the means by which matter is disposed for the receiving of form.

84–87

Having shown how potency and act are found in the intelligences, St. Thomas notices in (84) that (1) the potency in them is the source of the possibility of their plurality and (2) that our understanding of the nature of our possible intellect is what enables us to understand the potency which is the source of this possibility. If there were no potency in them, there could not be a plurality of them. And if we had not come to understand the potential character of our possible intellect, we would be unable to understand what the potency in them amounts to. Diverse grades of potency, therefore, determine the grades of their actuality, and their grades of actuality thus determined distinguish them from one another, thus plurifying them, so that the superior intelligences have more act and less potency. In (85) St. Thomas points out that the human soul is the lowliest of the intelligent substances, being related to intelligible forms in the way in which prime matter is related to sensible forms. In (86) he points out that the magnitude of the soul's potentiality, facing the realm of intelligible forms, is manifested by the fact that a quantified portion of matter is drawn to it to enable it to exist and to operate. This is done in such a way, however, that the soul's existence and operation are its own (see pages 141–146), although they are shared by, and performed with accompaniments in, the body. There is one thing, the man, composed of body and soul, and there is one existence, the soul's. Although it is communicated to and shared by the body, this existence is independent of the body, except for its beginning (see page 222, [93] in the text of the treatise; also pages 225–227, 232). In (87) St. Thomas points out that there are forms other than the soul, more potential than it, lowlier than it. These forms exist and operate only in and through matter. But here too, as among the intelligent substances, there is a grading: from the sensitive through the vegetative, down to the forms of the elements, where activity is simply that activity which is necessary for preparing matter for the receiving of sensible and corporeal forms.

IF THERE WERE NO POTENCY IN THE INTELLIGENCES, THERE COULD NOT BE MANY OF THEM.

Whatever exists, and is such that there is absolutely no potency in it, exists as Pure Act. And Subsistent Existence is Pure Act.

Consider that the existence of an essence-existence composite is related to all else in the thing (even to the form of the thing, in the case of a matter-form composite; even to the form which *is* the thing, in the case of a simple substance like an intelligence) as act to potency; it is related to absolutely nothing else in the thing as potency to act. Existence has rightly been called the act of acts and the perfection of perfections; existence has rightly been described as what is most formal in a thing, as the ultimate act in a thing.[12] Now, if existence is the act of all acts in an essence-existence composite, if existence is related to nothing in the thing as potency to act, what must be true of that existence which is found in reality in a pure or separated or subsistent state? It is clear that it must be an act absolutely devoid of potency, i.e., it must be Pure Act. As we wrote above (page 183), "Subsistent Existence alone is Pure Act, for it alone is related to nothing as recipient to received." There is nothing which Subsistent Existence could receive or acquire; there is nothing which could be added to Subsistent Existence, for there is no potency in Subsistent Existence. Subsistent Existence is Actuality or Perfection in a state of absolute and unacquired fulfillment.

Thus, if there were no potency in an intelligence, it would be Pure Act, and hence Subsistent Existence. But we have seen that Subsistent Existence can be but one. If, therefore, there were no potency in the intelligences, there would be but one of them; or, perhaps more accurately, it would *not* be one of *them,* for it would be God. This is what St. Thomas means when he says in (84) that it would be impossible to find multitude in the intelligences if there were no potency in them.

The intelligences are distinguished from one another, and plurality thus arises, according to varying degrees of potency and act. The superior intelligence has more of act and less of potency, whereas the lower intelligence has more of potency and less of act. No two intelligences have the same degree of act; they cannot, for this would require that they be distinguished from one another by virtue of a distinction of matter, and each would thus be an individual of a same species. But this is impossible, for among the intelligences, as we have seen, there are as many species as there are individuals; and this is so because there is no matter in them (see pages 158–159).

The Potentiality of Our Possible Intellect, and That of the Intelligences

It is one thing to say that the intelligences are distinguished from one another according to varying degrees of potency and act. It is another thing to see what these degrees amount to, how the potency in them is to be understood. Everything we understand about immaterial things, whether these be human souls or the intelligences, is understood from, or in terms of, our understanding of what is given to us in the material world.

In terms of a reference to our understanding of substantial change (see pages 61–67), we come to understand that the human soul is completely immaterial, i.e., such that prime matter is not a part of what it is, such too that it does not depend on prime matter for its existence and proper activity. We base this conclusion on the indisputable fact, given to men in introspection, that human understanding is nothing other than the acquisition of—i.e., the production by abstraction and with dependence on sense perceivable things—and the possession of absolute forms (see pages 141–146). Thus, to say that the human soul is completely immaterial is to point to the fact that it produces and possesses absolute forms. And to say that the human soul is engaged in an act of knowing is to say either that it is producing these forms or that it is in possession of them (having produced them).

In terms of a reference to our understanding of the complete immateriality of the human soul, we come to understand the immateriality of the intelligences. From the fact that they are held to be in possession of absolute forms, they must be said to be completely immaterial. But from the fact that an intelligence is not the form of a body, it is free from what is peculiar to *human* knowing. It cannot therefore be said to have produced these absolute forms by abstraction and with dependence on sense perceivable things. Thus, to say that an intelligence is completely immaterial is to point only to the fact that it is in possession of absolute forms. And to say that it is engaged in an act of knowing is to say only that it is in possession of these forms. It is clear why Averroes can say that the human soul is related to intelligible forms in the way in which prime matter is related to sensible forms; each is the lowliest in its realm. Prime matter is a potentiality for *all* sensible forms; the human soul, for *all* intelligible forms. But there is this difference: whereas there can never be a time in which prime matter is not in possession of some sensible form, since prime matter is not a substance but only a part of a substance, there is a time in which the human soul is not in possession of any intelligible form, the time of infancy. And this is why Aristotle can compare the human soul to a blank tablet on which nothing has been written.

What, now, does it mean to say that a superior intelligence, one which is closer to Subsistent Existence, has more act and less potency? If the Pure Act which is Subsistent Existence is such that it is related to nothing as recipient to received, then to say that a superior intelligence has more act and less potency is to say that there are fewer things to which it is related as recipient to received. All things not God are related to their existence as a recipient to something received from God (see pages 183–184). Among intelligent things the human soul is related to the multiplicity of the intelligible forms it possesses as a recipient to something received from sensible things, at least in part. Since an intelligence cannot know all things in knowing its own essence (only God can know all things in knowing His own essence, for only God's essence comprehends all things), it must be in possession of intelligible forms whereby it knows those things which it does not know in knowing itself. And since an intelligence does not produce these intelligible forms by abstraction and with dependence on sensible things, these intelligible forms must be produced in it by some immaterial substance, either itself or another. It cannot itself produce them, for its essence does not comprehend those things of which these intelligible forms are the likeness. Another, therefore, must produce these intelligible forms, another whose essence does comprehend those things of which these forms are the likeness. An intelligence which knows by means of a lesser number of intelligible forms is, for that reason, an intelligence related to fewer things as a recipient to something received. So that an intelligence which knows by but one intelligible form would be the supreme creature, dependent on God in such a way that it depends on no creature for anything at all.

It is to be noticed that when one says that an intelligence is related to the intelligible forms it possesses as potentiality to actuality, the potentiality-actuality relation is to be taken in the third sense described above (pages 183–184); that is, it is to be taken to mean only that the intelligence possesses something on which it of itself has no claim, in the sense that what it possesses is over and above, and hence not identical with, its essence. All reference to *change,* hence to *before and after change,* is to be eliminated.

To make the preceding clearer, it will be helpful to consider that there are two intellectual powers in the human soul. One of these is the knowing or understanding power. This is the one which has come to be called the possible intellect. This is the power by which we grasp absolute forms. This is the power

one ordinarily has in mind, unless he specifies otherwise, when
one speaks of the human intellect. But this one is not enough.[13]
For the forms or natures of material substances, which are the
substances we know, do not subsist in the real world as
immaterial and actually intelligible entities. Rather, they are
only potentially intelligible. And this is why one is led to see
the necessity of a second intellectual power in the human soul,
a power which does not know or understand, but a power
which makes it possible for the human soul to know or
understand. This power has come to be called the agent
intellect. Its function is to abstract, i.e., to make actually
intelligible what is only potentially intelligible in the real
world. This done, the possible intellect can grasp it. It is clear
that the abstracting power is related to the understanding
power as agent to patient, as something in a state of actuality to
something in a state of potentiality; and it is from this relation
that the former has come to be called the agent intellect, and
the latter the possible intellect.

The Lower Forms and the Way in Which They Rise Above Matter

We wrote above (page 145) that the complete immateriality of
the human soul can be described as a complete immateriality
which is at the same time partial. By way of explaining this
partial character we pointed out that man's soul is the substantial form of man's body, and that, as the form of a living body,
it is the source of vegetative and sensitive activities, which take
place with a dependence on the matter which is man's body.
Thus, the human soul is not immaterial in all its powers or
parts. It is independent of matter, to some extent, in its
intellectual power or part; not so in its other powers or parts.

It is in these other parts that the human soul is like the lower
forms, like the sensitive soul which is the form of animals, like

the vegetative soul which is the form of plants, like the forms of inanimate things down to the forms of the most basic material constituents of all physical things.

The point of (87) will become clearer if one pursues the following outline consideration. Although these lower forms exist only in matter and perform their operations through or by means of it, these operations rise above matter in different ways. The lowest forms are those whose operations do nothing other than to bring about changes which result in a combining of the things involved in such a way that no one of them survives with the identity it had before the change. For example, hydrogen and oxygen bring about a change which results in their being combined in such a way that neither of the two survives with the identity it had before the change. What results is water, which is neither hydrogen alone nor oxygen alone, but something with a power to perform operations by utilizing the powers of both. Water has an identity all its own different from that of hydrogen alone, different from that of oxygen alone, an identity which we judge in terms of its operations. Water's identity is rooted in water's form. Water's form needs matter previously in possession of hydrogen's form and oxygen's form. Water's form is nothing other than the power of a certain sort of matter—namely, hydrogen and oxygen combined in a certain ratio—to perform certain sorts of operations.

There are other forms, next in line, whose operations reveal them to be in some sense dominating forms. These operations bring about changes which result in a combining of the things involved in such a way that one of them survives with the identity it had before the change, and the other of them ceases to be. And this happens in such a way that the ceasing to be of the latter is identically the continuing to be of the former. These are the forms of those things we call living things. The forms of living things dominate the matter of those things which they use as food, and not only in the sense that each living thing thereby preserves itself in being but also in the sense that it uses food to produce other living things like itself. The identity of the living thing is rooted in the living thing's form. A living thing's form needs matter previously in possession of the form of food; not just any matter serves as food—e.g., a bar of iron does not, although iron properly disposed does. Soul—simply another word for "a living thing's form"—is nothing other than the power of a certain sort of matter—namely, food—structured in a certain way to perform certain sorts of operations, the fundamental one of which is the use of food. This is what Aristotle was concerned to point out when he defined soul as the first actuality of a natural organized body.[14] What we mean here by "food structured in a certain way" is what Aristotle meant by "natural organized body."

There are still other forms, next in line, whose operations reveal them, too, to be dominating forms, but dominating in a subtle sort of way when compared to the forms whose operations have to do with the use of food. These are the forms of those things which we call sensitive things. These operations bring about changes which result in a different sort of combining of the things involved. Whereas in the use of food only one of the things involved survives with the identity it had before the change, here both survive, each with its own identity, and one with something of the identity of the other, as when we see an exterior object. That is, the thing with the form which is said to dominate achieves another identity, an identity in addition to its own, that of the thing which is said to be dominated. And this it achieves by producing within itself something of the form which is the source of the identity of the other. The things involved combine in the sense that one affects the other in a way such that the other reacts by producing a change within itself; the one which is dominated affects the dominating one in such a way that the latter reacts by producing within itself something of the form of the former. These things are therefore combined as regards form, but not as regards matter, as is the case in the use of food. The form which dominates does not dominate the other in point of matter; it does not physically possess and destroy the other. It dominates the other in point of form, which is simply to say that it reproduces within itself something of the form of the other, and, having produced it, possesses it. Domination here is something like the relation which obtains between two women who appear at a party, each wearing the original and exclusive gown worn by the other; the only difference here is the fact that domination by exclusive garb is a mutual domination. Rather than producing another like itself, as is the case in one of the uses of food, the living thing in this case produces another like the thing which it dominates; and this other it produces *within* itself.

The sensitive soul, like the soul which uses food, also needs a matter properly structured and constituted, i.e., a natural organized body in which to exist and through the qualities of which it performs its proper activity, the activity of dominating other things in point of form. The sensitive soul is nothing other than the power of a certain sort of matter to perform dominating activities of a certain sort. The activity of seeing, for example, is such a dominating activity. It takes place in and by means of the bodily organ called the eye, an organ with a certain structure relating iris, lens, retina, optic nerve, proper brain center etc., an organ composed of certain combinations of the basic material constituents of physical things, of certain combinations of bits of matter whose forms are the lowest of forms (see page 193), some of which combinations constitute the chemistry of the rods and the cones, others of which are the sources of the electrical impulses which relay stimulation from the retina through optic nerve to proper brain center. By the activity of seeing, an activity emanating from the power of a certain sort of bodily organ, the sensitive thing produces within itself something of the form of the thing seen. We say "*something of* the form" to indicate that the form is produced not in all its aspects, but only in its visible aspects. The production of other aspects—e.g., audible, tangible—is left to other activities.

In the *Summa of Theology*[15] we find what can be taken as a clarifying summary of the above. St. Thomas is there concerned to point out how the operations of the three types of soul—the intellectual, the sensitive, and the vegetative—rise above the operations of what he calls the whole of corporeal nature. By the "whole of corporeal nature" he means those things which we described above (page 193) as things with the lowest of forms, those things which we call inanimate things. He begins by pointing out that the whole of corporeal nature, the whole range of inanimate things down to the basic material constituents, is related to souls of all types as their subject and their instrument, i.e., as that in which they exist and through which they operate. Then he points out that there is an operation of soul which so far exceeds the whole of corporeal nature and its operations that it is not even performed through a corporeal organ. This is the operation of the intellectual soul, the operation of understanding. There is another operation of soul, lower than the first, which is performed through a bodily organ, but not through any corporeal quality. This is the operation of the sensitive soul. And although corporeal qualities like hot and cold, moist and dry (and, we might add, like the chemistry of the rods and the cones, and the source of the electrical impulses which relay stimulation to the proper brain centers) are required for the operations of the sensitive soul, they are required only for the proper constitution and disposition of the organ, for the disposition by which the sensitive soul reacts and produces within itself something of the form of the sensed object. The lowest of the operations of soul is that which is performed through a bodily organ and which requires corporeal qualities not only for the proper disposition of the organ but also as the means by which it physically destroys and possesses the other. But even this lowest of the operations of soul rises above the operations of inanimate things. For the living thing survives its being combined with food with the identity it had before the change; this is not so in the combining changes undergone by inanimate things.

Thus, inanimate things are things which have, and can have, only one form, their own. And since being is consequent upon and measured by form, they have a very limited sort of being; and even this limited being they lose in the combining changes they undergo. Things at the vegetative level also have, and can have, but one form, their own; but they do not lose it in at least some of the combining changes in which they are involved. Things at the sensitive level are things which can have forms in addition to their own, but only those forms which are sensible. Lastly, things at the intellectual level are things which can have forms other than their own, and these are not restricted to the sensible realm. These forms are intelligible forms. The being of the human soul is, therefore, quite unlimited; the human soul can produce and possess the forms of all things, both sensible forms and intelligible forms. And this is why it has been said that the human soul is in some way all things: *anima est quodammodo omnia.*[16]

LOOKING BACK

At the beginning we wrote (page 14) that "the clarificatory function of metaphysics has at least this twofold orientation: (1) toward lessening a certain indeterminateness and incompleteness in human knowledge and (2) toward metaphysics itself for which it elaborates meanings suitable for scientific procedures," i.e., for the doing of metaphysics as a science. We also wrote (page 14) that metaphysics "elaborates these meanings in a way such that they represent some sort of continuity in terms of an extension" and that "extended meanings of this sort, especially those which are extensions of the meanings of words used in the discourse of everyday life, are very valuable because they are extensions of what everybody already knows in some way." We have attempted, in the course of this interpretation, to clarify the meanings of a word used in everyday life—namely, the word "being"—and to elaborate a suitably metaphysical meaning for it. We considered, by way of clarifying its meanings, that the word "being" means *what is,* and *what is* means first of all *what is out there,* and secondly *what is true.* We considered that *what is out there* is primarily *substance,* and we pointed out that the primary concern of metaphysics is about *substance.* Then we considered how essence is found in diverse substances: in physical substances, in the human soul, in the intelligences. This consideration was in fact, whatever else it also was, an attempt to elaborate a suitably metaphysical meaning for the word "being," which turned out to be *substance which is such that existence is other than its essence.* This meaning is not only metaphysically suitable—i.e., such that it is independent of sensible matter *and* realized extramentally apart from matter (as far as we know, at least in the human soul)—but it also turned out to be metaphysically fruitful. Thus, this meaning showed successfully that *all beings* (other than the First) have a relation of dependence on the First, hence that there *is* a First, i.e., that God exists. This meaning also yielded a description of God, namely, a substance such that existence is identical with its essence, which we saw to be fruitful in showing a property of God, that He can be but one.

FURTHER REMARKS ON BEING AS FIRST CONCEIVED BY THE INTELLECT

The distinction between essence and existence which figures in the metaphysically suitable meaning of the word "being" elaborated above (pages 163–172), and the distinction between signifying *as a whole* and signifying *as a part* which figures in the discussions of chapter three, offer us further and most useful means for taking another look at being as first conceived by the intellect.

(1) *The word "being" signifies as a whole.* When what is first conceived by the intellect is given the name "being," to which is attached the meaning *what exists,* what is first conceived by the intellect is signified as a whole. This is clear from the fact that the word "being" can be predicated *directly* of things, i.e., by means of "is" as opposed to by means of "has." Not only can "being" be predicated of the ultimate genera, say of substance, but it can also be predicated of everything of which the ultimate genera can be predicated, down to the individual, say Socrates. We can say *Socrates is a being,* just as we can say *Socrates is a substance,* or *a body,* or *an animal;* each of these signifies as a whole. If it can be said that *Socrates is a being,* then being and Socrates must be the same whole, for a part cannot be predicated *directly* of its whole; i.e., we cannot say that a whole *is* its part (see page 85). Obviously "being" and "Socrates" do not have the same meaning; "being" means simply *what exists,* and this expresses determinately only part of what "Socrates" expresses, but it leaves unexcluded what it does not express.

But what is first conceived by the intellect can also be signified as a part, as by "beingness" or "entity." "Man" and "manness" (or "humanity") represent intellectual under-

standings of a *same* content or intelligibility, but "man" signifies this content without excluding anything which is found in
individual men, whereas "manness" signifies this content only;
it positively excludes anything not of the content. So, too,
"being" and "entity" represent intellectual grasps of a *same*
content, but differently signified; and in a way which corresponds to the way in which "man" and "manness" signify what
they signify. Just as "manness" disengages the formal content
of the meaning of "man," so too does "entity" disengage the
formal content of the meaning of "being." And just as "manness," though signifying as a part, is nonetheless something
composed (see pages 112–113), so too "entity," though signifying as a part, is nonetheless something composed. "Entity"
expresses neither existence alone nor essence alone, but both;
just as being expresses neither *exists* alone nor *what* alone, but
both together, i.e., *what exists*. And just as "manness" cannot be
predicated directly of the individual, or "substantiality," or
"bodiliness," or "animality," also "entity" cannot be so predicated. But one can say *Socrates has entity*, for a whole can be
said to have a part. And what one says in saying that *Socrates
has entity* is that *Socrates has both essence and existence*.

(2) *The integral parts of the meaning to which we attach
the word "being."* In (1) above we spoke of part and of
whole; we said that "being" signifies as a whole what it
determinately expresses, whereas "beingness" or "entity"
signifies it as a part. Though each signifies it differently, each
expresses the same meaning, the same intellectual grasp,
namely, *what exists*, or *something-there*. "Part," in this context,
is used to designate formal content, or intellectual grasp, or
what is determinately expressed (as opposed to what is unexpressed, though not excluded; what is unexpressed but unexcluded is the other part).

Here we shall speak of part in another sense. We shall speak
of part in the sense of *integral part of formal content*, of

intellectual understanding, of a determinately expressed meaning. Since an intellectual understanding can be signified as a whole or as a part, it is clear that we can speak of the integral parts of the intellectual grasp to which we attach the word "being," as well as of the integral parts of the intellectual grasp to which we attach the word "beingness" or "entity." But we will be speaking of the same integral parts, because we are speaking of the same intellectual grasp.

What are these integral parts? They are conveniently revealed if one considers that what the word "being" means is often expressed as *what exists*. The integral parts of the meaning which we attach to "being" are two: one represented by the word "what" of the phrase *what exists*, the other represented by the word "exists" of that same phrase. This is nothing other than to say that essence (designated by "what") and existence (designated by "exists") are the integral parts of the meaning, or intellectual grasp, to which we attach "being." One must be careful to notice that to conceive *being*, i.e., *essence-existing*, is not in and by that very conceiving to assert that any given thing exists (see pages 163–165).

When, therefore, the intellect first conceives *being* as *essence-existing*, the intellect conceives at once essence and existence, at once *that which we later call essence* and *that which we later call existence* (see page 29). Since being is what is first conceived by the intellect, and since all other concepts are had by way of addition to the concept of being, it is easy to see that essence and existence are conceived after, and by way of addition to, being, even though to grasp being is to grasp at once both essence and existence. When the intellect first conceives being, it must necessarily be the case that the intellect conceives at once both essence and existence. For things are intelligible only to the extent that they are actual, and things are actual by essence and existence at once.

(3) *Being as first conceived represents an indistinct con-*

ceiving of essence and existence. In (2) we spoke of the integral parts of the concept of being, of the meaning we attach to "being." The concept of being, then, is a whole. We shall speak now of how we can know a whole.

We can know something in which several things are contained but know it *without* having a proper and distinct knowledge of the many things contained in it. To know a thing in this way is to know it *indistinctly.* We can have such knowledge of a universal whole, and we have such knowledge of a universal whole *before* we have distinct and proper knowledge of it. To have some distinct and proper knowledge of a universal whole is to have some distinct knowledge of its parts, i.e., of its subjective parts or of something which is less universal. For example, to know animal indistinctly is to know animal as animal; to begin to know animal distinctly is to begin to know man, horse, dog, etc.[17] The same thing is to be noted about concepts signified as a whole and as a part. The same thing, too, is to be noted about a concept and its integral parts.

As regards the concept of being and its integral parts, when the intellect first predicates (by words, images, sensations, or gestures) what it has first conceived—namely, *being* or *essence-existing*—of a sensible thing, it knows indistinctly the sensible thing—i.e., its essence and its existence—but the intellect has nonetheless grasped the thing at once by its essence and its existence. Since the intellect's grasp is an indistinct grasp, the essence and the existence of the thing are distinguished or known distinctly, and named or worded, *only later on.* Thus, in knowing *being* about a thing, all we know is that the thing is out there (see pages 4–5). It is not until later that we realize explicitly that what exists out there must have an essence, i.e., a principle by which it exists out there. We begin to realize this when we realize that there are certain things which depend totally for whatever they are upon their being thought or talked about by us, like the make-believe characters in stories. When we have realized this, we have begun to differentiate essence from existence as components of the meaning of the word "being." We do not, in simply knowing *being* about a thing, know any of the characteristics of its essence, or, therefore, do we know anything about the relation which existence out there has to the thing's essence. We come to know the characteristics of its essence one by one as our experience with things grows, and then by inspecting these characteristics we discover that existence out there is not among them, that existence out there is *per accidens* in relation to the essence of the thing (though we come to understand that existence out there is *per se,* in another sense, in relation to the essence, since essence alone is the proper subject of existence) (see pages 163–166). It is at this point that we begin to see clearly the difference between the meaning of "being," on the one hand, and being, on the other.

As regards the concept of being signified as a whole and as a part, when the intellect first grasps a sensible thing as a being or as an essence-existing, we have in fact grasped the sensible thing by its *beingness* or its *entity;* but beingness is known distinctly, and named or given a word only later on. To know beingness distinctly means *both* to have formed and named the concept of being, *and* to have disengaged it, i.e., beingness as the formal content, the determinately expressed part, of the concept of being (as opposed to that which is unexpressed, but unexcluded, namely, *all* the characteristics of the *essences* of things).

We must note that a concept may have integral parts which are such that one of them is more universal than the concept itself. For example, the concept *man* has the integral parts *rational* and *animal. Animal* is an integral part of the concept *man,* and it is an integral part which is more universal than man. The concept of being, clearly, can have no such integral part, for being is the most universal possible concept. Thus, essence and existence are integral parts of the concept of be-

ing in the way in which matter and form are integral parts of
the concept *composite substance*. Essence and existence are
not integral parts of the concept of being in the way in which
animal and rational are integral parts of the concept of man.

(4) *Being as first conceived and the judgment of
existence*.   There is a view which attributes to the judgment of
existence a role in the formation of the intellect's first concept,
namely, *being*, or *essence-existing*, or *something-there*.[18] It is
claimed (1) that the judgment of existence (i.e., a singular
existential judgment, or a judgment of the form *x exists*, where
x is some individual sensible thing here and now being perceived by sense) and the concept of being are so related that
each depends on the other. The concept of being is prior to the
judgment of existence in the order of material or subjective
causality, and the judgment of existence is prior to the concept of being in the order of formal causality.[19] The intellect
"forms its first idea (that of being) while uttering its first judgment (of existence), and utters its first judgment while forming its first idea," so that the concept of existence is the result,
not of the process of simple apprehension alone, but of judgment as well.[20] It is also claimed (2) that the concept of existence is conceived in and with the concept of being, that it
cannot completely be detached or isolated from the concept
of being, and that this simply amounts to saying that the concept of existence cannot be detached from the concept of
essence.[21] It is claimed (3) that only essences are the object
of the first operation of the intellect, simple apprehension, and
that existence is the object of the second operation of the
intellect, judgment.[22]

These claims seem to say

(a) that the concept of being as well as that of existence is
the result, not of simple apprehension alone, but of judgment as
well, since the concept of existence is said to be conceived
inseparably in and with the concept of being.

(b) that the concept of essence, as well as that of being, is prior in the order of material causality to the judgment of existence (and thus that the judgment of existence is prior in the order of formal causality to the concept of essence, as well as to the concept of being), since essences are said to be the object of the intellect's first operation, that of simple apprehension.

(c) that essence grasped by the intellect's first operation, and existence affirmed and grasped by its second operation, furnish the content of the concept of being. Point (c) follows from (a) and (b) just above.

(d) that the formation of the concept of being, the formation of that of essence, and the judgment of existence are simultaneous, i.e., that there is no temporal priority and posteriority involved. The intellect simultaneously grasps all three: being, essence, and existence.

There is a serious difficulty in this view, at least in the way in which it is expressed, arising from (1) the insistence that there are concepts (namely, those of existence and being) which result, not from simple apprehension alone, but from judgment as well, and (2) from the use of the notions of material priority and formal priority. The judgment of existence is formally prior to the concept of essence, it is claimed (see just above point [b]). Does this mean that the judgment of existence and the concept of essence are the form and the matter—i.e., the formal constituent and the material constituent, respectively —of the concept of being? If this is what it means, a difficulty arises concerning how the judgment of existence can be of the content of a concept. If the judgment of existence is of the content of the concept of being, then to conceive being is, *in and by that very conceiving*, to judge that something exists. This is clearly not the case. Moreover, since all other concepts are had by way of addition to the concept of being in a way such that the concept of being is of the content of all our concepts, but not vice-versa, then to form any concept is, *in and by that very forming*, to utter the judgment of existence, to judge that something exists. This, too, is clearly not the case. One would want, thus, a precise understanding of the meaning of "material priority" and of "formal priority," since the distinction between the two appears to be a cardinal one in this view.

Let us say, in view of the immediately preceding, that what is intended by this view is not that the judgment of existence is the formal constituent of the concept of being, but simply that what this judgment asserts of its subject—namely, existence—is the formal constituent of the concept of being. But on this interpretation, "formal priority of the judgment of existence" is being used to convey, and very misleadingly, nothing other than what has traditionally been conveyed by the expression *ens sumitur ab esse*, i.e., being is taken from existence. This Latin expression is talking about the meaning of the *word* being, as opposed to being in the real world. It is to be understood in the sense in which one understands the expression "the difference is taken from the form." The expression *taken from,* as we explained above (page 95), "is used apropos of a word which functions as designating a whole, but in terms of, or as determinately expressing only, something which belongs to, and is therefore not the same as, the whole, whether a part or whatever." To say "this is a being" is the equivalent of "this has existence," for "being" signifies as a whole, but as determinately expressing only what belongs to, and is hence not the same as, the whole; and this latter is what "existence" signifies.

It is to be noticed that $\dfrac{\text{"existence"}}{\text{"being"}} : \dfrac{\text{"human soul"}}{\text{"man"}}$, whereas $\dfrac{\text{"entity"}}{\text{"being"}} : \dfrac{\text{"humanity"}}{\text{"man"}}$. That is, whereas "entity," like "humanity," though signifying as a part, is nonetheless composed; "existence," like "human soul," neither signifies as a part nor is composed; like "human soul," "existence" signifies a part, and what it signifies is simple.

There must, therefore, be something which leads to this way of describing the concept of being, to claiming that the concept of being depends on the judgment of existence in the order of formal causality. It appears to be this: these men have not understood the proper function of judgment, even though they describe it correctly. They describe it correctly when they say that judgment is what is pronounced in the words *ita est*, thus it is.[23] But they have not understood the description, for they explain it to mean that judgment restores simply apprehended essences to the existence from which the intellect has detached them by its abstracting activity. And they take this to be the equivalent of saying that the function of judgment is an existential function,[24] that its function is to affirm existence.[25] Essences, they claim, and only essences, are open directly to the intellect in simple apprehension, where "directly" means *without the aid of judgment;* whereas existence is not. Existence is not an essence, they are fond of pointing out, and hence is not directly open to the intellect in simple apprehension. It is nonetheless, they affirm, directly open to the intellect, but only in judgment. Once the intellect has asserted existence in a judgment, existence is open to simple apprehension; so too is being. The intellect can now *conceive* existence, and inseparably in and with the conceiving of being.

But it is simply not the case that the function of judgment is, unqualifiedly, to affirm existence. For sometimes what is done in judgment is precisely that, but sometimes something different. To make this clear one must consider that the goal of the human intellect is to grasp things as they are in their completeness. And it is in part because of the natural weakness of the human intellect *as a conceiving intellect* that it needs the operation of judgment. For the role of judgment is simply to join together that which is found together, but which the human intellect has not conceived together. But this happens either (1) because of the natural weakness of the human intellect or (2) because of the objects themselves which are conceived. In the case of what is not conceived together because of (1), the human intellect by an interior effort of its own—i.e., without needing the aid of sense observation (nor of introspection)—can come to join together what it has not conceived together. And this it does by discovering the necessary connections which obtain among such separate conceptions, e.g., between the conception *plane figure bounded by three straight lines* and the conception *plane figure with an exterior angle equal to the sum of the opposite interior angles*. Thus, when the intellect pronounces that *a plane figure bounded by three straight lines is* (*necessarily*) *a plane figure with an exterior angle equal to the sum of the opposite interior angles,* it is clear that it is judging, that it is saying *ita est;* but it is also clear that it is not asserting existence. In the case of what is not conceived together because of (2), the human intellect cannot achieve the joining by an interior effort of its own. The intellect needs aid from the senses or from introspection; it needs such aid because there is no necessary connection among these separate conceptions; e.g., between the conception of *plane figure bounded by three straight lines* and that of *white,* or between the conception of *man* and that of *white.* Here again, when the intellect pronounces that *this plane figure bounded by three straight lines* (given here and now to sense observation) *is white,* or when it pronounces that *this man is white,* it is clear that it is judging, saying *ita est;* but it is also clear that it is not asserting existence.

When, then, does the intellect, confronting the world of sensible things, assert existence in a judgment? Only in those cases of objects not conceived together because of (2), in which one of the conceptions is that of existence and the other is that of the essence of a natural substance. The essence and the existence of a natural substance are not conceived together, *not because* of the natural weakness of our intellect, but *because* of the object itself, the natural substance, whose essence is conceived. The fact is, nonetheless—a fact given in sense observation—that the essences of natural substances and their existences are found together, i.e., that natural substances do exist. It is when it pronounces *ita est* about this fact that the intellect asserts existence. And this it does *not simply* by an interior effort of contemplating the essence of the natural substance and the fact of its existence, since there is no necessary connection between the two; but with aid from sense observation, on the basis of evidence provided by the senses. To be sure, what has just been described must be taken at the level of indistinctness (see pages 201–204).

The claim that existence is not an essence, and hence is not directly open to the intellect in simple apprehension, is an ambiguous claim. If it is taken to mean that the fact of the existence of a natural substance is not of the understood content of its essence (see page 159, [77] in the text of the treatise), then it is an acceptable claim. But if it is taken to mean that the intellect cannot *conceive* existence (or therefore *conceive being*) unless it has affirmed and grasped existence in a judgment,[26] it is an unacceptable claim. For it is as obvious that existence cannot be affirmed in a judgment unless it has been conceived, as it is that anything else cannot. For to judge is simply to pronounce *ita est* about a joining of concepts which are not conceived together, but which are nonetheless conceived prior (at least analytically) to the joining and to the *ita est*. It is the function of the intellect to conceive within itself all things. Yet not only does it not *in one conceiving* lay hold of all things but it also does not *in one conceiving* lay hold completely of a *single one* among them. This is so because of the two reasons mentioned above (pages 207–208); hence the need for the operation of judgment.

Apropos of the first claim (see page 204), this is to be said. Every predicate is related to its subject as form to matter. And this is why it can be said that in the proposition *x exists*

$$\frac{exists}{x} : \frac{form}{matter}.$$ There is also another matter-form relation in a judgment—namely,

$$\frac{\text{the pronouncing of } ita\ est\ \text{form}}{\text{the joining of predicate and subject: matter}}$$
$$\text{form}$$

—and this is the form which is essentially constitutive of a judgment. It is clear from this that if one claims that the pronouncing of *ita est,* which is most formally what it means to judge, is related to the *x* of the proposition [27] *x exists* as form to matter, in the sense that it supplies the formal constituent of the concept of *x* (the concept of *this being*),[28] then being as first conceived means *what is true,* for *ita est* means *it is so* or *it is true.* This amounts to attributing to a product of simple apprehension what belongs only to the products of judgment; far worse, it amounts to attributing to things what belongs to our way of knowing them. The concept of existence cannot, therefore, be the result of the process of simple apprehension along with that of judgment.

The point of the preceding paragraph will perhaps become clearer from the following consideration. The word "exists" in the proposition *x exists* has two uses, which are obscured by the grammatical form of *x exists.* These two uses are conveniently revealed by noticing that the proposition *x is a being,* though grammatically different from, is nonetheless logically equivalent to, *x exists.* Now the grammatical form of *x is a being* is such that the two uses of *exists* in *x exists* are not located in just one word; rather each of the two uses is located in a different word. In *x is a being* the word "is" functions as the explicitly formulated sign of the intellect's interior *ita est.* The word "being" functions as formally expressive of the existence which is being joined to the subject. In *x exists,* on the other hand, the *ita est* of the intellect has no separate verbal formulation, so that the word "exists" functions at once as sign of the *ita est* and as formally expressive of the existence which is being joined to the subject. It is easy not to notice this twofold burden of the word "exists," and to end up by attributing to things what belongs only to the interior act of our intellect.

Apropos of the *concept* of being, it is to be said that existence is its form, in the sense of its formal constituent, in the sense of what is conveyed by the expression *ens sumitur ab esse.* It is also to be said that what is meant by the word "essence" (as opposed to the essence of some thing, say man) is the material constituent of the concept of being.

The second claim (see page 204) is acceptable if it is interpreted as saying that what is first conceived by the intellect is indistinctly conceived. To conceive being is also to conceive existence and essence, but it is to conceive all three in an undifferentiated, and also "unworded," way (see pages 201–204; also page 29). There is another condition to be put on the acceptability of this claim, namely, that to conceive being and essence and existence be taken as conceiving that which we later refer to as what the *word* being means, what the *word* essence means, what the *word* existence means, as opposed to conceiving the being, essence, and existence of some real thing, say man.

Apropos of the third claim (see pages 204–205), two things are to be said. (1) The object of the first operation of the intellect is anything and everything in things which is the source of any and every sort of actuality. It is things as actual which move the intellect to produce them within itself in a concept. Things as possessing that actuality which is existence (this is always some sort of existence) move the intellect to produce them within itself in the concept of being: *habentia esse,* which, when later explicitly unfolded, becomes *habentia esse et essentiam.* Things as possessing that actuality which is *human existence* move the intellect to produce them within itself in the concept of man: *habentia esse quae habent etiam corpus et animam rationalem.* (2) The object of the second operation of the intellect is to pronounce *ita est* about any proposition [29] at all, including propositions in which the predicate concept is that of existence. The role of judgment is simply to join together that which is found together, but which the human intellect has not conceived together, whatever the concepts involved.

CHAPTER SIX

88. From the preceding it is clear how essence is found in diverse substances. For we find that they have essence in three different ways.

89. There is a thing, God, whose essence is his existence itself. And this is why we find some philosophers who say that God does not have a quiddity or essence, because his essence is not other than his existence. And from this it follows that he is not in a genus, because everything which is in a genus must have a quiddity which is other than its existence. And this is so since the quiddity or nature of a genus or species, in the case of those things which have a genus or species, is not multiplied according to the intelligible content of the nature; rather, it is the existence in these diverse things which is diverse.

90. Nor is it necessary, if we say that God is existence alone, for us to fall into the error of those who say that God is that universal existence whereby each and every thing formally exists. For the existence which God is, is such that no addition can be made to it. Whence by virtue of its purity it is an existence distinct from every existence. This is why, in the com-

mentary on the ninth proposition of the *Book on Causes*, it is said that the individuation of the First Cause, which is existence alone, is through its pure goodness. But as regards that universal existence, just as it does not include in its intelligible content any addition, so too neither does it include in its intelligible content any exclusion of addition, because if this were the case, nothing in which something is added over and above its existence could be understood to be.

91. Similarly, although God is existence alone, it is not necessary that the other perfections or excellences be wanting in him. Rather he has all the perfections which are in every genus. This is why he is called simply perfect, as the Philosopher and the Commentator say in book five of the *Metaphysics*. But he has these perfections in a more excellent way than all things because in him they are one, whereas in other things they have diversity. And this is so because all these perfections belong to him according to his simple existence. If some one could perform the operations of all the qualities through some one quality, he would have every quality in that one quality; so too God has all these perfections in his existence itself.

Chapter six of *On Being and Essence* briefly summarizes what has already been seen apropos of how essence is found in all substances: how it is found in God, how in created intellectual substances, how in composed substances. This summary, accompanied by certain clarifications apropos of God ([90] to [91]) and of human souls (93), is given to provide a take-off point for continuing the last of the three tasks set down in the introduction. Chapter six, thus, considers how God and the created intellectual substances are related to the logical intentions, genus, species, and specific difference.

88–91

In (88) St. Thomas indicates that he intends to summarize what he has already discussed as regards the essences of all substances. In (89) he begins his summary with God, stating that in God essence is identical with existence, and noticing that some philosophers have expressed this by saying that God has no essence, meaning no essence which is other than existence. And this is why, he points out, God is not in a genus. In (90) he shows that his position on the identity of essence and existence in God does not entail a pantheism. And in (91) he shows that to maintain that God is existence alone does not entail depriving God of the other perfections or excellences.

God Cannot Be in a Genus.

As regards the Divine Essence in relation to the three logical intentions, we shall begin by considering why the Divine Essence cannot be in a genus, i.e., why it cannot have a genus. The fundamental reason for this is the way in which essence is found in God: *what God is* is Existence, i.e., the Divine Essence is Existence.

As St. Thomas notices elsewhere,[1] there are two ways in which something can be contained in a genus: (1) simply or properly, i.e., in the way in which a species is contained in a genus, or (2) reductively, i.e., in the way in which principles and privations are contained in a genus; e.g., *the point* and *unity* are in the genus quantity, not as species, but as principles of the genus; and blindness is in the genus in which we find sight, of which blindness is the privation.

What St. Thomas shows here in (89) is that the Divine Essence cannot be in a genus as a species. Elsewhere [2] he also shows that God cannot be in a genus as a principle. The argument of (89) amounts to the following. God's essence is existence, as we have seen, and such a thing can be but one; i.e., there cannot be a plurality of subsistent existences. But in a genus there must be more than one, and the essence of each of the many must have something in common. For example, Fido, John, and this horse have this in common that they are animals. But many things cannot have this in common that they are subsistent existences. Hence, God cannot be in a genus. It is clear from what we have just said why St. Thomas writes that "everything which is in a genus must have a quiddity which is other than its existence," for if it did not, its quiddity would be existence, and it could be but one.

Elsewhere St. Thomas offers other arguments for the same claim. For example,[3] if God were in a genus, being would be a genus, for He would necessarily be in the genus *being*. But being cannot be a genus (see pages 115–118). Therefore, God cannot be in a genus. Why would God necessarily be in the genus *being* if He were in a genus? This is so because whatever is placed in a genus is placed therein by reason of something of its essence, that of its essence which it possesses in common with the other things in the same genus. But God's essence is simply existence, so that if He possessed something in common with other things (i.e., if He were in a genus), it would have to be existence which He possessed in common. Now, just as all things which possess *animality* in common are placed in the genus *animal,* so too all things which possess *existence* in common (this would mean all things, including God) would be in the genus *being.* But being cannot be this genus, for all things which have existence in common do not have existence as identical with their essence.

A second example,[4] if God were in a genus, one could argue that He would be either in the genus of substance or in the genus of some accident (since *being* cannot be a genus). Clearly, He cannot be in the genus of some accident, for an accident cannot be the First Being and the First Cause. Nor can He be in the genus of substance, for if He were, the genus of substance would be existence (which it is not), since God's essence is existence. It would follow that the essence of every thing in the genus of substance would be existence, and consequently that no substance would be caused by another. It would follow, further, that every substance would be but one substance, one and the same substance, namely, God. Thus, God cannot be in a genus.

From the preceding it is clear that God cannot have a specific difference, for a specific difference is that whereby species of a same genus differ from one another, and God cannot be a species in a genus, as we have just seen. This is also clear, namely, that a definition of God formulated in terms of genus and specific difference is impossible. It is also apparent that a definition of God formulated in terms of causes, whether intrinsic or extrinsic, is impossible, since God has no causes. This, too, is clear, namely, that there can be no demonstration about God *as about the subject of a science,* for the definition of a thing is the middle term of such a demonstration; and there can be no definition of God, either in terms of causes or in terms of genus and specific difference. All demonstrations apropos of God are demonstrations formulated in terms of what we know about His effects.[5]

That the Divine Essence is not in a genus reductively *as a principle* is evident from the fact that the *scope* of those principles which are reduced to a genus does not exceed what is in that genus; e.g., the point is the principle of continuous quantity *only,* and unity is the principle of discrete quantity *only.* But God is the principle of *all beings in all genera.* Thus, God is not contained in a genus *as a principle.*[6]

We must note here that if a thing is a caused thing, the essence of the thing is other than existence. Such a thing is able (at least able), therefore, to be in a genus, for such a thing can have something of its essence in common with another caused

thing (if there exists another caused thing). Such a thing is
definable, therefore, *both* in terms of its cause(s), since it has
a cause(s), *and* in terms of its genus and specific difference, at
least in the sense that it is able to have a genus and a specific
difference. This is *not* to say that *we* can define it.

It is clear from the preceding that one cannot apply to God
the question, How is such-and-such an essence related to the
logical intentions? in either of the two senses which we distinguished for it above (see page 120). For (as regards the
second sense of the question) God's essence is such, being
Subsistent Existence, that there is nothing in It which could be
the source of the content of a concept about It which
(concept) could be called a genus or a species or a difference.
Hence (as regards the first sense of the question) there is no
question about how God's essence must be taken in order that
It be called a genus or a species or a difference. Or, if one wants
to maintain that the question can be applied to God, one will
have to admit that the proper way to answer it, in either of its
senses, is by pointing out that God cannot be a genus or a
species or a specific difference, i.e., that God can have no
relation to these logical intentions.

THE EXISTENCE SAID OF GOD AND THAT SAID OF CREATURES

It is easy to see the weakness of the following argument:
physical things, human souls, and the intelligences are beings,
i.e., they have *in them* that actuality which is existence. But
God is existence. Therefore, God is *in the things just named*
that actuality which is their existence.

The weakness of the argument lies in the equivocal use of
the word "existence." The existence which is commonly or
universally said of all things other than God is grasped and
expressed by the intellect as without any addition, but it is not
found extramentally without addition. For example, *animal*

cannot be found without the differences *rational* or *irrational,* although animal is grasped by the intellect without grasping rational or irrational. And yet, although animal is grasped without rational and irrational, it is nonetheless not grasped except as with an openness to their addition. If no difference could be added to animal, it would not be a genus; or, more generally, if nothing could be added to animal, it would not be something universal.

So, too, the *existence* which is commonly or universally said of all things other than God when it is said of them that they are *beings*—this existence is grasped and expressed by the intellect as without any addition, although it is not found extramentally without addition. Being as it is found extramentally is either *material being* or *immaterial being,* and each of these adds to being. And further, although *being* is grasped without grasping material being as differentiated from immaterial being, being is nonetheless not grasped except as with an openness to their differentiated addition, for if they could not be added to being, being would not be something universal. This is why St. Thomas writes, "just as it [e.i., universal existence] does not include in its intelligible content any addition, so too neither does it include in its intelligible content any exclusion of addition, because if this were the case, nothing in which something is added over and above its existence could be understood to be." The *existence which God is,* on the other hand, is without addition not only as it is grasped by our intellect but also as it is found in reality; and, further, not only is it without addition but it is also without any openness to the possibility of addition. This is why St. Thomas writes that "the existence which God is, is such that no addition can be made to it."

If one does not distinguish these two senses of the word "existence," and considers only that something common or universal is restricted to a species or even to an individual *by*

reason of an addition to it, it is not difficult to want to conclude
that the divine existence, *to which no addition is made,* is
something common to all things. If, on the other hand, one
considers these two senses of the word "existence," it is easy to
see that the divine existence cannot be something common to
all things. One will understand, by reason of the very fact
that the divine existence neither has nor can have anything
added to it, that it is an existence distinct from all other
existences; this is why it can be said that the Divine Essence is
individuated by the purity and unmixed character of the
existence which It is.[7]

Consider, too, the following. First, it is clear that a principle
is naturally prior to that of which it is the principle. Now there
are some things in which their existence has a principle; for
example, the form of a thing is a principle of the thing's
existence, as is the agent. If, therefore, the divine existence
were the existence of each and every thing, it would follow that
God, who is existence, would have a cause. But Pure or
Subsistent Existence is uncaused.[8] Secondly, in all things not
God essence and existence are other. In God, however, essence
and existence are not other, and this is why God can be but
one. If, therefore, God were the formal existence of all things,
God's existence would be the essence of all things, and all
things would be but one.

There are some in our day who refuse to apply directly to
subsistent being the expression *different from creatures,* claiming that such a refusal "is required to forestall an accusation of
pantheism, namely, that the admission of an infinite being
leaves no room whatsoever for the existence of finite beings."[9]
This claim (like the claim that the existence which God is, is
that whereby creatures intrinsically and formally exist, to
which St. Thomas refers in [90]) has a root in the failure to
notice the distinction between the existence which God is and
the existence found in all creatures. It is easy to see that the

admission of an infinite being is quite compatible with the existence of finite beings, for whereas the existence which is said of God is not open to the possibility of addition, the existence which is said of creatures is so open. This compatibility is exactly what St. Thomas has in mind when he writes in (90), "if this were the case [i.e., if the universal existence said of creatures included in its intelligible content any exclusion of addition, as is the case with that said of God], nothing in which something is added over and above its existence could be understood to be."

Is God the Least Perfect of All Things?

It is better to be than not to be; better to be alive than simply to be; better still to be wise than to be alive. Thus, to be appears to be the least of all perfections; to exist is to be just this side of nothing. If the preceding is so, is not God the least perfect of all things, since His essence is simply to be, simply to exist, simply existence?

The question just asked can be answered in at least three ways:

(1) Since God is Subsistent Existence, God is an actuality absolutely devoid of potentiality. From this it follows that there is nothing which Subsistent Existence could receive or acquire; there is absolutely nothing which could be added to Subsistent Existence; Subsistent Existence "has it all," we might say. To put it more appropriately, Subsistent Existence is Actuality or Perfection in a state of absolute and unacquired fulfillment (see page 188). There is no perfection which God does not possess. It is easy to see, therefore, since there is no perfection which God does not possess, that God "possess all the perfections which are in every genus," as St. Thomas writes in (91).

(2) Since God is the principle of *all beings in all genera*

(see page 217), it is easy to see that whatever other perfections He possesses, He possesses the perfections of all genera of beings. The cause is at least as perfect as its effect.

(3) The existence *which God is* is without addition not only as grasped by our intellect but also as found in reality, and not only is it without addition in reality but it is also without any openness to the possibility of addition (see page 219), for the existence *which God is* is Subsistent Existence. To say that to be alive is better than simply to be is to speak of an existence which, although grasped by our intellect as without addition, is nonetheless not found extramentally except with additions, and which is grasped only as with an openness to these additions. To speak of such an existence is to speak of the existence which is common to all things not God. It is not to speak of the existence which God is; it is not to speak of Pure Actuality without the possibility of any addition.

92. Essence is found in a second way in created intellectual substances. Existence in them is other than their essence, although essence is without matter. Whence their existence is not absolute, but received, and therefore limited and confined to the capacity of the recipient nature. But their nature or quiddity is absolute, not received in any matter. And this is why it is said in the *Book on Causes* that the intelligences are unlimited from below and limited from above, for they are limited as regards their existence, which they receive from above; but they are not limited from below because their forms are not limited to the capacity of a matter receiving them.

93. And this is why, as has been said, there is not found among such substances a multitude of individuals in

one species, with the exception of the human soul on account of the body to which it is united. And although its individuation depends on the body as upon the occasion for its beginning because it does not acquire its individuated existence except in the body of which it is the actuality, it is not necessary that its individuation be lost when the body is taken away because that existence, since it is absolute, always remains individuated once the soul acquires it by being made the form of this individual body. And this is why Avicenna says that the individuation and multiplication of souls depends on the body as regards its beginning, but not as regards its termination.

94. And because quiddity in these substances is not the same as existence, they are orderable within a predicament. And this is why they have a genus, a species, and a difference, although their proper differences are hidden from us. For even in the case of sensible things, the essential differences themselves are not known; whence they are signified through accidental differences which rise out of the essential ones, as a cause is signified through its effect; this is what is done when *biped,* for example, is given as the difference of man. But the proper accidents of immaterial substances are unknown to us; whence their differences cannot be signified by us either through themselves or through accidental differences.

95. But we must notice that the genus and the difference of these substances are not taken in the same way in which the genus and the difference of sensible substances are taken. In the case of sensible substances the genus is taken from that which is material in the the thing, whereas the difference is taken from that which is formal in it. Whence Avicenna says at the

beginning of his book *On the Soul* that form in things composed of matter and form is the simple difference of that which is constituted by it; but not in such a way that the form is the difference, but because the form is the principle of the difference, as the same writer says in his *Metaphysics*. And this sort of difference is called a simple difference because it is taken from what is part of the quiddity of the thing, namely, from the form. But since immaterial substances are simple quiddities, their difference cannot be taken from what is part of the quiddity, but from the whole quiddity. This is why Avicenna says, at the beginning of *On the Soul*, that only those species have a simple difference whose essences are composed of matter and form.

96. Similarly, their genus too is taken from the whole essence, but in a different way, for separated substances agree with each other in immateriality, and differ from each other in grade of perfection, according as they withdraw from potentiality and approach pure actuality. The genus is taken from that in them which follows upon their being immaterial; for example, intellectuality or something of this sort. But the difference, which is unknown to us, is taken from that in them which follows upon their grade of perfection.

97. And it is not necessary that these differences be accidental because they are determined by greater and lesser perfection which does not diversify a species. For grades of perfection in the reception of a same form do not diversify a species, as whiter and less white in participating whiteness which is of the same nature. But a diverse grade in the forms or natures themselves which are participated does diversify a species. For example, nature proceeds by grades from plants to animals by way of certain things which are midway

between animals and plants, according to the Philosopher in book seven of *On Animals*. Nor, similarly, is it necessary that intellectual substances be divided always by two true differences, because this cannot come about in the case of all things, as the Philosopher says in book eleven of *On Animals*.

98. Essence is found in a third way in substances composed of matter and form. Here it is *both* the case that existence is received and limited because they have existence from another; *and* that their nature or quiddity is received in designated matter. And so, they are limited both from above and from below. And because of the division of designated matter, the multiplication of individuals in one species is here possible. As regards the question how the essence of these substances is related to the logical intentions, we have explained that above.

92–98

In (92) to (98) St. Thomas continues and completes the summary begun in (88). Created intellectual substances, both the intelligences and human souls, have an essence other than existence, although their essence is "without matter," as he puts it here in (92). He means, of course, that they are completely immaterial, as is clear from discussions in chapter five, even though the expression "without matter" can at times be taken to mean immaterial only in the sense that matter is not a part of what the thing is. There is thus a sort of infinity or limitlessness in these substances along with an accompanying finiteness. They are finite in the sense that their existence is other than their essence, an existence received [10] into and therefore limited by the confining capacities of the essence; their existence is not an absolute existence, but some *sort* of existence, the sort determined by the essence. The essence of created intellectual substances, on the other hand, is absolute in the sense that it is not received into any matter; it is therefore infinite in the sense that it is not limited to the confining capacities of matter. Among the confining capacities of matter are those which are rooted in matter's *per se* indivisibility, from which it follows that if more than one thing has matter, they must have it as quantified and circumscribed; from which it follows in turn that such things are confined to being in place, and that all the forms they receive, whether physical or cognitive, are received as individual forms. There is also the confining capacity which is rooted in the purity of matter's potentiality, namely, confinement to a being threatened by the inherent possibility of ceasing to be.

It is impossible that there be a multitude of intellectual substances in a same species, except for the human soul. And this is so because the human soul is the form of a body, as well as being the source of intelligent activity. But the individuation of human souls, points out St. Thomas in (93), depends on the body only in the sense that the soul first begins to be in the body, i.e., when the man, composed of body and soul, first begins to be. But since the soul's existence is an absolute existence, it is not necessary that the soul cease to exist at the ceasing to be of the man (see pages 151–152), which is to say that it is not necessary that the soul cease to be an individual, since its absolute existence is an individuated existence. The absolute existence which St. Thomas attributes to the human soul is clearly not absolute existence in the sense in which he attributes it to God; the absolute existence of the human soul is simply its existence completely independent of matter; the human soul remains distinct from its existence.

Unlike God, who can have no relation to the logical intentions (see pages 215–218) because His essence is identical with existence, the created intellectual substances are orderable within a predicament or category, precisely because their essence is other than existence. And this is why, St. Thomas explains in (94), they have a genus, a species, and a difference. But this is not to say that *we* can so order them. We cannot, for we cannot come to an understanding of their differences. And this is so because they are completely outside our experience, being given to us neither in sense observation nor in introspection.

In (95) to (96) St. Thomas argues that the genus of the separated substances cannot be taken from that part which is matter, or difference from that part which is form, since separated substances have not these parts. Both genus and difference are taken from the whole essence, but differently.

In (97) he points out that the differences, unknowable by us, among the separated substances are essential, not accidental, differences. For the separated substances do not participate more or less perfectly in a form of the same nature; rather the form which is each substance is of itself of a different nature. And this is why it is often said that substances which are not composed of matter and form are individuated, hence specifically diversified (since the individual here is the species), *by virtue of themselves,* as opposed to being individuated by something other than themselves, as is the case with composed substances, whose essences are individuated by designated matter. He notices further that it is not impossible that there be some separated substances which are not divided by two true differences, as it sometimes happens in the physical world. For example, the insectivorous plant *Dionaea muscipula,* commonly known as Venus's-flytrap, is neither simply—i.e., truly (this is the sense of "true" in the expression "true difference")—a plant, nor simply or truly an animal. In its visible features it is most certainly a plant; in its manifestations of sensitive activity, that of touch at least, it is most certainly an animal. Though the Venus's-flytrap has not a true difference, the composite difference which it does have is nonetheless essential, not accidental. Similarly, it is not impossible that there exists a separated substance which differs essentially from another in the way in which the Venus's-flytrap differs from a true plant or from a true animal. Nonetheless, even here these differences are not discoverable by us.

In (98) St. Thomas completes the summary begun in (88). In substances whose essences are composed of matter and form there is the finiteness consequent upon the fact that their existence is other than their essence. There is also a further finiteness, consequent upon the fact that these essences are received in designated matter. Furthermore, numerical plurality is possible within a same species because of the division of designated matter. The relation of these essences to the logical intentions was discussed above.

A further discussion of two questions will help clarify some of the basic points made in this chapter: (1) the question of the relation of the separated substances to the logical intentions and (2) the question of the individuation of diverse sorts of substance.

The Separated Substances and the Logical Intentions

From the preceding it is clear that if a thing exists, and is not an essence-existence composite, it must *be* existence, and hence can be but one, and cannot be in a genus. Because the intelligences are essence-existence composites (even though their essence is pure form, i.e., form without matter), there can be many of them, and hence "they are orderable within a predicament," i.e., they can be distributed into species within the supreme genus of substance. Thus, the basic reason why the intelligences can be in a genus (ultimate or not) is the way in which essence is found in them. So, too, the basic reason why anything can be in a genus is the way in which essence is found in it. Anything not God can be in a genus precisely because it is an essence-existence composite.

But this must be noted. To say that the intelligences can be ordered in the predicament or category of substance is to say that they are such in themselves (they are essence-existence composites) that they are so orderable; it is *not* to say that *we* can so order them. We cannot so order them because their proper or essential differences are not known to us. Even in the case of sensible things, we do not know their proper or essential differences (the only exception appears to be man); we designate these unknown essential differences through accidental differences which in some way rise out of the essential principles of these things, and to that extent are *signs* of the unknown essential differences.[11] For example, when we say *biped* is man's difference, this is what we are doing, for *biped* is an accidental difference of man in the sense that there are things which are not men but which are bipeds.

Furthermore, even when we do know an essential difference, as we say we do in the case of *rational* apropos of man, we cannot know the difference in terms of itself. For *rational* has meaning for us only by virtue of our introspective contact with that *thought activity of the soul which is reasoning;* to be rational means to be able to reason or, perhaps better, to have a reasoning soul. But the *reasoning activity* is no part of *what* man is; it is an accident (predicamental), whereas man is a substance. Nor is reasoning activity part of a part (human soul) of what man is, and for the same reason, i.e., reasoning is an accident, whereas the soul is something substantial. Now, man differs properly from other sorts of substances by virtue of something substantial.[12] It is clear, therefore, that the *reasoning activity* is that by which *we* differentiate men from other sorts of things. We use the *reasoning activity*, which arises out of the human soul, to designate the human soul in the way in which we designate a cause by its proper effect. And we do this because we have no introspective contact with the soul, from which it follows that we cannot know it in terms of itself. And this is what it means to say that we cannot know the difference of a substance in terms of itself. But in the case of immaterial substances we can know neither their accidental differences nor their proper activities; they are completely outside our experience, being given to us neither in sense observation nor in introspection.

This too must be noted, namely, "that the genus and the difference of these substances are not taken in the same way in which the genus and the difference of sensible substances are taken." In the case of sensible things the difference is taken from what is *part of the quiddity* of the thing, namely, from the form of the thing. In the case of man, for example, the difference is taken for the human soul, which is a rational soul. In the case of the immaterial substances the difference cannot be taken from what is part of the quiddity, since the quiddity is simple; it must be taken from the whole quiddity.

As regards the genus, in sensible substances it is taken from what is *part of the quiddity,* namely, from that which is as matter in relation to the form from which the difference is taken, e.g., in man the genus is taken from flesh and bones, which are the matter of the rational soul; not, however, from flesh and bones considered as the proper matter of the rational soul (i.e., not from *human* flesh and *human* bones), but from flesh and bones seen with an openness for, an indetermination toward, both rational soul and irrational soul; from flesh and bones as found commonly in animals. But in immaterial substances the genus, like the difference, must be taken from the whole quiddity, since the quiddity is simple.

Although both difference and genus are taken from the whole essence, each is taken differently. The genus is taken from that which the intelligences have in common, for what is common is related to them in a way similar to the way in which matter is related to composed substances—e.g., immateriality, intellectuality—whereas the differences, which are unknown to us, are taken from the grade of perfection which is in each of the intelligences, and according to which they are distinguished from one another, and according to which they approach or fall short of Pure Actuality.

From the preceding it is clear that *we* cannot formulate a definition of an intelligence in terms of genus and specific difference. It is clear also that a definition of the intelligences in terms of the *intrinsic* causes matter and form is impossible, for they have no matter and form. Further, it is easy to see that *we* cannot define the intelligences in terms of their *extrinsic* causes, even though they have extrinsic cause(s), for their extrinsic cause(s) would be some other intelligence(s), or God. That in terms of which we define something must be *more knowable to us* than that which we are defining. Hence, we cannot have demonstrations about an intelligence as about the subject of a science, for the definition of a thing is the middle term of such a demonstration.

THE INDIVIDUATION OF DIVERSE SORTS OF SUBSTANCE

From what we have seen in various discussions above, it is clear that the way in which essence is found in diverse substances is what determines *both* whether there can be one or more than one of them *and* how a substance is distinguished from all other substances, thus giving rise to plurality. To be concerned with how a substance is distinguished from all others is to be concerned with the problem of individuation (with *at least one aspect* of the problem of individuation; see pages 78–79 and pages 233–235).

Essence as found in God is existence, i.e., *what God is* is existence. It is because God's essence is existence that there can be but *one* God (see pages 170–172). It is because God's essence is existence that it neither has nor can have anything added to it, and this is why the existence *which God is* is not something common to all things, but rather a *unique* existence *distinct* from all other existences (see page 220); this is why God is a being distinct from all other things. God's individuation is accomplished by virtue of *what He is*, by virtue of the purity and subsistent character of the existence which He is.

Essence as found in created intellectual substances, in the intelligences and in human souls, is not existence. Created intellectual substances are essence-existence composites, and this is why there can be a plurality of them (see pages 187–189). Further, essence as found in the intelligences is such that matter is no part of it, nor does essence in them depend on matter in any way, which is why there cannot be many individual intelligences of a same specific essence. The intelligences are distinguished from one another as species from species; each intelligence is a subsistent species, a species unmixed with dividing matter. The individuation of an intelligence is accomplished by virtue of *what the intelligence is*, by virtue of the purity and subsistent character of the form or species which it is.

Essence as found in human souls is such that matter is no part of it and such that *to some extent* it is independent of matter, but the human soul also depends on matter *to some extent*. A human soul depends on the matter which is the human body *not only* for the performance of its vegetative and sensitive activities *but also* for the *beginning of its existence*, a condition which explains why there are *many human souls*, many individual souls of a same specific nature, as many human souls as there are human bodies. This is why it has been said that the human soul depends on matter for the *beginning of its individuation*. But, because of the extent to which the human soul is independent of the matter which is the human body—i.e., to the extent of its intellectual operations—the human soul *once individuated* (by the dividing matter of the human body) remains always individuated, and independently of the body. This is why St. Thomas writes, citing Avicenna, "the individuation and multiplication of souls depends on the body as regards its beginning, but not as regards its termination." The individuation of a human soul is accomplished *in the beginning* by the designated matter of a human body; the individuation of a human soul once accomplished is forever maintained by virtue of *what the human soul is,* by virtue of the purity and subsistent character of the form which it is.

Essence as found in composed substances is not existence. Composed substances are essence-existence composites, and this is the reason why there can be a plurality of species of them. Further, essence as found in composed substances has matter as part of it, and this is why there can be many individual composed substances of a same specific nature. The individuation of a composed substance, *individuation within a same species,* is accomplished by the division of designated matter.

In what we have written thus far in this section we have been concerned with but one aspect of the problem of individuation, the *distinction* of a substance from all other substances, a condition which gives rise to plurality. *In the context of composed substances* it is not difficult to ask a number of different questions, each of which can be said to bear on a different aspect of the problem of individuation *in that context.*

(1) What, intrinsic to individuals of a same species, accounts for the *possibility of a plurality* in that species? If the problem of individuation is approached with this question in mind, the answer will be quantified matter, or matter as quantified. (See pages 75–80; and page 148.)

(2) What, intrinsic to the individuals of a same species,

accounts for the *factual plurality* in that species? If the problem of individuation is approached with this question in mind, the answer will be designated matter, or matter as designated. (See pages 75–80; page 148.)

(3) What, intrinsic to individuals of a same species, is that in virtue of which we, *human knowers*, distinguish these individuals from one another *in our knowledge?* If the problem of individuation is approached with this question in mind, an acceptable answer appears to be individual sensible matter, or matter as sensible and individual, i.e., the unique set of sensible accidents found in the matter of a given composed individual. Someone may ask, How can we distinguish identical twins? Since designated matter is part of individual sensible matter (see pages 149–150), we can fall back on the *circumscription* proper to matter as designated when all sensible qualities are identical. We can distinguish these twins by noticing that one is *here* and that the other is *there;* it is clear that the one's being *here* and the other's being *there* are consequent upon the *circumscription* of the quantified matter of each. If we cannot fall back on the circumscription proper to matter as designated, then we did not have twins to begin with.

(4) What, intrinsic to individuals of a same species, accounts for the fact of the continued (temporal) identity of each individual? If the problem of individuation is approached with this question in mind, an acceptable answer appears to be the identity of the substantial form. Someone may claim that it is one's *awareness, through memory,* of himself as the identical source *throughout life* of a multiplicity of diverse acts of intellection, volition, emotion, etc., which explains the temporal identity of the *human individual.* It is a fact that *awareness through memory* is what puts each man into contact with the fact of his temporal identity. It is much like saying that it is by means of our senses that we are put into contact with the fact of the existence of, say, this tree. But just as being in contact

with the existence of this tree is not equivalent to knowing what a tree is, so too being aware through memory of one's temporal identity is not equivalent to knowing what this identity is, i.e., what constitutes it. Thus, awareness through memory puts us into contact with a fact, but does not explain the fact. Besides, awareness through memory is an activity, and as such is an accident; and an *accident* cannot be constitutive of the identity of a *substance*.

Apropos of physical individuals other than men, one would have some special problems arising out of the fact that their temporal identity is not given to us in an *introspective awareness through memory* as is our own. Their temporal identity is differently, if at all, accessible to us. There is a further problem. Before one could even ask the question about temporal identity, one would first have to have faced the problem of determining where one individual ends and another begins. Is the earth or some given planet an individual, or is the whole solar system the individual? Is a stone an individual, or is it just one part of that individual which is the planet earth? Is the cell of the sponge the individual, or is that aggregate of cells which we call the sponge the individual? Is the electron the individual, or is it the atom?

In the context of the intelligences, what accounts for the *possibility of a plurality* of them is the essence-existence composition which is in them; what accounts for the *factual plurality* of them is the grade of perfection found in the pure and subsistent form which each is. We do not know the unique accidents of any intelligence, and this is why we do not *in our knowledge* distinguish them one from another, as we do composed substances in terms of the unique sensible accidents of each of them. The intelligences do not exist in time, for they are entirely independent of matter; and hence one cannot ask, What in an intelligence accounts for the fact of its continued temporal identity?

Apropos of God, not only is there no factual plurality but

also is there no possibility of a plurality, nor are there any accidents in God, nor does God exist in time. There are no accidents in God because accidents are related to substance as actuality to potentiality, and there is absolutely no potentiality in God. And God does not exist in time because only that exists in time which depends on matter.

We should like to say the preceding in just one more way. Composed substances are individuals *of* a species. Human souls, too, are individuals *of* a species, and this is so because of the bodies of which they are the substantial forms. Intelligences, too, can be said to be individuals, but *not* individuals *of* a species (since there is no matter in them); the intelligences are individuals which *are* species, subsistent species. And God, too, can be said to be an individual, but *not* an individual *of* a species, since there is no matter in Him, nor an individual which *is* a species, since He cannot be in a genus. Can God, then, be said to be an individual which *is* a genus, a subsistent genus, as one might want to say at this point? Clearly not, for in that case He would have to be an essence-existence composite. When it is said that God is an individual, this and only this is being said: God's essence is *unique,* and hence *distinct* from all other essences, *in this* that it neither has nor can have anything added to it, for *what God is* is Subsistent Existence, and Subsistent Existence is Pure Actuality devoid of all potentiality.

THE HUMAN SOUL AND THE LOGICAL INTENTIONS

It may be helpful to make some clarifying comments apropos of the question of the relation of the human soul to the logical intentions: genus, species, and specific difference. For in his treatment of this question in (94) to (97) St. Thomas' statements were aimed at *all* created intelligent substances, and in such a way that they were directed primarily at the angels, and via the angels at the human soul. Witness what he does in (92) to (93). In (92) he points out, among other things, that created intellectual substances (*all* of them) are not limited from below because their forms are not received into matter, so that (93) there is not found among such substances a plurality of individuals in a same species, *with the exception of the human soul because of the body of which it is the form.* Thus, having made what looked like a general statement about *all* created intellectual substances, St. Thomas notices that it holds only for the angels, and not for human souls.

One must notice that the human soul has the twofold character of being (1) the form of a body and (2) a subsistent form.[13] As the form of a body, it belongs in the genus of substance only reductively, as a principle, which is to say that if the whole, the man, is in the genus of substance, so are its parts, but each differently: the whole properly—i.e., as a species—and the parts reductively. As a subsistent form, the human soul belongs in the genus of substance properly, i.e., as a species. Considered as a subsistent form, therefore, it is related to the logical intentions in the same way as the angels. That is, (1) it is orderable within the predicament of substance; (2) it has a genus, a species, and a difference; (3) its difference is unknowable to us in itself, although it is knowable in terms of our introspective contact with our thought activity, from which we can describe the human soul as being the lowliest of the intelligent substances, as being related to all intelligible forms in the way in which prime matter is related to all sensible forms; and this description can be taken as the difference of the human soul by way of distinguishing it from all angels; [14] (4) its genus cannot be taken from matter, or its difference from form, but both from the whole essence (although each differently, as was explained on page 230), since its essence is not composed of matter and form.

CHAPTER SEVEN

99. What remains now is to see how essence is in accidents; how it is in all substances has been discussed.

100. And because essence, as has been said, is that which is signified by the definition, it is necessary that accidents have essence in the way in which they have definition. They have an incomplete definition because they cannot be defined unless a subject is placed in their definition. And this is so because they do not have existence in themselves free of a subject.

101. But just as a substantial existence results from matter and form when they are composed, so from an accident and a subject results an accidental existence when the accident comes to the subject. And this is also why neither substantial form nor matter have a complete essence because it is necessary to place in the definition of substantial form that of which it is the form; and so its definition is formulated by the addition of something which is outside its genus, just like the definition of an accidental form. Whence, also, the body is placed in the definition of the soul by the natural philosopher, who considers the soul only insofar as it is the form of a physical body.

102. But there is this difference between substantial and accidental forms. Just as substantial form does not have existence in itself, separately from that to which it comes, neither does that to which it comes, namely, matter. And thus from the conjunction of the two results that existence in which a thing subsists in itself, and from them is produced something essentially one; and because of this an essence is the result of their conjunction. Whence, although the form considered in itself does not have the complete nature of an essence, it is nonetheless part of a complete essence. But that to which an accident comes is a being complete in itself and subsisting in its own existence. And this existence naturally precedes the accident which supervenes. And this is why the supervening accident does not, by its conjunction with that to which it comes, cause that existence in which a thing subsists, and through which the thing is a being in itself. It causes, rather, a certain second existence, without which the subsisting thing can be understood to be, just as what is first can be understood without what is second. Whence something essentially one is not produced from an accident and a subject, but something accidentally one. And this is why an essence does not result from their conjunction, as from the conjunction of form and matter. And this is why an accident neither has the nature of a complete essence, nor is it part of a complete essence. But just as it is a being in a qualified way, so too does it have essence in a qualified way.

103. Now, whatever is said to be most fully and most truly in any genus is the cause of the things which are posterior in that genus; for example, fire, which is unsurpassed in heat, is the cause of heat in hot things, as it is said in the second book of the *Metaphysics*.

This is why substance, which has first place in the genus of being, having essence most truly and most fully, must be the cause of accidents, which participate in the nature of being secondarily and in a qualified way.

104. But this happens in diverse ways. For, since the parts of substance are matter and form, certain accidents follow principally on form, certain others follow principally on matter. There are forms whose existence does not depend on matter, for example, intellectual souls; but matter does not have existence except through form. Whence some of the accidents which follow on form are such that they share nothing with matter; for example, to understand, which does not take place through a bodily organ, as the Philosopher proves in the third book of *On the Soul.* But some other of the accidents following on form are such that they do share something with matter; for example, to sense. But no accident follows on matter which shares nothing with form.

105. Among those accidents which follow on matter we find a certain diversity. For some accidents follow on matter according to the ordering which it has to a special form; for example, male and female among animals, the diversity of which derives from matter, as is said in the tenth book of the *Metaphysics.* Whence these accidents do not remain on the removal of the form of animal, except equivocally. Other accidents follow on matter according to the ordering which it has to a general form. Thus, on the removal of the special form they still remain in the matter; for example, the blackness of an Ethiopian's skin is from the mixture of the elements and not from his soul; and this is why it remains in him after death. And because each and

every thing is individuated by matter and placed in a genus or species by its form, accidents which follow on matter are accidents of the individual, and it is according to these that individuals of a same species differ from one another.

106. But accidents following on form are the proper attributes of the genus or of the species. Whence they are found in every thing which participates in the nature of the genus or of the species. For example, man's ability to laugh follows on the form because laughter takes place by reason of the fact that a man's soul has grasped something.

107. It should also be noticed that sometimes the essential principles cause accidents in a state of perfect actuality, as heat in the case of fire which is always actually hot. But sometimes they cause accidents which are only aptitudes, their completion being received from an exterior agent; for example, transparency in the air, which is completed by some exterior light-emitting body. And in such things the aptitude is an inseparable accident, but the completion, which comes from some principle which is outside the essence of the thing, or which does not enter the constitution of the thing, is separable; for example, being moved and things of this sort.

Chapter seven of *On Being and Essence* completes the second and third tasks of this treatise, for it considers how essence is found in accidents (in [99] to [107]), and how accidents are related to the logical intentions: genus, species, and specific difference (in [108] to [112]). The first task of this treatise, *as it applies to accidents,* was considered above in chapter one (see page 21, [4] in the text of the treatise) and in chapter two (see page 49, [12] in the text of the treatise). It can be summarized in this way: "being" is used to mean *what is,* and "what is" is used first of all to mean *what is there,* posteriorly to mean *what is true.* And when used to mean *what is there,* it is used first of all to designate substances, posteriorly to designate accidents.[1]

99–107

In (99) St. Thomas states his intention to consider how essence is found in accidents. He begins in (100) by pointing out that since it is the function of a definition to signify the essence of a thing, accidents must have essence in a way which corresponds to the way in which they are defined. Clearly, if a *definition* is a statement of *what a thing is,* a consideration of the features of the content of the definition is equivalent to a consideration of the features of the essence. Now, the content of the definition of an accident has this feature, namely, that it always includes a subject which is other than the accident itself, and on which the accident depends. This is what it means to say that accidents have an incomplete definition. Accidents, therefore, have an incomplete essence. It is to be noticed that the consideration just outlined does not amount to saying that *such-and-such is so* (i.e., that accidents in the real world have an incomplete essence) because *I understand it to be so* (namely, in the definition of accident, which definition is in the intellect), for this is another instance of a context in which *for something to be understood to be so* is also *for it to be so* (see pages 167–168). Thus one can say *both* that accidents have an incomplete essence because they have an incomplete definition *and* that accidents have an incomplete definition because they have an incomplete essence. The sense of this quasi-equivalence is this: we *know* that accidents have an incomplete essence because we *know* that they have an incomplete definition, but we give them an incomplete definition because they have an incomplete essence. And it is why we give them incomplete

definitions which St. Thomas is explaining in the closing statement of (100): "And this is so because they do not have
existence in themselves free of a subject."

In (101) St. Thomas points out that the incompleteness of
the essence of an accident is similar to the incompleteness of
the essence of matter and of form. For just as what exists is
neither the matter alone nor the form alone, but rather the
composite by virtue of the conjunction of matter and form, so
too what exists is neither the accident alone nor the substance
alone, but the substance by virtue of the conjoined accident.
There is, of course, this difference: whereas the composite of
matter and form exists with a substantial existence—i.e., in an
unqualified way—the substance with conjoined accident exists
with an accidental existence, i.e., in a qualified way. For
example, when one says *Socrates is,* he is designating Socrates'
unqualified existence; and when one says *Socrates is white,* he
is designating one of the many qualified existences of Socrates.
The incompleteness of the essence of an accident can also be
pointed up by considering that for *whiteness to be* is for
Socrates (or some other substance) to be white. Thus, just as
the definition of an accident includes something which is other
than the accident itself, so too do the definitions of matter and
of form include something which is other than either. And this
is why the philosopher of nature includes *natural organized
body* in the definition of the soul.

Having pointed out in (101) in what way substantial and
accidental forms are similar, St. Thomas explains in (102) how
they differ. The difference can be summarized by saying that
whereas a substantial form is not a complete essence, though it
is a part of a complete essence, an accidental form is neither a
complete essence nor part of a complete essence. In (103) St.
Thomas notices that substance, since it has first place in the
genus of being, must be the *cause* of accidents. In (104) to
(107) he is concerned with pointing out the diverse ways in

which a substance causes accidents: some by virtue of matter and form in conjunction, some by virtue of form alone, none by virtue of matter alone; some as proper attributes of a genus or a species, some as unique features of a given individual; some in a state of intrinsically fulfilled actuality, some in a state such that they need fulfillment from an extrinsic source.

ACCIDENTS HAVE AN IMPERFECT DEFINITION BECAUSE THEY HAVE AN IMPERFECT ESSENCE.

At the beginning of chapter two of *On Being and Essence* St. Thomas wrote that "essence is in substances truly and properly, in accidents only in some way with qualification" (see page 49, [12] in the text of the treatise). To say that essence is in substances *truly and properly* is to say that a substance has a *perfect* essence, and to have a perfect essence means at least two things: (1) to be a thing such that it exists *simply,* such that it is an *ultimate existing subject,* and (2) to be *complete* or *total* in the perfection of some given species.[2] The second of these is useful for pointing out what it means to say that a *substantial form* has an imperfect essence; a substantial form is not complete or total in the perfection of some given species; a substantial form is but *part* of the perfection of a given species, the other part being the matter. The first of these is useful for pointing out what it means to say that an *accidental form* (or accident) has an imperfect essence; an accident does not exist simply, it is not an ultimate existing subject; this is another way of saying that essence is "in accidents *only in some way with qualification.*" The first of these is useful, too, for pointing out why it is said that a *substantial form* has an imperfect essence; a substantial form, like an accidental form, does not exist simply, is not an ultimate existing subject; every form, substantial or accidental (excepting the human soul to the extent of its immaterial activities), depends on another as on a subject in which to exist.

Since a definition states *what a thing is*, the definition of a thing which has a *perfect* essence will include only that thing's own intrinsic principles or perfections. The definition of a thing which has an *imperfect* essence notes this imperfection by including that, outside the things intrinsic perfections, on which the thing depends, whether as on a subject or an actuality. Thus, definitions of things are in terms of the causes of these things. And definitions by intrinsic causes are better than definitions by extrinsic causes; this is so because a definition states *what a thing is*, and we know *what a thing is* more properly in knowing it by what is *in it* than in knowing it by what is outside it. In the case of a composed substance, what is *in* it is its matter and its form: the matter which has survived in it from that out of which it came to be, and the form by which it differs from that out of which it came to be. These two, matter and form, constitute the intrinsic perfection of a composed substance.

In the case of an *accident* of a composed substance, if we can speak of what is *in* it, we must not think that it has a matter and a form; an accident has no intrinsic causes. To speak of what is in it is to speak only of what the accident itself is, for the accident is a form, a form such that matter is no part of what it is, a form such that (unlike a substantial form) it does not come to be in matter as in a subject, a form such that it comes to be in a complete substance as in a subject. The substance in which an accident comes to be is related to that accident as matter is related to substantial form. Just as matter must be such by its nature that it can acquire and maintain the substantial form received in a change, so too the substance must be such by its nature that it can acquire and maintain the accident received in a change. Thus, we can speak of a form and of a matter *both* in the case of a substance *and* in the case of an accident, but it is only in the case of a substance that both the matter and the form are *intrinsic* causes. In the case of an accident the form can be said to be *intrinsic to,* though *not* an

intrinsic cause of, the accident in the sense that it is identical
with the accident itself; the matter, however, is an *extrinsic*
cause, for the matter is the substance (*ultimately* the substance) in which the accident exists, and apart from which the
accident does not exist. Only that can be defined by intrinsic
causes which has them, and an accident does not have them
(or does a substantial form).

Thus, it is possible for a composed substance to be defined in
a way such that the elements of the definition are not elements
of the essence; this occurs when the definition is formulated in
terms of the extrinsic causes on which the substance depends.
But it is also possible, since a substance has a *perfect* essence,
for it to be defined in a way such that the elements of the
definition are elements of the essence; and this happens when
the definition is formulated in terms of the intrinsic causes on
which the substance depends (see pages 71–72). But in the
case of anything which has an *imperfect* essence, it cannot be
defined in a way such that all the elements of the definition are
also elements of the essence. And thus something other than
the thing itself appears in the definition, *either* a subject as in
the case of substantial forms and accidental forms—for example, *natural organized body* in the definition of soul as the
first actuality of a natural organized body, and *nose* in the
definition of snubness as *curvature of the nose*—*or* an actuality,
for example, substantial form in the definition of prime matter
as the *potentiality for substantial form.*

AN ACCIDENT IS NEITHER A COMPLETE ESSENCE NOR IS IT PART OF A COMPLETE ESSENCE.

In the immediately preceding we saw that a substantial form
and an accidental form have something in common, namely,
that each has an imperfect essence, each depends on a subject
for existence, which subject is placed in their definition.

We must now notice a difference between a substantial form and an accidental form. Although a substantial form is not a complete essence, it is nonetheless *part* of a complete essence. A substantial form does not exist alone, i.e., apart from the matter which is its subject; this is why it is said that it is not a complete essence. Nor does the matter exist alone, i.e., apart from the substantial form; each can be said to depend, in its own way, on the other. *What exists* is the matter-form composite; it is the matter-form composite which is the complete essence, and something essentially one.

An accidental form, on the other hand, is neither a complete essence nor part of a complete essence. For an accident is acquired by, and hence presupposes, *what is already a complete essence,* namely, the matter-form composite which is something essentially one. Thus, the union of an accident and subject does not result in an essence, does not result in something essentially one, since the accident presupposes a substance already constituted, and therefore already something essentially one. The union of an accident and subject constitutes something accidentally one, for the accident is no part of what the substance (the substance which the accident presupposes) is, and the substance is no part of what the accident is (although the substance is placed in the definition of the accident, as we have seen on pages 243–246).

It may be helpful to notice that there are two senses in which an accident can presuppose a substance: (1) by nature *only* and (2) temporally as well as by nature. To make this clear one should consider that a newly generated substance is accompanied, from the instant it first begins to be, by a set of accidents which remain with it as long as it exists; e.g., the powers of nourishment and of sensation. Such accidents presuppose a substance by nature only; there is no temporal priority of the substance over such accidents. The conjunction of a substantial essence and such accidents can sometimes be said to constitute something essentially one, or *per se* one, in the sense of the second mode of *per se,* but only when the accidents are the proper attributes of some genus or species, and not when they are the unique accidents of some individual. But there is another set of accidents which do not accompany the substance from the instant it first begins to be, a set of accidents which the substance acquires (and loses at times, as well) subsequent to its generation; e.g., in man, the height of 4 ft. 6 in. Such acquired and lost accidents presuppose a substance temporally as well as by nature. The conjunction of a substantial essence and such accidents always results in something only accidentally one.

SUBSTANCE, HAVING FIRST PLACE IN THE GENUS OF BEING, IS THE CAUSE OF ACCIDENTS.

In this section we shall (1) point out what it means to call being a *genus* and (2) identify the *senses of cause* in which a substance is cause of its accidents.

Apropos of (1), if one is speaking about being (real being) *as divided into the ten ultimate genera,* then substances are the primary instances of being; and among substances the intelligences are the primary instances of being. If one is speaking of *all being* (real being) *without the qualification of being divided into the ten ultimate genera*—i.e., without any qualification—then that thing whose essence is existence is the primary instance of being. When one calls being a genus, *in pointing out that substance is what has first place in this genus and is therefore cause of the accidents which exist in it,* genus is not to be taken as that to which one can add specific differences, for being cannot be a genus in this sense (see pages 115–118). Genus is to be taken only as something common or universal [3] which can be contracted to something less common or universal by means of an addition, without considering the character of the universal being contracted, i.e., without considering whether its content represents a grasp of *what things are* or not. A genus properly speaking represents a partial grasp of *what things are; being* does not.

Apropos of (2), if a substance is cause of the accidents which exist in it, substance *cannot* be an *intrinsic* cause; substance cannot be said to be the matter or the form *out of which* an accident is constituted, for substance is no part of what an accient is. This is so, even though a substance can be said to be a material cause of its accidents, for it is an *extrinsic* material cause (see page 243 and page 245). Further, an accident is not something composed of matter and form; an accident is simply a form, and matter is no part of what a form is; an accident has no intrinsic causes. If, therefore, a substance is cause of the accidents which exist in it, it is an *extrinsic* cause.

If a substance is an extrinsic cause of the accidents which exist in it, it is either (in addition to being an *extrinsic material* cause) a final cause or an efficient cause, or it is both (from different viewpoints). It is not difficult to see that it is both.

That it is a final cause of the accidents which exist in it is clear from the following. The secondary (or less primary) always exists on account of, or for the sake of, the primary (or more primary). That is more primary which is more actual. Thus matter exists for the sake of substantial form, and by way of the form for the sake of the composed substance; without its matter and its form the composed substance is not complete. Thus both matter and form exist for the sake of the completion of the composite. Similarly, accidents, which are beings secondarily, exist on account of substance, which is being primarily. Accidents exist for the completion of the substance in which they are found.[4] Of course, whereas matter and substantial form are *intrinsically and primarily* completive of a composed substance, accidents are only *extrinsically and secondarily* completive.

That a substance cannot be an efficient cause of all the accidents which exist in it is clear from the fact that some of its accidents are obviously caused by *extrinsic agents,* most obviously those accidents which detract from the perfection of a thing; e.g., in a man, the new shape which his body takes on because his legs have been amputated. But the accidents which accompany a substance from the instant it first begins to be and which remain with it as long as it exists, the accidents which are neither acquired nor lost by a substance subsequent to its generation—these accidents can be said to be caused *as by an efficient cause* by the substance in which they exist. For an accident cannot be the efficient cause of itself (nothing can be the efficient cause of itself), and the presence and absence of such accidents in a substance following on the presence and absence, respectively, of the substance itself points clearly to such accidents in the *generated* substance. Yet it *is* to say that the substance is the *sole* efficient cause of these accidents; obviously the *generating* substance also is an efficient cause of such accidents in the *generated* substance. Yet it *is* to say that the generated substance is an efficient cause in a special sense: the generated substance *is* an efficient cause—i.e., accounts for the continuance in being of the accidents—whereas the generating substance *was* an efficient cause, i.e., accounts in some way for their having been brought into being. Or, in some cases the generating substance is the sole cause of the production of these accidents, whereas the generated substance *along with the generating substance* is the cause of their continued being. Nor is this to say that such accidents are the only accidents caused by a substance as by an efficient cause; for example, a man is obviously the efficient cause of his *acts of thinking,* which obviously come and go and do not remain.

Thus, a substance is the material cause (*extrinsic*) of all its accidents inasmuch as it is receptive of them, inasmuch as it is the subject in which they exist. It is the final cause of some of its accidents inasmuch as it is perfected or completed by them; obviously it is not final cause of those which detract from its completion, like the new shape which a man's body takes on because of an amputated arm. Lastly, it is the efficient cause of some of its accidents to the extent that it is productive of them or to the extent that it accounts for their continued being, but some of the accidents of a substance are produced by extrinsic agents.

The Different Ways in Which a Substance Is Efficient Cause of Its Accidents.

Having seen the senses of cause in which a substance can be said to be cause of its accidents, we shall consider further, following St. Thomas in (104) to (107), the role of a substance *as efficient cause* of its accidents.

If a composed substance is the efficient cause of its accidents, it causes these accidents by its matter and its form. For these two, its matter and its form, constitute the total perfection of the substance. But we must note that a thing can exercise an efficient causality only according to the status of its actuality. First of all, it can exercise efficient causality only if it actually exists, for it is the function of an efficient cause to make something actually to be. And secondly, its efficient causality corresponds to the way in which it actually exists. For example, if the thing depends on a subject for its actuality, its efficient causality is exercised with a dependence on that subject. If a thing is independent of another as of a subject—i.e., if it is subsistent—so is its efficient causality independent of a subject.

Since the form is what differentiates the term toward which

of a change from the term from which, those accidents of a newly generated substance (the term toward which) whereby it can be differentiated from the term from which have their fundamental efficient cause in the form. If the form is such that it depends for its existence on the matter which has survived in the term toward which from the term from which, the efficient causality of the form apropos of the differentiating accidents is an efficient causality exercised with a dependence on that matter. For example, the power of nourishment as well as the activity of nourishing is rooted in the form of a thing as in its efficient cause, but in the form *as depending* for its existence on the matter. If, on the other hand, the form is such that it does not (at least to some extent, as in the case of the human soul) depend on matter for its existence, the efficient causality of the form in relation to the differentiating accidents is a causality exercised independently of the body; the human soul is efficient cause of the power of understanding and of the acts of understanding independent of the human body.

Since the matter is what survives in the term toward which of a change from the term from which, those accidents of a newly generated substance (the term toward which) which it has *in common* with the term from which have their basic efficient cause in the matter. But matter cannot exist without form; hence whatever accidents are rooted in matter are rooted in matter *as dependent* for its existence on form. The efficient causality of matter apropos of these common accidents is an efficient causality exercised with a dependence on form. For example, the color of a Negro's skin is caused by matter according to the relation which it has to a form, but to a *general form,* a form which is more universal than the form of man; this color is caused by certain combinations of certain sorts of particles of matter and is found even in nonliving things. Thus, at the death of the Negro the color of what is no longer his skin remains properly that color, for that color does not depend on the relation which his body has to his soul. But there are other sorts of accidents, deriving from matter, which cease to be at the ceasing to be of the substance in which they exist; these accidents, thus, are *not* possessed *in common* by the term from which and the term toward which. These are accidents which derive from matter's ordering to a less general form or even to the form of some species. For example, male and female in animals are caused by matter according to the relation which it has to the form of animal, so that at the death of the animal the animal cannot be properly called a male or a female (just as the animal cannot be properly called an animal, but rather a corpse).

We must notice that matter is not only the source of the common accidents of which we have been speaking. Matter is also the source of the unique set of accidents whereby an individual differs from all other individuals; this is matter considered as individuating principle; this is matter according to the relation which it has to a given individual substantial form. It is to be noticed that to speak here of matter as individuating principle is not to speak of matter as that which accounts for the possibility or for the fact of numerical plurality within a same species. It is to speak of that *in the individuals* of a same species whereby we, human knowers, can tell them apart (see page 234, [3]), which presupposes the fact, and the possibility, of their numerical plurality.

Thus, matter can be considered as having a relation to a generic form, to a specific form, and to an individual form. According to these diverse relations matter is the efficient cause of certain generic accidents, specific accidents, and individual accidents. If matter is taken in itself, apart from the forms to which it has an ordering, it is clear that so taken it cannot be the efficient cause of any accident, for matter has actuality by virtue of form, and a thing can behave as an efficient cause only to the extent that it is something actual.

Apropos of the accidents which follow on form, it is to be noticed that they are the proper attributes of the genus or of the species; and this is why they are found in every thing which has the nature of the genus or of the species. For example, the sense of touch is found in every animal. But not every animal is a male, and this is why being a male is said to follow on matter, rather than on the form; so, too, apropos of female.

Lastly, it is to be noticed that sometimes the essential principles of a substance cause accidents which are fully actual; and sometimes only partially actual, in which case the completion of the actuality needs an exterior agent, or, perhaps better, accidents which have actuality in some respects and potentiality in other respects. For example, an infant when born is actually quantified, but at the same time it is in a state of potentiality as regards the quantity of adulthood, for which it depends, at least in part, on extrinsic sources. Being quantified is thus an inseparable accident, but *this* given circumscription is not. And an eye is actually a power for sight, but the actuality of seeing depends in part at least on extrinsic agents. Thus, the power of sight is an inseparable accident; not so the actuality of seeing.

108. It should be noticed, further, that the genus, the species, and the difference of accidents are taken in a way which differs from the way in which those of substances are taken.

109. In substances something essentially one results from the substantial form and matter, a certain nature results from their conjunction, a nature which is properly placed in the predicament of substance. This is why concrete names of substances which signify the composite are properly said to be in a genus, as species or

genera; for example, man or animal. But the form, or
the matter, is not in a predicament in this way, though
each is in a predicament by reduction, as principles
are said to be in a genus. Something essentially one
does not, on the contrary, result from an accident and
its subject. Whence the result of their conjunction is
not a certain nature, to which the intention of genus
or species may be attributed. Whence names of accidents expressed concretely are not placed in a predicament as species or genera; for example, white or
musical, except by reduction. They are placed in a predicament only according as they are signified in the
abstract; for example, whiteness and music.

110. And because accidents are not composed of matter and
form, their genus cannot be taken from matter and
their difference from form, as in the case of composed
substances. Rather, their first genus must be taken
from their way of existing itself, according to which the
word "being" is diversely predicated of the ten genera
according to a priority and posteriority; for example, an
accident is called quantity from the fact that it is the
measure of substance, and quality according as it is
the disposition of substance, and so with the other accidents, according to the Philosopher in the fourth
book of the *Metaphysics*. But their differences are
taken from the diversity of the principles by which
they are caused. And because proper attributes are
caused by the proper principles of the subject, the subject is placed in their definition to function as the difference if they are defined in the abstract, which is the
way in which they are properly in a genus; as when it
is said that snubnosedness is the turned-up-ness of the
nose. But the converse would be the case if their definition were taken according as they are said con-

cretely. For in this way the subject is placed in their definition as a genus because they are then being defined after the manner of composed substances, in which the genus is taken from matter; as when we say that a snub nose is a turned up nose.

111. We have a similar case if one accident is the principle of another, as action and passion and quantity are principles of relation. And this is why the Philosopher divides relation according to these in book five of the *Metaphysics.*

112. But because the proper principles of accidents are not always manifest, we sometimes take the difference of accidents from their effects; as when *concentrating* and *diffusing* are called the differences of color. These effects are caused by the abundance and the scarcity of light, which cause the diverse species of color.

113. And so it is clear how essence is in substances and in accidents, and how it is in composed substances and in simple ones, and how the universal intentions of logic are found in all of these, with the exception of the First Principle, which is infinitely simple, and to which, because of its simplicity, belongs the notion neither of the genus nor of the species, nor consequently definition. With this, let the discussion, its tasks achieved, be brought to a close.

108–113

In (108) to (112) St. Thomas completes the third task of this treatise, for he considers how accidents are related to the logical intentions: genus, species, and specific difference. In (108) he notices that accidents are not related to these logical intentions in the same way as substances are. In (109) he points out *how the essence of an accident must be taken* [5] in order that it be called a genus or a species. It must be taken signified in the abstract, as by "whiteness" as opposed to "white"; and this is so since the result of the conjunction of a subject and an accident is not something essentially one, not an essence. Substances, on the contrary, are taken signified as a whole, and therefore also concretely (see page 121); and this happens because the result of the conjunction of substantial form and matter *is* something essentially one, *is* a certain essence. In (110) St. Thomas points out *what in the essences of real things furnishes,* in the case of accidents, *the content* [6] of those first intentions which can be called genera and specific differences. It is clear that the genus of an accident cannot be taken from matter and that its difference cannot be taken from form, for an accident is not composed of matter and form. Their "first genus," their ultimate genus, is taken from the ways in which they exist in relation to substance; these ways are reflected in the ways in which the word "being" is analogically predicated of things in the ten genera. The differences of the accidents are taken from the diversity of the principles which cause them. When accidents are defined in the abstract, the principles of the causing subject are placed in the definition to function as the difference. When, however, they are defined in the concrete, the causing subject is placed in the definition to function as a genus; and this is so since such definitions are patterned after definitions of substances. In the definition of a substance, the genus is taken from matter; and so, when accidents are defined after the fashion of a substance, their causing subject functions as a genus because it is related to them as their matter (though *extrinsic;* see pages 245–246). In (111) he points out that sometimes the proximate cause of one accident is another accident; action, passion, and quantity are the proximate causes of relations. For example, begetting is the proximate cause of the relation of fatherhood; and conceiving, of motherhood. In such cases the causing accident functions as the difference when the defined accident is defined in the abstract. And this is why one can differentiate or divide relations in terms of action, passion, and quantity. In (112) he notices that the proper *causes* of accidents are not always evident to us, so that we often differentiate accidents in terms of their effects. This often happens apropos of substances as well, as we have seen (pages 228–230). In (113) he gives a brief summary of the treatise and brings it to a close.

Genus, Species, and Difference in the Case of Accidents

Having seen how essence is found in accidents with a dependence on substance, we shall consider now, following the argument of (109) to (112), how accidents are related to the logical intentions: genus, species, and difference.

Substances are related to these logical intentions in one way, accidents in another:

(1) In the case of substances something essentially one, an essence, results from the conjunction of matter and form. It is this essence, this essential unity of matter and form, which is placed in the category of substance properly, i.e., as a species or a genus. *Expressed concretely, and as a whole,* as by the name *man* or *animal,* it is this essence which is placed in the category of substance, for expressed *as a part,* an essence can be neither a species nor a genus (see page 121). As regards the matter and the form which constitute the essence of the substance, neither the one nor the other belongs in the category of substance as a species or a genus; they are placed in the category only reductively, *as principles* of what is properly in the category.

But in the case of an accident something essentially one does not result from its conjunction with a substance. The result of their conjunction is not an essence, is *not* some *one* essence, to which one or other of the above-named logical intentions could attach. And this is why an accident *expressed concretely* (we do not add *and as a whole,* since what the accident expresses is no part of *what that substance is* which is signified by the concrete form of the name of the accident) is not properly placed in a category, i.e., as a species or a genus. An accident *expressed concretely* is signified as inhering in some substance,[7] and hence some substance is signified, or perhaps better, co-signified. For example, *white* means *something white,* and the word "something" refers to a substance; and what substance is, is no part of what accident is. Of course, an accident *expressed concretely* may be placed in a category *reductively,* i.e., by ignoring the substance which is signified. If the accident is expressed in the abstract, as by the word "whiteness," it does not signify anything other than what it is in itself, and it is not signified as inhering in some substance. Indeed, an accident expressed abstractly is signified as though it itself *were* a substance;[8] it does not signify anything which is *per accidens* in relation to it. And this is why, when abstractly expressed, it is properly placed in a category, for whatever is properly placed in a category must not signify what is *per accidens* in relation to it.

(2) In the case of substances which are composed of matter and form, their genus is taken from the matter, their difference from the form. But in the case of accidents this cannot be done, for accidents are not composed of matter and form; accidents are simply forms. The *primary or ultimate genus* of an accident, like that of a substance, is taken from the way in which it exists, which way of existing happens to correspond to, and is thus well manifested by, the way in which the word "being" is predicated analogically of the ten ultimate genera, i.e., according to an order of priority and posteriority. (We say "happens to correspond to" because predicating according to an order of priority and posteriority does not always correspond to the priority and posteriority in the way in which things exist; see page 51; pages 53–54.) For example, for a substance to be a

being is for it to be an independently existing subject; for quantity to be a being is for it to be the measure or extended-ness of an independently existing subject; for quality, the disposition of an independently existing subject.

The *differences* of accidents are taken from the diversity of principles (the proper principles or constituents of the subjects on which they depend for their existence) by which they are caused; but the subject, considered in terms of its causing prin-ciples, has the role of a difference in the definition of its proper accidents *only when* the accident is expressed abstractly, i.e., in the way in which it falls properly into a category. For example, *snubness*[9] can be defined as the *turned-up-ness of the nose*. Snubness is not just any kind of turned-up-ness, but a distinctive kind; it is turned-up-ness *of the nose*. The expression *of the nose* clearly has the role of a difference. When the accident is expressed concretely, its subject has the role of a genus in the definition of the accident. Such defini-tions of accidents are very much like the definitions of com-posed substances, in which the genus is taken from the matter. For example, a *snub* [10] can be defined as a *turned up nose;* a snub is not just any sort of nose, for it is a *turned up* nose; the word "nose" clearly plays the role of a genus.

It is to be noted that an accident is properly defined only when the subject which causes [11] the accident, and which is included in its definition, is the *proximate* cause of that accident. This is similar to the way in which a substance is properly defined only when the genus included in its definition is the *proximate* genus; e.g., rational *animal*, and not rational *body*, is man's proper definition. If the proximate cause of the accident is the composed substance itself, this should be included in the definition; if the proximate cause is another accident, this other accident should be included (in this case one should define the accident which is proximate cause by pointing, in turn, to *its* proximate cause, etc. until one comes to an accident whose proximate cause is the substance itself alone). For example, the proximate causes of relations are actions, passions, and quantity. The relation *fatherhood* is proximately caused by the action which is generation, and this is why that action is included in the definition of this relation.

We must notice that the proper principles, the proximate causes, of accidents are not always manifest to us; in such cases we take the differences of these accidents from their proper effects if these are more knowable to us than the accidents themselves which we are trying to define. For example, we can distinguish diverse kinds of color by means of diverse wavelengths (this is obviously *not* the meaning of St. Thomas' *concentrating* and *diffusing*), which are related to something in the colored things themselves as proper effects to a cause. Generally speaking, to define a thing is to know that thing by its causes, which must in some way be more known to us than the thing itself. If the effects of the thing to be defined are more knowable to us than its causes, our definition will be formulated in terms of these effects. And, of course, to the extent that a thing has no causes it will be defined in terms of its effects. It is because God has no causes at all that He can be defined only in terms of His effects. It is because the human soul has no intrinsic causes that we define it in terms of its effects, its activities. Although the human soul has an extrinsic cause, it is unknowable to us in terms of itself.

THE ULTIMATE GENERA

We considered briefly on page 40 the use of the word "being" apropos of substances and accidents. Of the ten ultimate or supreme genera (or categories, or predicaments) one is the genus of substance; the other nine are accidents: quantity, quality, relation, action, passion, where, when, disposition, habitus. It was not our purpose there to say something about the meaning of each of the ten supreme genera; rather it was our purpose simply to distinguish accident, in an easy and beginning way, from substance. We say "in an easy and beginning way," since what we said there by way of describing accident applies only to quantity, quality, and relation.

In this section we shall try to understand why being can be divided into the ultimate genera according to *diverse ways of predicating;* secondly, we shall divide being into its ultimate genera by using the diverse ways of predicating.

Commenting on Aristotle's *Metaphysics,* St. Thomas points out why it is that the ultimate genera of being are also called *predicaments;* they are called predicaments because they represent a division of being (real being) by means of diverse ways of *predicating* [12] "being." That is, they represent a division of being which we can come to understand by way of considering diverse ways of predicating "being." This is not to say that real things exist in different ways because we predicate "being" of them in different ways; it is rather the case that we predicate "being" of them in different ways because things exist in different ways, and because we have discerned these differences; and having discerned these differences, we have made our ways of predicating correspond to the ways of existing. St. Thomas points out that the ultimate genera are also called predicaments immediately after he states why being cannot be divided into lesser universals by the addition of differences, as is the way in which a genus is divided into its species. Being cannot be divided in this way because being has no differences of the sort which a genus has (see pages 115–118). There is nothing outside being except nothing, and nothing obviously cannot be a contracting difference. Therefore, being must be divided into lesser universals by differences of a different sort, by differences which are within being, i.e., by the different ways in which real things exist.

Perhaps this can be said more clearly. The word "being," unlike a genus, does not express anything of *what* a thing is, or anything of any of the diverse ways in which a thing exists, not even a minimally partial grasp of *what* a thing is, or of any of the diverse ways in which it exists (this is so since the meaning of the word "being" is taken from the *existence* of a thing, and existence is no part of what a thing is). Therefore, whatever is added to the meaning of the word "being" by way of contracting it to a lesser universal must be expressive of something of *what* things are, of something of the *essences* of things, i.e., of something of some one or other of the diverse ways in which real things exist; otherwise the addition will express nothing, and nothing cannot differentiate and contract being. If, therefore, we look at the diverse predicates we attribute to real things when we are expressing something about *what they are*—i.e., something about any of the diverse ways in which they exist—and if we arrange or order these diverse expressions in a way such that our ordering yields a set of diverse expressions *each of which* is the most universal possible or the least detailed possible in relation to another set of predicates, we shall have, in identifying these least detailed possible expressions, divided being into its ultimate genera.

Thus, any predicate *which is said of real things,* and which is less universal than the predicate *being,* is a predicate which expresses something of the *essences* of real things, i.e., something about some one or other of the diverse ways in which these things exist. Since *being* has no specific differences (only nothing is outside being, and nothing cannot be a difference of being), being is divided into its ultimate genera by means of a consideration and an ordering of those predicates which express what is *within* being, those predicates which express nothing other than *being* or *what is* itself, an ordering of them which identifies the most universal possible among them.

It should be clear from the preceding why one can divide

being into the ultimate genera according to diverse ways of predicating without falling into the error of saying that *such-and-such is so* because *I understand it, and therefore predicate it, to be so.* These ways of predicating are so related to the ways of existing that they correspond to them. The fact is that we—everyone or almost everyone—have discerned these different ways of existing and have thereupon conformed our ways of predicating to the discerned differences, although both the discerning and the conforming were achieved without paying explicit attention to either. And still, from another point of view, it can be said that our ways of predicating just *happen* to correspond to these ways of existing, in the sense that this does not always happen, as we have already seen (see pages 51, 53–54, 259). Further, since to speak of ways of existing is simply to speak of *essences,* it is clear that we have here another instance of a context in which *for something to be understood to be so* (which can be manifested in ways of predicating) is also *for it to be so* (see pages 167–168; 241–243).

Apropos of dividing being into its ultimate genera by using diverse ways of predicating, consider the following.[13] When one looks at what he predicates (we are speaking of predicates less universal than *being*) of individual things like Socrates, one will see quite readily that what he predicates falls into three easily discernible groups, according to three easily discernible relations which it has to the subject of which it is predicated. The first of these relations has to do with *what a thing is;* the second and the third, with the *other* of the diverse ways in which a thing exists.

(1) What he predicates expresses something which belongs to the essence of the subject, e.g., as in *Socrates is a man.* If we consider such predicates, it is easy to see that *substance* is a part of the meaning of all of them, and *that part* which is the most universal or least detailed expression of *what* Socrates is;

and this is why what "substance" expresses is said to be an ultimate genus.

(2) What he predicates expresses something which is not of the essence of the subject, but *which exists in* the subject, e.g., as in *Socrates is five feet nine inches tall* and *Socrates is thinking*. Whatever exists in a subject exists in it either primarily because of the matter of the subject or primarily because of the form of the subject (see pages 251–254); there are no other possibilities as far as the substance itself goes, for there are only two intrinsic constituents, its matter and its form. If we take predicates like *being five feet nine inches tall*, it is easy to see that *being quantified* is part of the meaning of all of them, and *that part* of their meaning which represents their most universal or least detailed expression. Socrates' *being quantified* is rooted in some way in the matter which is part of what Socrates is, for if a thing has matter, it must be a quantified matter (see pages 139–141). If we express Socrates' *being quantified* in an abstract way, as by the word "quantity," this excludes what is *per accidens* in relation to it (i.e., the substance of Socrates, which is *per accidens* in relation to what quantity is), and yields another ultimate genus. In a similar way, Socrates' *thinking* can be reduced to *quality*, another ultimate genus, but a genus which, unlike quantity, is rooted in the form (soul) which is part of what Socrates is. *Quantity* and *quality* exist in Socrates *absolutely*, but if we consider predications like *Socrates is a father* and *Socrates is taller than Plato*, we can reduce these to an ultimate genus such that what it expresses *exists in* Socrates, not absolutely, but in reference to something other than Socrates; this is the ultimate genus *relation*. Relations are ultimately rooted either primarily in the matter or primarily in the form of a thing; there are no other possibilities.

(3) What he predicates expresses something which is neither of the essence of the subject, nor exists in the subject, but

which is *extrinsic* to the subject and from which the subject is denominated, i.e., worded or given a name. (Of course, to call a substance *quantified,* or *qualified,* or *related* is to denominate the substance from something which is in a sense extrinsic, for neither quantity nor quality nor relation belong to *what* the substance is; none of these are among the intrinsic constituents of the essence of the substance.)

Some extrinsic denominations are applicable to all composed substances; one is applicable only in the case of men. Apropos of those which are applicable to all composed substances, consider these predications:

1. Socrates *is being carried* to the hospital by Plato.
2. Plato *is carrying* Socrates to the hospital.
3. Socrates *is at the post office.*
4. Socrates *is sitting* on the floor.
5. Socrates was at the lake *at noon.*

No. 1 exemplifies the category *passion,* an extrinsic denomination of something from an efficient cause, or from what is being done to or for it by an efficient cause, here the carrying. No. 2 exemplifies the category *action,* an extrinsic denomination of an agent cause from the recipient of the effect produced, or from what the agent is doing to or for the recipient, here the carrying. No. 3 exemplifies the category *where,* an extrinsic denomination from other place-occupying things to which it is related in place. No. 4 exemplifies the category *disposition,* an extrinsic denomination of some thing A from other place-occupying things to the parts of which the parts of A have a relation. No. 5 exemplifies the category *when,* an extrinsic denomination from time, which is the measure of the motion which a composed substance undergoes.

It is to be noticed that the extrinsic denominations which are applicable to all composed substances are applicable to them precisely because they are matter-form composites. It is because of the potentiality of their matter that they are acted on (*passion*); it is because of the actuality of their forms that they act on others (*action*); it is because they are quantified that they exist in place (*where*) and have *disposition* of their bodily parts in place (and it is because they have *matter* as part of what they are that they must be quantified); it is because of the potentiality of their quantified matter that they are in a state of motion, of which time (*when*) is the measure.

Apropos of the extrinsic denomination applicable in the case of man alone, consider the propositions

1. Socrates *is well dressed*.
2. Socrates *is armed* for a long and hard fight.

In the case of animals other than men nature has provided them with means of self-preservation which are bodily parts, for example, thick or hairy hides as a covering, claws and teeth for defending themselves, hooves to enable them to walk without injury to their feet. Thus, to describe a lion as *well armed* (referring to his teeth and claws) is not to denominate the lion from something extrinsic; rather it is to denominate the lion from what are parts of his substance. But in the case of man we find *reason* in the place of what are natural endowments in other animals; by reason man fashions for himself his self-preservatives, that is, his clothing, his shoes, his arms. Socrates' *being well dressed*, or his *being armed*, exemplifies the ultimate genus *habitus*. Man fashions by reason not only his self-preservatives, but beautifiers and ornaments as well, for example, as in *that young lady is exquisitely made up* and *that bride is strikingly jeweled*.

We must note that the ultimate genus *habitus* functions at times as an extrinsic denomination even in the case of animals other than men, and even in the case of inanimate objects like the walls of houses, but only in those instances in which these things fall into man's use, for example, as in *my horse is beautifully saddled, the donkey is expertly shod,* and *that wall is most appropriately decked out.*

THE INDIVIDUATION OF ACCIDENTS

St. Thomas does not in *On Being and Essence* take up in an explicit way the question of the individuation of accidents. One would want an answer to this question if only for the sake of completeness, for St. Thomas did treat of the individuation of all substances. The individuation of composed substances is rooted in designated matter (see page 74, [22] to [23], in the text of the treatise; also page 137, [75], and page 225, [98]); that of the human soul is rooted in the body of which it is the form (see page 222, [93]); that of the intelligences is rooted in the purity and subsistent character of the form which each is (see page 137, [75], and page 222, [92] to [93]); that of God is rooted in the purity and subsistent character of the Existence which He is (see page 213, [90]). (See also pages 231–236.)

It is to be noticed that St. Thomas did offer, in (61) to (62) of the treatise, more than a strong hint at an answer to the question of the individuation of accidents. In that context he was not in fact concerned with the individuation of accidents, but with pointing out the defect in Averroes' argument for the claim that there is one intellect in all men. An intellectually grasped form can be considered in two ways: (1) as representing things in the real world and (2) as produced by and existing in an individual intellectual soul. Taken in the first way, the intellectually grasped form is something universal. Taken in the second way, the intellectually grasped form is something individual. It is an *individual accident* produced by and *existing in an individual* soul. What St. Thomas was pointing out there is but an application of his general thesis that accidents are individuated by the substances *in which they exist.*[14] (And this, in turn, is but an application of his more general and twofold thesis that (1) subsistent forms are individuated by virtue of themselves—i.e., by virtue of their purity and subsistent character—and (2) nonsubsistent forms—i.e., forms which exist in a subject—are individuated by the subject in which they exist; and this is the case whether the forms belong to the category of substance or to that of accident.)[15]

Whatever reality an accident has depends on substance; so too does its individuation. And although the reality of accidents depends on substances other than simply those in which they exist, their individuation depends only on those in which they exist. But it is to be noticed that accidents can depend on the substances in which they exist in different ways: as on a final cause, as on an agent cause, as on an extrinsic material cause (see pages 248–251). It is in virture of this last sort of dependence—i.e., as on an extrinsic material cause—that *all* accidents are individuated. For an accident *to be individuated* is for it *to exist in* an individuated substance. Accidents which exist in the composite of matter and form, like quantity and color, are individuated by the composite; those, like the intellect and thought activity in the case of man, which exist only in the soul, are individuated by the soul. Thus, that which individuates accidents is ultimately that which individuates the substances, or the essential parts thereof (we have in mind the human soul, which is *alone* the subject *in which certain sorts of accidents exist*), in which they exist, whether these substances are composed or simple.

NOTES

NOTES TO PREFACE

1. For a listing, and brief historical discussion, of commentaries on *On Being and Essence* see Martinus Grabmann, "De Commentariis in Opusculum S. Thomae Aquinatis *De Ente et Essentia,*" *Acta Pont. Academiae Romanae S. Thomae Aq. et Religionis Catholicae,* Nova Series, Vol. V, 1938; pp. 7–20. Grabmann gives special attention to the commentary of Conrad of Prussia, which, as far as he has determined, is the historically first commentary on *On Being and Essence,* having been composed prior to July 1323, the date of the canonization of St. Thomas Aquinas, and thus within 50 years of his death in 1274.

2. *S. Thomae Aquinatis Sermo seu Tractatus "De Ente et Essentia."* Edidit Ludovicus Baur, Editio Altera Emendata (Monasterii, 1933). Typis Aschendorff.

3. *S. Thomae Aquinatis Opusculum "De Ente et Essentia,"* Editio Tertia (Marietti, 1957).

4. *Le "De Ente et Essentia" de S. Thomas d'Aquin.* Texte établi d'après les manuscrits parisiens. Introduction, Notes et Études historiques. Par M.-D. Roland-Gosselin, O.P. (Kain, Belgique: Le Saulchoir, 1926).

5. *"On Being and Essence" by St. Thomas Aquinas,* Translated with an Introduction and Notes by Armand Augustine Maurer, C.S.B. (Toronto: The Pontifical Institute of Medieval Studies, 1949).

270

1. The first task lays, in effect, the foundations for avoiding errors like those of Parmenides and Melissus, for avoiding frustrating ambiguities and unintelligibilities like those of Heidegger, and for avoiding rejections of metaphysics as a science of being as being like that of R. G. Collingwood.

2. This is done with a view to rising as quickly and as economically as possible to an account of the existence and of the characteristics of God. One begins to see, in pursuing this task, what sorts of pursuits are necessary, and what sorts are not, for rising to a knowledge of the existence and characteristics of God.

3. This task will help one to avoid attributing to things what belongs to our knowledge about them, i.e., to the way in which we know them; also, to avoid attributing to our way of knowing things what in fact belongs to them.

4. For example, *In I Metaph.*, lect. 2, n. 46; *In IV Metaph.*, lect. 6, n. 605; *De Verit.*, q. 1, a. 1, c.; *S.T.*, I–II, q. 94, a. 2, c.

5. *S.T.*, I–II, q. 94, a. 2, c.

6. See, for example, texts cited in footnote 4 just above.

7. J. Maritain, *Existence and the Existent,* Eng. trans. by Galantiere and Phelan (New York: Pantheon, 1948), p. 25, including footnote 12.

8. This is to be taken in the context of *learning* a language; obviously not in the context of adding to a language.

9. *In XI Metaph.*, lect. 1, n. 2146.

10. See *In IV Metaph.*, lect. 1, n. 533.

11. *De Pot.*, q. 7, a. 9, c. See also *In IV Metaph.*, lect. 4, nn. 574–577; *In I Post. Anal.*, lect. 20, nn. 170–172; *S.T.*, I, q. 28, a. 1.

NOTES TO CHAPTER ONE

1. See, for example, *In I Phys.*, lect. 1, n. 8.

2. See, for example, *In I Phys.*, lect. 1, n. 8; *In I Post. Anal.*, lect. 4, n. 43; also *In I Metaph.*, lect. 2, nn. 45–46, where some details are added.

3. *In I Metaph.*, lect. 2, nn. 45–46.

4. *In I Metaph.*, lect. 2, n. 46.

5. See, for example, *On Being and Essence by St. Thomas*

Aquinas, Translated with an Introduction and Notes by Armand Maurer, C.S.B. (Toronto: The Pontifical Institute of Medieval Studies, 1949), p. 26, footnote 1.

6. See *In V Metaph.,* lect. 9, for a discussion of many uses of the word "being."

7. See *S.T.,* I, q. 3, a. 4, ad 2; *ibid.,* q. 48, a. 2, ad 2; *C.G.,* I, ch. 12; *De Pot.,* q. 7, a. 2, ad 1; *De Malo,* q. 1, a. 1, ad 19, ad 20; *In I Sent.,* d. 19, q. 5, a. 1, ad 1; *In II Sent.,* d. 34, q. 1, a. 1, sol.; *ibid.,* d. 37, q. 1, a. 2, ad 3; *Q.Q., Quodl.* 9, a. 3, c.

8. *In V Metaph.,* lect. 9, n. 885.

9. *Ibid.,* n. 889.

10. Throughout *In VII Metaph.;* for example, lect. 5, n. 1378.

11. See pages 61–67, especially pages 64–65, for the notion of substantial form.

NOTES TO CHAPTER TWO

1. See, for example, *C.G.,* I, ch. 34.

2. See *S.T.,* I, q. 13, a. 10, c.; *ibid.,* a. 6, c.

3. See *In IV Metaph.,* lect. 1, nn. 535–543.

4. See *In VIII Metaph.,* lect. 1, n. 1682.

5. *In IV Metaph.,* lect. 1, n. 546.

6. See *In I Phys.,* lect. 12–lect. 13, for an inductive analysis of change; in *In VII Metaph.,* lect. 2, nn. 1285–1290, one finds the metaphysician's argument for the matter in substantial change, which argument is not an inductive analysis.

7. *C.G.,* IV, ch. 65.

NOTES TO CHAPTER THREE

1. For a fuller consideration of the expression "taken from," see pages 94–95.

2. For a fuller consideration of the expression "taken from," see below pages 94–95.

3. See *In Boetii De Trin.,* q. 4, a. 2, c.

4. See *In V Metaph.,* lect. 7, n. 862.

5. See *In V Metaph.,* lect. 7, n. 862.

6. See above, page 47, the paragraph beginning: "In (8) we

are told that essence is something which constitutes the total determination or identity. . . ."

7. The relation of $\frac{C}{D}$, as formulated here, is perhaps a more precise way of expressing what we called above, in outlining the contents of chapter three (see page 83), the relation of the un-expressed-but-unexcluded to the expressed. It might also be better expressed as the relation of the unexpressing-but-unexcluding to the expressing.

8. See the immediately following paragraph.

9. See above, pages 86–88.

10. See *In Boetii De Trin.*, q. 4, a. 2.

11. See *In XI Metaph.*, lect. 1, n. 2196; also *In V Metaph.*, lect. 9, n. 889.

NOTES TO CHAPTER FOUR

1. In fact, the third task is pursued and completed only by showing how essence (not how both being and essence) is related to these logical intentions. See above pp. 60–61, the section headed: *To investigate the essence of a thing is to investigate its being.*

2. Those features of a thing which are included in its definition are said to belong to it *per se* in the first mode, e.g., rational and animal to man. Those features of a thing which, though not included in its definition, belong to it precisely because of its definition, its *whole* definition, are said to belong to it *per se* in the second mode, e.g., the feature expressed by the words *plane figure with an exterior angle equal to the sum of the opposite interior angles* to triangle; the feature expressed in the Pythagorean Theorem to right triangle. Such features are also described as belonging to a thing *always* and *necessarily,* and *only* to that thing. Sometimes the difference between these two modes of *per se* is described in terms of the subject and the predicate of a proposition, so that if the predicate is the definition of the subject, or some element placed in its definition, we have the first mode of *per se*. If, on the other hand, the subject is placed in the definition of the predicate, the predicate being a proper accident of the subject, we have the second mode of *per se*.

3. See page 48, the paragraph beginning, "In (11). . . ."
4. See page 47, the paragraph beginning, "In (9). . . ."
5. See *In Boetii De Trin.*, q. 5, a. 2, especially the *corpus* and *ad 4.*

NOTES TO CHAPTER FIVE

1. See *S.T.*, I, q. 50, a. 2, c.
2. See *S.T.*, I, q. 75, a. 5, c.; see also *ibid.*, q. 2, c.
3. *S.T.*, I, q. 75, a. 6, c.
4. See *S.T.*, I, q. 75, a. 2, ad 3. See also above, pages 144, 146.
5. See *De Principiis Naturae*, in *Opuscula Philosophica*, ed. Marietti (1954), p. 125, n. 356.
6. See above, page 48, for the sense in which things which are not real things can be said to have an essence.
7. See *In III Phys.*, lect. 4.
8. See Cajetan, *In De Ente et Essentia* (ed. Laurent), p. 141, n. 90, first paragraph.
9. For a brief discussion of the sort of middle term which is adequately universal for the doing of metaphysics see above, pages 14 and 147.
10. In the *Summa of Theology*, I, q. 2, a. 3, c., he explicitly infers from it that there would be no first mover, hence neither any moved mover, nor the thing observed to be in motion.
11. As an example of such a charge, see C. J. F. Williams, "*Hic autem non est procedere in infinitum:* . . . ," *Mind*, Vol. LXIX, No. 275 (July, 1960) pp. 403–405. The whole of his charge is actually contained in his first paragraph, which is as follows: "The flaw in this argument [i.e., in the argument for *hic non est procedere in infinitum*] is its use of the term *moventia secunda* in an attempt to prove the impossibility of an infinite series of causes. For not until we know that such a series is impossible can we know that all movers are properly described as "a first mover" or as "second movers." This, however, is precisely what the argument assumes. It equates "movers other than a first mover" and "second movers." It fails to recognize the possibility of a third class of movers, those, namely, which belong to an infinite series of moved movers. Thus to presuppose the impossibility of the infinite series in the premises of the argument is to commit *petitio principii*."

12. See, for example, *S.T.*, I, q. 4, a. 1, ad 3; *ibid.*, q. 8, a. 1, c.; *De Pot.*, q. 7, a. 2, ad 9.

13. See, for example, *S.T.*, I, q. 79, a. 3; *ibid.*, q. 54, a. 4.

14. See Aristotle, *De Anima*, Bk. II, ch. 1; in particular 412 b 3–6; see also 414 a 4–26, where Aristotle is stressing, by way of correcting the views of certain others, the need of a *certain sort* of body of which soul is the soul.

15. *S.T.*, I, q. 78, a. 1, c.

16. See, for example, *S.T.*, I, q. 16, a. 3, c.; *ibid.*, q. 80, a. 1, c.; *ibid.*, q. 84, a. 2, ad 2. See also Aristotle, *De Anima*, 431 b 19–23; and *In III De Anima*, lect. 13, n. 787.

17. See *S.T.*, I, q. 85, a. 3, c.

18. See, for example, Jacques Maritain, *Existence and the Existent*, pp. 10–26, especially section 7, pp. 22–26.

19. *Ibid.*, pp. 25–26.

20. *Ibid.*, p. 23.

21. *Ibid.*, pp. 24–25.

22. *Ibid.*, pp. 17–18; pp. 22–23.

23. *Ibid.*, p. 12.

24. *Ibid.*, pp. 11–12; p. 16.

25. *Ibid.*, p. 16.

26. *Ibid.*, p. 26.

27. The word *proposition* is here being used as a convenient shorthand way of designating what the judgment judges, i.e., the joining of two concepts which are not conceived together.

28. Jacques Maritain, *op. cit.*, p. 26, lines 5–6.

29. See just above footnote 27.

NOTES TO CHAPTER SIX

1. *S.T.*, I, q. 3, a. 5, c.

2. *Ibid.*

3. *Ibid.*; see also *C.G.*, I, ch. 25.

4. *C.G.*, I, ch. 25.

5. See *S.T.*, I, q. 3, a. 5, c.; also *C.G.*, I, ch. 25.

6. *S.T.*, I, q. 3, a. 5, c.

7. See *C.G.*, I, ch. 26.

8. *Ibid.*

9. See Fr. Owens, "Elucidation and Causal Knowledge," *The New Scholasticism*, XXXVII (1963), pp. 69–70.

10. The words *received, receiver*, and *recipient* are often used by

St. Thomas in the context of the potentiality-actuality relation, and in the way indicated by this proportion:

$$\frac{\text{the receiver (or recipient)}}{\text{the received}} : \frac{\text{potency}}{\text{actuality}}.$$

See above pp. 183–184 for the sense of the word *potentiality* or *potency* as attributable to the separated substances.

11. See *In VII Metaph.*, lect. 12, n. 1552.

12. See *S.T.*, I, q. 77, a. 1, ad 7; see also: *ibid.*, q. 29, a. 1, ad 3; *ibid.*, I–II, q. 49, a. 2, ad 3; *De Verit.*, q. 10, a. 1, ad 6; *De Pot.*, q. 9, a. 2, ad 5.

13. See *In II Sent.*, d. 3, q. 1, a. 6, c.

14. *Ibid.*

NOTES TO CHAPTER SEVEN

1. See above, pages 31–38; page 40, (2); pages 52–54.

2. See *In II De Anima*, lect. 1, n. 213.

3. See *In X Metaph.*, lect. 8, n. 2092.

4. See *S.T.*, I, q. 77, a. 6, c.

5. See above, page 120, for the two senses of the question, How is an essence related to these logical intentions?

6. See preceding footnote.

7. See *In VII Metaph.*, lect. 1, n. 1255.

8. See *ibid.*, n. 1254.

9. It is to be noticed that the English word *snubness* does not function like the Latin word *simitas*, for "simitas" includes the *nose* in a way in which "snubness" does not. "Simitas" includes the *nose*, functioning as difference, in the way in which what "man" expresses includes what "rational" expresses, i.e., it includes it, but without expressing it and without differentiating it from the genus animal. The English "snubness," thus, does not say as much as the Latin "simitas" does. On the other hand, the English contrivance *snub-nosedness*, which was used in the translation in (110), expressly includes the *nose*, whereas the Latin *simitas* does not. Thus, whereas "snubness" says too little, "snubnosedness" says too much. There is no English word, descriptive of noses, which functions like "simitas."

10. Again, the English "snub" does not function like the Latin "simum." Like "snubness" in relation to "simitas," "snub" in relation to "simum" does not say enough. The English "snub nose," on the

other hand, which was used in (110) to translate "simum," says too much, since it explicitly expresses *nose*. As in the case of "simitas," there is no English word, referring to noses, which functions like "simum."

11. For the different senses in which a substance can be cause of an accident see above, pages 248–254.

12. *In V Metaph.*, lect. 9, n. 890.

13. See *ibid.*, nn. 890–892; *In III Phys.*, lect. 5, n. 322.

14. See *S.T.*, I, q. 29, a. 1, c.; *ibid.*, q. 39, a. 3, c.; *ibid.*, II–II, q. 24, a. 5, ad 1; *ibid.*, III, q. 77, a. 2, c.; *In I Sent.*, d. 9, q. 1, a. 1, c.; *De Pot.*, q. 9, a. 1, ad 8.

15. See *In IV Sent.*, d. 12, q. 1, a. 1, q. 3, 3 and ad 3; *S.T.*, I, q. 3, a. 2, ad 3; *De Pot.*, q. 9, a. 3, ad 5; *De Spirit. Creat.*, a. 5, ad 8; *ibid.*, a. 8, ad 4, ad 13.

INDEX

Accident (predicable), 16
Accident(s) (predicamental), or accidental form, depend on substances, 50
  not an intrinsically complete existent, 72
  and their essence, 238, 239, 242
  and substantial form, 238–239, 243, 246–248
  and their form and matter, 240
  following on form, 241, 254
  has an imperfect essence, 244
  has no intrinsic causes, 245
  and an *extrinsic* material cause, 246
  not a complete essence, 246–248
  an accident and a substance, 247
  genus, species, and difference of, 254
  expressed by *concrete* names, 255–259
  not composed of matter and form, 255, 257
  and their causing principles, 255–256, 257, 260
  genus of, 255, 259
  differences of, 255, 260
  and their differences, 256, 258, 261

Accidents (*Continued*)
  as forms, 259
  properly defined, 260
"Act of existing," *viii*
Adequately universal middle term, 14, 147, 172
Analogical word, defined, 53
  priority and posteriority, 53–54
Analytically first, vs. temporally first, 3
an est, 47
Angels, 35–36, 147
Aristotle, 12, 47, 275
Averroes, 71, 102, 127, 131, 190, 268
Avicebron, 135, 138
  distinction of things, 139–141, 183
Avicenna, 1, 45, 47, 70, 71, 88, 107, 108, 109, 113, 119, 124, 131, 159, 223, 224, 233

Baur, Ludovicus, text of, *viii*, 270
"Because" (the word), 51
Being, a *genus*, 248–249
  and ultimate genera, 262–263
Being, as first conceived by the intellect, 1, 3–8, 200–201
  with vs. without essence, 9

279

Regress, infinite, 176–181
vs. infinite series, 182
Roland-Gosselin, Fr., text of, *viii*, 270

"Say" (the word), 52
Second intentions, 16–20, 54–56
and intellect's operations, 19–20
are there, 35
relations between genus and difference are, 102
Sense knowledge, vs. intellectual knowledge, 3–4
Separated substances, 135
Sight, and light, 9, 67
Signifying, 86–87
Simple substance, defined, 67
vs. a composed substance, 137–138
its essence, 158–159
plurality of, 159
and pure act, 159
Snubness, defined, 246, 260
"snubness" and "simitas," 276–277
Something-there, 4, 6–7
Soul, defined, 72, 92, 238, 243, 246
Soul(s) (human), beings or things, 35–36
created by God (def.), 72
and matter-form composition, 135
immaterial, 135, 141–147
existence of, 146–147
need of senses in thinking, 146, 153
incorruptible, 151–154
a *subsistent form*, 151, 237
separated from the body, 153–154
lowest grade among intellectual substances, 185
and intelligible forms, 185–187
a blank tablet, 186, 190
in some way all things, 197

Soul(s) (*Continued*)
individuation of, 223, 226
absolute existence of, and of God, 226
no introspective contact with, 230
has a twofold character, 237
and logical intentions, 237
Species, 1
expresses the whole of what a thing is, 16
that which is a species vs. what it is to be a species, 18–19
is there, 35
taken from matter and form, 93
genus and essences of, 101–102
and individual, 106
signified, 106, 107, 111–113
"Species" (the word), uses of, 133
Specific essence, and individual essence, 81, 84
and generic essence, 81
Subject of a science, 57–58, 132
Subsistent Existence, 188
Substance(s), simple and composed, 49
prior to accidents, 54
a complete essence, 72, 244
complete existent, 72
have essence in three different ways, 213
cause of accidents, 240, 248–254
properly in a genus, as species or genera, 254–255, 258
"Substance" (the word), an analogical word, 54
Substantial form, not complete existent, 72, 238
defined, 238
and accidental form, 238–239, 243
an imperfect essence, 244
no intrinsic causes, 246
Sweetness, 71